SURY
MENT
GENT
XAM

OTHER TITLES OF INTEREST FROM LEARNINGEXPRESS

Police Sergeant Exam, 3rd Edition

Police Officer Exam, 4th Edition

State Trooper Exam

Corrections Officer Exam

Probation Officer/Parole Officer Exam

9 Steps to a Great Federal Job

TREASURY ENFORCEMENT AGENT EXAM

3rd Edition

LEARNING EXPRESS®

NEW YORK

Library of Congress Cataloging-in-Publication Data:
Treasury enforcement agent exam.—3rd ed.
    p. cm.
    ISBN 978-1-57685-709-0
    1. Civil service—United States—Examinations. 2. United States. Dept. of
the Treasury—Officials and employees. I. LearningExpress (Organization).
HJ268.T74 2009
363'.28—dc22

                                                          2009021315

ISBN 978-1-57685-709-0

Printed in the United States of America

9 8 7 6 5 4 3 2 1

Third Edition

For information or to place an order, contact LearningExpress at:
    2 Rector Street
    26th Floor
    New York, NY 10006

Or visit us at:
    www.learnatest.com

Contents

Contributors

The following individuals contributed to the content of this book:

Byron Demmer is a freelance writer with a degree in Economics living in Middleport, New York.

Valerie Demmer is a freelance writer with a degree in Business living in Middleport, New York.

Michael Foster is a freelance writer with a master of science degree in Forensic Science, a bachelor's degree in Criminal Justice Administration, and a bachelor of science degree. He is a former Senior Special Agent with the U.S. Customs Service and a Senior Special Agent (retired) from DHS/ICE.

Jordan Lanini is currently obtaining a degree in Environmental Engineering from Iowa State University in Ames.

Jo Lynn Southard has Juris Doctor and master of law degrees from the University of Iowa. She is an adjunct professor in the Andover College Paralegal Studies Department and a freelance writer living in Portland, Maine.

Pat Stevens is a test development specialist with an MFA from the University of Iowa living in Iowa City, Iowa.

Shirley Tarbell is a test development specialist and writer living in Portland, Maine.

TREASURY ENFORCEMENT AGENT EXAM

1 ▶ BECOMING A TREASURY ENFORCEMENT AGENT

CHAPTER SUMMARY

This chapter will describe the career of a Treasury Enforcement Agent. It will explain the agent's typical duties and responsibilities in each of the treasury bureaus, guide you through the hiring process, and give you helpful explanations and tips to use along the way.

I f you are looking for a job in which you can truly make a difference, in which every day can be an adventure and you can have the satisfaction of knowing that your work contributes to the strength, security, and overall welfare of the United States, then becoming a Treasury Enforcement Agent may be the right career for you.

The federal government is the largest single employer in the United States, and when you join the ranks of federal employees, you can be sure you will have excellent benefits, a competitive salary, and job security. Some of the many perks include a good selection of health and life insurance programs, liberal cost of living allowances and geographic locality pay adjustments, generous personal and sick leave, and the availability of dependent care centers and fitness centers. Once you are hired, noncompetitive promotion potential exists up to the GS-12 level, and a comfortable retirement is provided by the Federal Employees' Retirement System.

But competition for a Treasury Enforcement Agent job is intense, and the application process can be daunting. So let's take a look at what will be required of you by each of the agencies that use the Treasury Enforcement Agent Exam and how you can gain an edge in the selection process.

The Agencies

The agencies that use the Treasury Enforcement Agent Exam are:

- Department of Homeland Security:
  U. S. Secret Service (USSS)
  U. S. Customs and Immigration Enforcement (ICE)
- Department of the Treasury:
  Internal Revenue Service (IRS)
- Department of Justice:
  Bureau of Alcohol, Tobacco, Firearms, and Explosives (ATF)

Salary and Benefits for Special Agent Positions

Salary and benefits are essentially the same for all special agent positions.

Salary

Salaries for special agents are based on the federal government's special rates for law enforcement officers at the GS-5 through GS-9 grade levels and the general schedule for the GS-11 and above grade levels. Applicable locality pay adjustments may apply depending on the duty location. Beginning salaries are determined by a combination of education and experience. The following ranges listed can be used as a guide:

GS-5: $33,333–$41,442
GS-7: $37,941–$47,985

Besides this salary, special agents are also eligible to receive Law Enforcement Availability Pay (LEAP) after the successful completion of training and certification. Under the LEAP program, agents receive an additional 25% of their base pay due to their availability to work irregular and unscheduled hours beyond the normal 40-hour workweek and the frequent requirement for them to do so.

Benefits

Benefits include vacation and sick leave, dependent care and employee support programs, a retirement plan, participation in health and life insurance plans, and appropriate cost-of-living/geographic locality pay.

A closer examination of the duties, training, and qualifications demanded by each agency will help you decide which type of job is right for you. It will also prepare you for the variety of challenges presented by the application process for each one.

The U.S. Secret Service

The U.S. Secret Service was created on July 5, 1865, as a federal bureau under the Department of the Treasury. At that time, its main function and purpose was to suppress the counterfeiting of U.S. currency. In 1901, the functions of the U.S. Secret Service were expanded to include the important responsibility of protecting the president of the United States. This responsibility has since been expanded to include protection of:

- The president and immediate family
- The vice president and immediate family
- Former presidents and their spouses for life and their children until age 16
- Visiting heads of foreign states and governments and spouses traveling with them
- Major presidential and vice-presidential candidates and spouses

The U.S. Secret Service's investigative responsibilities have also expanded. In addition to investigating counterfeiting, many more investigative areas have been added. These include investigation of financial crimes relating to banks, access devices (including credit/debit cards), identity theft, computers, telecommunications, and telemarketing.

Description of Duties

Special agents of the U.S. Secret Service are charged with two main duties: protection and investigation. During the course of their careers, special agents carry out assignments in both of these areas.

Protection

Special agents are legally authorized to protect the president and vice president (or other officer next in the line of succession to the presidency) and their immediate families; the president-elect and vice president-elect and their immediate families; former presidents and their spouses and minor children; visiting heads of foreign states or governments and their spouses; other distinguished foreign visitors to the United States; official representatives of the United States performing special missions abroad; and major presidential and vice-presidential candidates and their spouses.

Investigation

The U.S. Secret Service is charged with investigation of and enforcement of laws against:

- Counterfeiting
- Forgery
- Crimes associated with financial institutions

Preventing counterfeiting of the currency and securities of the United States and of foreign governments is still a main duty of special agents. The Secret Service is also charged with investigating the counterfeiting of certain government identification documents and devices.

Enforcing laws against forgery is a similarly important task. Forged or stolen Social Security checks, retirement pensions, savings bonds, and other federal government disbursements result in the loss of millions of dollars each year. The Secret Service is responsible for investigating these crimes.

The Secret Service also investigates crimes associated with financial institutions, including bank fraud, theft involving access devices, fraud involving credit and debit cards, telecommunication and computer crimes, fraudulent identification crimes, fraudulent government and commercial securities crimes, and electronic funds transfer fraud.

Training

Special agents in the Secret Service undergo especially rigorous training, including extensive training in federal law enforcement and state-of-the-art investigative procedures. All agents receive ten weeks of general investigative training at the Federal Law Enforcement Training Center (FLETC) Glynco, Georgia, and 11 weeks of specialized instruction at the U.S. Secret Service training facilities in the Washington, DC, area. Besides classroom study, agents receive on-the-job training through advanced in-service training programs. Training includes but is not limited to:

- Criminal, constitutional, and civil law
- Rules of evidence
- Courtroom etiquette
- Report writing
- Comprehensive courses in protection
- Criminal investigation procedures
- Surveillance techniques
- Undercover operations
- Use of scientific devices
- Emergency medicine
- Firearms
- Self-defensive measures, arrest techniques, and control tactics
- Extensive physical fitness and conditioning
- Protective and defensive driving measures

After successful completion of the training program, agents are assigned to one of the many U.S. Secret Service offices around the country.

Qualifications

To qualify, an applicant must:

- Be a U.S. citizen between the ages of 21 and 37 at the time of appointment
- Pass the written test
- Meet one of the following education and/or experience qualification requirements:
  - A bachelor's degree from an accredited college or university **or**
  - A minimum of three years experience in criminal investigations or law enforcement **or**
  - A combination of education and related experience
- Undergo a series of in-depth interviews
- Submit to a drug test for illegal drugs and receive a negative result
- Submit to a physical examination and meet the requirements of the position as outlined under medical and physical requirements
- Have vision no worse than 20/60 (uncorrected) in each eye, which must be correctable to 20/20
- Initiate paperwork for, and receive a favorable suitability determination on, a full background investigation
- Complete a polygraph test

Applicants with a minimum of one to five years of work experience are generally considered highly qualified. Applicants with a bachelor's degree may qualify with work experience unrelated to criminal investigations, but the experience should demonstrate responsible full-time employment status.

How to Contact the U.S. Secret Service

www.secretservice.gov
1-888-813-8777

U.S. Immigration and Customs Enforcement

As the nation's main border agency, the duty of the U.S. Immigration and Customs Enforcement (ICE) is to ensure that all goods enter and leave the United States in accordance with U.S. laws and regulations. This responsibility includes:

- Enforcing U.S. laws intended to prevent illegal trade practices
- Protecting the American public and environment from the introduction of prohibited hazardous and noxious products
- Assessing and collecting revenues in the form of duties, taxes, and fees on imported merchandise
- Regulating the movement of persons, carriers, merchandise, and commodities between the United States and other nations while facilitating the movement of all legitimate cargo, carriers, travelers, and mail
- Interdicting narcotics and other contraband
- Enforcing certain provisions of the export control laws of the United States

Description of Duties

Within the U.S. Immigration and Customs Enforcement agency, the criminal investigators (special agents) of the Office of Investigations are charged with enforcing a variety of statutes in the United States Code and for investigating violations.

Investigation and Enforcement

ICE special agents have enforcement authority over crimes such as:

- Narcotics smuggling
- Money laundering
- Child pornography
- Trade fraud

- Illegal traffic of arms or components of nuclear, chemical, or biological weapons
- Immigration violations (special agents in the Immigration and Customs Enforcement agency have unique border search authority)
- Cyber-smuggling

Successful investigations of violations depend upon the application of a broad range of investigative methods, including:

- Development and use of informants
- Physical and electronic surveillance
- Examination of a variety of records including, but not limited to, those of:
  - Importers/exporters
  - Banks
  - Couriers
  - Manufacturers
- Conducting of interviews
- Doing interagency liaison and multi-jurisdictional investigations
- Completion of application for and conducting of search warrants

An ICE special agent may be given a wide variety of assignments in both domestic and foreign posts, and has exposure to all investigative areas.

Training

Special agents in the U.S. Immigration and Customs Enforcement agency are required to complete a basic training course. Acceptance into the position requires that selectees successfully complete a 20-week course of specialized training at the Immigration and Customs Law Enforcement Training Center in Brunswick, Georgia, which includes training in the investigative techniques previously described.

Qualifications

To qualify, an applicant must:

- Be a U.S. citizen under the age of 37
- Meet one of the following education and/or experience qualification requirements:
  - A bachelor's degree from an accredited institution in any field of study **or**
  - Three years responsible experience in criminal investigation or law enforcement **or**
  - An equivalent combination of experience and education
- Pass the written test
- Submit to a drug test for illegal drugs and receive a negative result
- Submit to a physical examination and meet the requirements of the position
- Initiate paperwork for, and receive a favorable suitability determination on, a full background investigation

How to Contact U.S. Immigration and Customs Enforcement

www.ice.gov

To learn about positions available at ICE, go to www.usajob.gov.

Internal Revenue Service

The purpose of the IRS is to collect tax revenues in a way that is most cost-effective to the public, and to assure public confidence in its integrity and impartiality. The Criminal Investigation (CI) division enforces the statutes that relate to tax fraud and related financial crimes; its mission is to encourage and achieve, directly or indirectly, voluntary compliance with the internal revenue laws. CI also fights computer crime, which includes unlawfully obtaining evidence from electronic databases and files and unauthorized disclosure of return information via electronic media.

The task of the IRS also includes undercover and other assignments designed to detect noncompliance. The Internal Security function is responsible for ensuring the highest standards of honesty and integrity at all levels of the IRS itself. To this end, it conducts criminal and administrative investigations of IRS employees and nonemployees who might be engaged in crimes and misconduct associated with the operation of the IRS.

Description of Duties
Investigation and Enforcement

IRS criminal investigators (special agents) are intensely involved in eliminating money-related crimes and are required to have a knowledge of accounting in order to understand complex financial reports. As duly sworn law enforcement officers, they investigate complex cases involving the following:

- International money laundering
- Narcotics
- Organized crime
- Tax evasion
- Healthcare fraud
- Savings and loan scandals
- Corruption
- Embezzlement
- Fraud
- Drug trafficking

Internal Security

The IRS internal security inspector (special agent) is charged with investigating federal crimes, including the following:

- Bribery
- Extortion and conspiracy
- Illegal drug activity

- Thefts and embezzlements
- Impersonations
- Assaults and threats against IRS employees
- Unauthorized disclosure of tax information

These special agents conduct probes into certain high-risk integrity areas to weed out corruption and preserve public confidence in our tax system.

Training

Special agents in the Internal Revenue Service are required to complete basic training. Acceptance to a position requires that selectees successfully complete a formalized course of required technical training at the Federal Law Enforcement Training Center according to the standards of the Internal Revenue Service, which include training in the investigative techniques previously described.

Qualifications

To qualify, an applicant must:

- Be a U.S. citizen under the age of 37
- Meet one of the following education and experience requirements:
  - A bachelor's degree from an accredited institution in any field of study **or**
  - Three years of responsible experience in accounting or business **or**
  - An equivalent combination of experience and education **or**
  - A certified public accountant (CPA) certificate
- Special agents working in the IRS Criminal Investigation division must have taken at least 15 semester hours in accounting and nine semester hours in the following, or closely related, fields: finance, economics, business law, tax law, or money and banking
- Pass the written test
- Have a driver's license
- Submit to a drug test for illegal drugs and receive a negative result

- Submit to a physical examination and meet the requirements of the position as outlined under medical and physical requirements
- Initiate paperwork for, and receive a favorable suitability determination on, a full background investigation

How to Contact the Internal Revenue Service

Visit the general site at www.irs.gov. Call a location near you to speak to a special agent for more information regarding a career in IRS Law Enforcement. You can find the nearest location by going to www.jobs.irs.gov.

To apply for an IRS position online, go to https://careerconnector.jobs.irs.gov.

Bureau of Alcohol, Tobacco, Firearms and Explosives

The Bureau of Alcohol, Tobacco, Firearms and Explosives (ATF) is charged with vital responsibilities aimed at preventing terrorism and fighting violent crime and thus protecting the public. The ATF enforces the federal laws relating to illicit tobacco and alcohol, firearms, explosives, and arson by taking direct action and by cooperating with other agencies to:

- Prevent crime and violence through enforcement and regulation
- Do community outreach
- Provide fair and effective industry regulation
- Support and assist federal, state, local, and international law enforcement
- Provide innovative training programs in support of criminal and regulatory enforcement functions

Description of Duties
Investigation and Enforcement
Special agents at the ATF investigate violations of federal laws relating to explosives, arson, firearms, and illicit liquor and tobacco. These investigations involve surveillance, participation in raids, interviewing suspects and witnesses, making arrests, obtaining and serving search warrants, and conducting searches for physical evidence.

Agents work closely with other federal, state, and local law enforcement agencies to fight crime and violence. At the end of investigations, they review all evidence, write case reports, and testify for the government in court.

Training

Selectees must complete basic training and are required to successfully complete a formalized course of technical training at the Federal Law Enforcement Training Center according to the standards of the ATF.

Qualifications

To qualify, an applicant must:

- Be a U.S. citizen
- Be at least 21 years of age, but under 37 at the time of appointment
- Pass the written test
- Have a driver's license
- Fill out an applicant questionnaire and pass a special agent assessment test
- Pass a full field background investigation and polygraph test
- Undergo a full panel interview
- Possess the proper experience or education requirements
- Meet the following physical requirements for the position:
  - Passing a comprehensive medical examination by a licensed physician before appointment
  - Having distance vision without correction testing at least 20/100 in each eye, correctable to 20/30 in one eye and 20/20 in the other
  - Having hearing within required levels
  - Having weight in proportion to height
  - Passing a drug screen for illegal substances

How to Contact the ATF

202-927-8610 or 202-927-5690 (agent applications only)
Bureau of Alcohol, Tobacco, Firearms and Explosives
Personnel Division
650 Massachusetts Avenue NW, Room 4100
Washington, DC 20226

Job Vacancies and Exam Periods

Job Listings through the OPM
The Office of Personnel Management (OPM) updates a list of federal job vacancies daily. If you have a touch-tone phone, you can access this information 24 hours a day, seven days a week by calling the OPM's automated telephone system, Career America Connection:

912-757-3000

The most user-friendly of the OPM resources, however, is its website:

www.opm.gov

You can also search for federal jobs, access information about pay scales, receive automated job alerts, download application forms, or apply online at www.usajobs.opm.gov.

Contacting the Hiring Agency Directly
Because the OPM is no longer responsible for overseeing hiring in most agencies, you can also get detailed job information directly from the agency in which you are interested, which will have its own personnel office and its own job list.

How to Apply

What to Submit
Applicants are required to submit the following initial paperwork when applying for positions:

- A completed Application for Federal Employment (SF 171) **or**
- An Optional Application for Federal Employment (OF 612) **and**
- A Declaration for Federal Employment (OF 306) **or**
- A Resume and a Declaration for Federal Employment (OF 306)

Filing Period
All openings have a *filing period* or *application window*, a specific time period during which applications will be accepted. Be sure you are aware of the filing period so that you do not miss the deadline. It could be weeks or even years before there's another filing period.

Application Forms
The SF 171, once required for all federal job applicants, is no longer a required OPM form. Rather than filling out the lengthy SF 171, applicants can now use the Optional Application for Federal Employment (OF 612), a short and easy-to-use form available online at www.opm.gov. A sample is reproduced at the end of this chapter.

Resume
You may also submit a resume instead of an OF 612 or SF 171. However, if your resume does not include the information that is requested on the OF 612 and in the job vacancy announcement, *you will not be considered for the job*. One vital piece of information people often neglect to include on resumes for federal jobs is their Social Security number. The OPM also requests that your resume or application be brief, so you should include *only* the relevant information. OPM's USAJOBS website also offers a resume builder that helps you create an online resume that contains all the

information required by government agencies. Go to www.usajobs.opm.gov to open an account and post your resume.

Following are the items that your resume must include in order for you to be considered:

Job Information

- Job announcement number
- Job title
- Grade(s) for which you are applying

Personal Information

- Full name and mailing address (including ZIP code)
- Daytime and evening phone numbers (including area code)
- E-mail address, if applicable
- Social Security number
- Country of citizenship
- Veteran's preference, if applicable

Education

You do not need to send a copy of your college transcript unless the job vacancy announcement requests it. However, on your resume, you should include:

- Name, city, state, and ZIP code, if possible, of your high school
- Date you earned your diploma or GED
- Name, city, state, and ZIP code, if possible, of any colleges or universities you attended
- Your major(s), minor(s), and GPA
- Type and year of degree(s) received
- Total number of credits you earned and whether those were earned in semester or quarter hours (if you did not receive a degree)
- Honors you received

Work Experience

Include the following information for all paid and unpaid work experience relating to the job vacancy:

- Job title
- Duties and accomplishments
- Name and address of employer
- Name and phone number of supervisor
- Dates employment began and ended (month and year)
- Number of hours per week
- Salary/wages
- Indicate whether your current supervisor may be contacted
- Indicate whether the job is a federal position

Other Qualifications

The OPM also requests that you provide dates for the following accomplishments. However, do NOT send documentation unless it is specifically requested.

- Job-related training courses you've taken (include course title and year)
- Job-related skills, such as foreign languages or computer software/hardware proficiency
- Current job-related certificates and licenses
- Job-related honors, awards, and special accomplishments, such as membership in a professional or honor society, leadership activities, publications, and performance awards

How to Pitch Your Skills

Since your application often determines whether you get called for the next part of the selection process, it's important that your SF 171, OF 612, or resume highlights how your accomplishments fit into the job requirements.

Some experts recommend that you also indicate the minimum grade level you will accept, keeping in mind that a step down in salary can get your foot in the door and be a stepping stone to regular promotions once you're in the system.

Remember that you will be rated primarily on related education and experience. Even voluntary experience counts, so list all that is relevant (but omit what is not). Look for key words in the job announcement (*teamwork*, for example) and highlight duties and accomplishments that demonstrate to the agency that you have those qualities. The more concrete evidence you provide regarding your qualification, the higher you are likely to be ranked.

Veterans' Preferences and How to Apply

If you've served on active duty in the military, you may be eligible for veterans' preference, which entitles you to an addition of five points—or ten points, if you are a disabled veteran—to your rating in the job selection process. To be eligible, you must show proof that you:

- Have been separated under honorable conditions **or**
- Have a Campaign Badge **or** an Expeditionary Medal (if you began serving after October 15, 1976) **or**
- Have a service-connected disability

To claim the five-point preference, you need to attach as proof of your eligibility a copy of your DD-214, Certificate of Release or Discharge from Active Duty, or other eligible form. For the ten-point preference, you must attach Standard Form 15, the Application for 10-Point Veterans' Preference, and the eligibility proofs it requires.

For more information regarding veterans' preference, go to www.opm.gov and select "Career Opportunities" and then "Veterans" under the employment-related information section.

Steps in the Hiring Process

Each applicant is reevaluated at each stage of the hiring process, and only the most highly qualified are advanced to the next stage, which includes the following steps.

Written Exam

Applicants who meet the education and/or experience requirements will be scheduled for the written test, which is designed to measure reasoning and analytical abilities. The test is approximately four hours in length. Applicants will receive a notice of results within two to three weeks after testing. Applicants who fail the test may retake it during the next open period. Passing scores range from 70 to 100 before the addition of veterans' preference points.

Submission of Further Information

If applicants meet the education/experience requirements and pass the written test, they may be invited for an interview. Prior to the interview, applicants will be asked to provide certain additional information including a resume or more detailed application, an official college transcript, verification of any veterans' preference claimed, and responses to questions relating to overall suitability for federal employment as a Treasury Enforcement Agent. Applicants may be eliminated at this point if information shows that they are ineligible or have a background that is unsuitable for employment or for performance of the required duties; these applicants will not be considered further for employment. Examples of background circumstances that might disqualify an applicant include:

- Employment discharge for cause
- A conviction for an offense that indicates a lack of integrity or respect for law enforcement
- Failure to pay a federal debt where there are no extenuating circumstances

Interview

Interviews for government positions almost always come *after* your agency has already determined that you are otherwise qualified for the job. These interviews often serve more as a final checkpoint in the hiring process than as a first step in the selection process as is the case in the private sector. Most interviewers will go into detail about the type of work the job entails, the benefits of the position, and the procedures of the agency. They will also probably ask questions that will help them ascertain how motivated, cooperative, intelligent, and logical you are, as well as what kind of work habits, goals, and personal values you have.

Give yourself an edge in the interview by showing some knowledge of the agency and its business. During your application process, seek out others in the position you desire. Find out what their work is like and what qualities are valued. If you know something about the position and the agency, you'll demonstrate your interest and your motivation—two characteristics employers value highly.

You'll also more likely to succeed if you're able to comfortably explain any gaps in your education or experience. Tell the truth; you'll be respected if you can admit to past failures or faults, especially if you can explain how you overcame, or plan to overcome, them.

Finally, you should be able to discuss your short- and long-term career goals. Clearly, if your goals are congruent with the goals of the department, you're in a better position to be hired. Here again your research—talking to people already working with the department—and your overall awareness of the business of the agency will help.

Medical and Physical Requirements

Following are the specific medical requirements for special agent positions. All applicants tentatively selected will be required to undergo a medical examination prior to actual placement in the position.

The hiring bureau will provide the required physical examination to the tentative selectees. If selected, the agent may also be required to undergo a periodic physical examination after employment to determine continued fitness for duty.

General Requirements

The duties of these positions have the following general requirements:

- Ability to do moderate to arduous physical exertion involving walking and standing
- Ability and willingness to use firearms
- Ability to withstand exposure to inclement weather
- Manual dexterity with comparatively free motion of fingers, wrists, elbows, shoulders, hips, and knee joints
- Arms, hands, legs, and feet that function well enough for applicants to perform the duties satisfactorily

Vision Requirements

For all positions, the applicant must have:

- Near vision, corrected or uncorrected, sufficient to read Jaeger type 2 at 14 inches
- Normal depth perception and peripheral vision
- The ability to distinguish shades of color by color plate tests

Visual acuity requirements for each bureau listed here are expressed in terms of the Snellen vision test:

- **U.S. Secret Service.** Uncorrected distant vision must test 20/60 in each eye, and corrected distance vision must test 20/20 in each eye
- **ATF.** Uncorrected distant vision must test 20/100 in each eye, and corrected distant vision must test 20/20 in one eye and 20/30 in the other
- **All other bureaus.** Uncorrected distant vision must test 20/200, and corrected distant vision must test 20/20 in one eye and 20/30 in the other

For all positions covered by this standard, applicants who have undergone laser vision correction or other types of surgery to correct vision defects may be disqualified *unless* they can pass special vision tests and an ophthalmologic exam.

Hearing Requirements

For all positions:

- Hearing loss, as measured by an audiometer, must not exceed 30 decibels (A.S.A. or equivalent I.S.O.) in either ear in the 500, 1,000, and 2,000 Hz ranges
- Applicants must be able to hear a whispered voice at 15 feet with each ear without the use of a hearing aid

Special Medical Requirements

Since the duties of these positions involve responsibility for the safety of others under difficult conditions, applicants must be emotionally and mentally stable. Any physical or mental condition that would hinder full, efficient performance of the duties of these positions or that would cause the individual to be a hazard to himself/herself or to others is disqualifying.

Other Evaluations and Conditions of Employment

General Qualification Checks

Because of the vitally important and sensitive nature of the responsibilities of special agents, all selectees must:

- Undergo an income tax record check before appointment and annually thereafter
- Undergo a firearms ability check at the time of appointment and on a periodic basis thereafter
- Carry firearms in the performance of the duties of the position
- Undergo drug testing at the time of appointment and submit to random drug testing thereafter
- Successfully complete a bureau-administered polygraph examination
- Successfully undergo a background investigation

The Treasury Enforcement Agent position requires an employee who not only meets all qualifications criteria and excels in all stages of the hiring process, but also meets certain citizenship standards. That's why you will be asked to fill out a Declaration for Federal Employment (OF 306). This form is used to determine your suitability for working for the federal government and to authorize a background investigation. You must answer personal questions on subjects such as loan defaults, felonies, and misdemeanors. Please note: Answering yes to questions does not automatically disqualify you, but your answers will be taken into consideration during the selection process.

You must also certify that all of the information you've provided is accurate and correct to the best of your knowledge. What you enter on your application will be checked. If investigators find you have falsified information in your application or resume, you may be subject to three possible consequences: you won't be hired; you'll be fired; and/or you may be jailed or fined.

These "checks" may significantly lengthen the hiring process, but they help ensure the safety and well-being of all the citizens who depend on these employees.

Selective Service Registration

All male applicants born after December 31, 1959, are required to complete a preemployment statement of Selective Service registration prior to employment. Failure to comply will prevent any further consideration of your application for employment.

U.S. Citizenship

Upon selection, applicants may be required to provide proof of U.S. citizenship as required by the Immigration Reform and Control Act of 1986.

Good Conduct

Department of the Treasury employees are required to fully comply with the Treasury Standards of Conduct and any established agency-specific standards. All Treasury Enforcement Agent applicants must exhibit impartiality, as demonstrated by the absence of statements or conduct evidencing hatred or prejudice on the basis of race, color, religion, national origin, sex, sexual orientation, age, or disability.

Motor Vehicle Operation

Applicants must possess a valid automobile driver's license at the time of appointment. Candidates must qualify after appointment for authorization to operate motor vehicles in accordance with applicable OPM regulations and related Department of the Treasury requirements.

Travel

This position requires overnight travel on a regular and recurring basis in order to accomplish the duties assigned.

Mobility

Selectees must be available for both temporary assignments and permanent reassignments as the workload and needs of the bureau dictate. Applicants must sign a mobility agreement as a condition of employment.

Sample Application

On the next four pages is a sample OF 612 application form similar to the one you will have to fill out for the positions discussed in this chapter.

You may apply for most Federal jobs with a résumé, an Optional Application for Federal Employment (OF 612), or other written format. If your résumé or application does not provide all the information requested on this form and in the job vacancy announcement, you may lose consideration for a job. Type or print clearly in black ink. Help speed the selection process by keeping your application brief and sending only the requested information. If essential to attach additional pages, include your name and job announcement number on each page.

- Information on Federal employment and the latest information about educational and training provisions are available at www.usajobs.gov or via interactive voice response system: (703) 724-1850 or TDD (978) 461-8404.

- Upon request from the employing Federal agency, you must provide documentation or proof that your degree(s) is from a school accredited by an accrediting body recognized by the Secretary, U.S. Department of Education, or that your education meets the other provisions outlined in the OPM Operating Manual. It will be your responsibility to secure the documentation that verifies that you attended and earned your degree(s) from this accredited institution(s) (e.g., official transcript). Federal agencies will verify your documentation.

  For a list of postsecondary educational institutions and programs accredited by accrediting agencies and state approval agencies recognized by the U.S. Secretary of Education, refer to the U.S. Department of Education Office of Postsecondary Education website at http://www.ope.ed.gov/accreditation/.

  For information on Educational and Training Provisions or Requirements, refer to the OPM Operating Manual available at http://www.opm.gov/qualifications/SEC-II/s2-e4.asp.

- If you served on active duty in the United States Military and were discharged or released from active duty in the armed forces under honorable conditions, you may be eligible for veterans' preference. To receive preference, if your service began after October 15, 1976, you must have a Campaign Badge, Expeditionary Medal, or a service-connected disability. Veterans' preference is not a factor for Senior Executive Service jobs or when competition is limited to status candidates (current or former career or career-conditional Federal employees).

- Most Federal jobs require United States citizenship and also that males over age 18 born after December 31, 1959, have registered with the Selective Service System or have an exemption.

- The law generally prohibits public officials from appointing, promoting, or recommending their relatives.

- Federal annuitants (military and civilian) may have their salaries or annuities reduced. Every employee must pay any valid delinquent debt or the agency may garnish their salary.

- Send your application to the office announcing the vacancy. If you have questions, contact the office identified in the announcement.

How to Apply

1. **Review** the listing of current vacancies.
2. **Decide** which jobs, pay range, and locations interest you.
3. **Follow instructions** provided in the vacancy announcement including any additional forms that are required.

   - You may apply for most jobs with a resume, this form, or any other written format; **all applications must include the information requested in the vacancy announcement as well as information required for all applications for Federal employment** (see below):
   - The USAJOBS website features an online résumé builder. This is a free service that allows you to create a résumé, submit it electronically (for some vacancy announcements), and save it online for use in the future.

Certain information is required to evaluate your qualifications and determine if you meet legal requirements for Federal employment. If your resume or application does not include all the required information as specified below, the agency may not consider you for the vacancy. Help speed the selection process - submit a concise resume' or application and send only the required material.

Information required for all applications for Federal employment:

Job Vacancy Specifics

- Announcement number, title and grade(s) of the job you are applying for

Personal Information

- Full name, mailing address (with zip code) and day and evening phone numbers (with area code) and email address, if applicable
- Social Security Number
- Country of citizenship (most Federal jobs require U.S. citizenship)
- Veterans' preference
- Reinstatement eligibility (for former Federal employees)
- Highest Federal civilian grade held (including job series and dates held)
- Selective Service (if applicable)

Work Experience

- Provide the following information for your paid and volunteer work experience related to the job you are applying for:
  - ► job title (include job series and grade if Federal)
  - ► duties and accomplishments
  - ► employer's name and address
  - ► supervisor's name and telephone number - indicate if supervisor may be contacted
  - ► starting and ending dates (month and year)
  - ► hours per week
  - ► salary

U.S. Office of Personnel Management
Previous edition usable

NSN 7540-01-351-9178
50612-101

OF 612
Revised June 2006

Page 1 of 4

Education

- High School
  - ▶ Name, city, and State (Zip code if known)
  - ▶ Date of diploma or GED
- Colleges or universities
  - ▶ Name, city, and State (Zip code if known)
  - ▶ Majors
  - ▶ Type and year of degrees received. (If no degree, show total credits earned and indicate whether semester or quarter hours.)
- Do not attach a copy of your transcript unless requested
- Do not list degrees received based solely on life experience or obtained from schools with little or no academic standards

Upon request from the employing Federal agency, you must provide documentation or proof that your degree(s) is from a school accredited by an accrediting body recognized by the Secretary, U.S. Department of Education, or that your education meets the other provisions outlined in the OPM Operating Manual. It will be your responsibility to secure the documentation that verifies that you attended and earned your degree(s) from this accredited institution(s) (e.g., official transcript). Federal agencies will verify your documentation.

For a list of postsecondary educational institutions and programs accredited by accrediting agencies and state approval agencies recognized by the U.S. Secretary of Education, refer to the U.S. Department of Education Office of Postsecondary Education website at http://www.ope.ed.gov/accreditation/.

For information on Educational and Training Provisions or Requirements, refer to the OPM Operating Manual available at http://www.opm.gov/qualifications/SEC-II/s2-e4.asp.

Other Education Completed

- School name, city, and State (Zip code if known)
  - ▶ Credits earned and Majors
  - ▶ Type and year of degrees received. (If no degree, show total credits earned and indicate whether semester or quarter hours.)
- Do not list degrees received based solely on life experience or obtained from schools with little or no academic standards

Other Qualifications

- Job-related:
  - ▶ Training (title of course and year)
  - ▶ Skills (e.g., other languages, computer software/hardware, tools, machinery, typing speed, etc.)
  - ▶ Certificates or licenses (current only). Include type of license or certificate, date of latest license, and State or other licensing agency
  - ▶ Honors, awards, and special accomplishments, (e.g., publications, memberships in professional honor societies, leadership activities, public speaking and performance awards) (Give dates but do not send documents unless requested)

Any Other information Specified in the Vacancy Announcement

Privacy Act Statement

The U.S. Office of Personnel Management and other Federal agencies rate applicants for Federal jobs under the authority of sections 1104, 1302, 3301, 3304, 3320, 3361, 3393, and 3394 of title 5 of the United States Code. We need the information requested in this form and in the associated vacancy announcements to evaluate your qualifications. Other laws require us to ask about citizenship, military service, etc. In order to keep your records in order, we request your Social Security Number (SSN) under the authority of Executive Order 9397 which requires the SSN for the purpose of uniform, orderly administration of personnel records. Failure to furnish the requested information may delay or prevent action on your application. We use your SSN to seek information about you from employers, schools, banks, and others who know you. We may use your SSN in studies and computer matching with other Government files. If you do not give us your SSN or any other information requested, we cannot process your application. Also, incomplete addresses and ZIP Codes will slow processing. We may confirm information from your records with prospective nonfederal employers concerning tenure of employment, civil service status, length of service, and date and nature of action for separation as shown on personnel action forms of specifically identified individuals.

Public Burden Statement

We estimate the public reporting burden for this collection will vary from 20 to 240 minutes with an average of 90 minutes per response, including time for reviewing instructions, searching existing data sources, gathering data, and completing and reviewing the information. Send comments regarding the burden statement or any other aspect of the collection of information, including suggestions for reducing this burden to the U.S. Office of Personnel Management (OPM), OPM Forms Officer, Washington, DC 20415-7900. The OMB number, 3206-0219, is currently valid. OPM may not collect this information and you are not required to respond, unless this number is displayed. Do not send completed application forms to this address; follow directions provided in the vacancy announcement(s).

THE FEDERAL GOVERNMENT IS AN EQUAL OPPORTUNITY EMPLOYER

U.S. Office of Personnel Management
Previous edition usable

NSN 7540-01-351-9178
50612-101

OF 612
Revised June 2006

Page 2 of 4

OPTIONAL APPLICATION FOR FEDERAL EMPLOYMENT - OF 612

Form Approved
OMB No. 3206-0219

Section A - Applicant Information

Use Standard State Postal Codes (abbreviations). If outside the United States of America, and you do not have a military address, type or print "OV" in the State field (Block 6c) and fill in the Country field (Block 6e) below, leaving the Zip Code field (Block 6d) blank.

1. Job title in announcement	2. Grade(s) applying for	3. Announcement number
4a. Last name	4b. First and middle names	5. Social Security Number

6a. Mailing address

7. Phone numbers (include area code if within the United States of America)

7a. Daytime

6b. City	6c. State	6d. Zip Code	7b. Evening

6e. Country (if not within the United States of America)

8. Email address (if available)

Section B - Work Experience

Describe your paid and non-paid work experience related to the job for which you are applying. Do not attach job description.

1. Job title (if Federal, include series and grade)

2. From (mm/yyyy)	3. To (mm/yyyy)	4. Salary per $	5. Hours per week

6. Employer's name and address

7. Supervisor's name and phone number

7a. Name

7b. Phone

8. May we contact your current supervisor?   Yes ☐   No ☐
If we need to contact your current supervisor before making an offer, we will contact you first.

9. Describe your duties, accomplishments and related skills (if you need to attach additional pages, include your name, address, and job announcement number)

Section C - Additional Work Experience

1. Job title (if Federal, include series and grade)

2. From (mm/yyyy)	3. To (mm/yyyy)	4. Salary per $	5. Hours per week

6. Employer's name and address

7. Supervisor's name and phone number

7a. Name

7b. Phone

8. May we contact your current supervisor?   Yes ☐   No ☐
If we need to contact your current supervisor before making an offer, we will contact you first.

9. Describe your duties, accomplishments and related skills (if you need to attach additional pages, include your name, address, and job announcement number)

U.S. Office of Personnel Management
Previous edition usable

NSN 7540-01-351-9178
50612-10
Page 3 of 4

OF 612
Revised June 2006

Section D - Education

Upon request from the employing Federal agency, you must provide documentation or proof that your degree(s) is from a school accredited by an accrediting body recognized by the Secretary, U.S. Department of Education, or that your education meets the other provisions outlined in the OPM Operating Manual. It will be your responsibility to secure the documentation that verifies that you attended and earned your degree(s) from this accredited institution(s) (e.g., official transcript). Federal agencies will verify your documentation.

For a list of postsecondary educational institutions and programs accredited by accrediting agencies and state approval agencies recognized by the U.S. Secretary of Education, refer to the U.S. Department of Education Office of Postsecondary Education website at http://www.ope.ed.gov/accreditation/.

For information on Educational and Training Provisions or Requirements, refer to the OPM Operating Manual available at http://www.opm.gov/qualifications/SEC-II/s2-e4.asp.

Do not list degrees received based solely on life experience or obtained from schools with little or no academic standards.

1. Last High School (HS)/GED school. Give the school's name, city, state, ZIP Code (if known), and year diploma or GED received:

2. Mark highest level completed: Some HS ☐   HS/GED ☐   Associate ☐   Bachelor ☐   Master ☐   Doctoral ☐

3. Colleges and universities attended.
   Do not attach a copy of your transcript unless requested.

			Total Credits Earned		Major(s)	Degree (if any), Year Received
			Semester	Quarter		
3a. Name						
City	State	Zip Code				
3b. Name						
City	State	Zip Code				
3c. Name						
City	State	Zip Code				

Section E - Other Education Completed

Do not list degrees received based solely on life experience or obtained from schools with little or no academic standards.

Section F - Other Qualifications

License or Certificate	Date of Latest License or Certificate	State or Other Licensing Agency
1f.		
2f.		

Section G - Other Qualifications

Job-related training courses (give title and year). **Job-related** skills (other languages, computer software/hardware, tools, machinery, typing speed, etc.). **Job-related** honors, awards, and special accomplishments (publications, memberships in professional/honor societies, leadership activities, public speaking, and performance awards). Give dates, but do not send documents unless requested.

Section H - General

1a. Are you a U.S. citizen?   Yes ☐   No ☐ →   1b. If no, give the Country of your citizenship

2a. Do you claim veterans' preference?   Yes ☐   No ☐ → If yes, mark your claim of 5 or 10 points below.

2b. 5 points   ☐ →   Attach your *Report of Separation from Active Duty* (DD 214) or other proof.

2c. 10 points   ☐ →   Attach an *Application for 10-Point Veterans' Preference* (SF 15) and proof required.

3. Check this box if you are an adult male born on or after January 1st 1960, and you registered for Selective Service between the ages of 18 through 25 → ☐

4. Were you ever a Federal civilian employee?   Yes ☐   No ☐ → If yes, list highest civilian grade for the following:

4a. Series	4b. Grade	4c. From *(mm/yyyy)*	4d. To *(mm/yyyy)*

5a. Are you eligible for reinstatement based on career or career-conditional Federal status?   Yes ☐   No ☐
   If requested in the vacancy announcement, attach *Notification of Personnel Action* (SF 50), as proof.

5b. Are you eligible under the ICTAP*?   Yes ☐   No ☐
   *ICTAP (Interagency Career Transition Assistance Plan): A participant in this plan is a current or former federal employee displaced from a Federal agency. To be eligible, you must have received a formal notice of separation such as a RIF separation notice. If you are an ICTAP eligible, normally you will be provided priority consideration for vacancies within your commuting area for which you apply and are well qualified.

Section I - Applicant Certification

I certify that, to the best of my knowledge and belief, all of the information on and attached to this application is true, correct, complete, and made in good faith. I understand that false or fraudulent information on or attached to this application may be grounds for not hiring me or for firing me after I begin work, and may be punishable by fine or imprisonment. I understand that any information I give may be investigated.

1a. Signature	1b. Date *(mm/dd/yyyy)*

Previous edition usable
U.S. Office of Personnel Management

NSN 7540-01-351-9178
50612-10
Page 4 of 4

OF 612
Revised June 2006

2 ▶ FEDERAL LAW ENFORCEMENT TRAINING

CHAPTER SUMMARY

In case you're wondering what will await you if you are accepted as a Treasury Enforcement Agent, this chapter describes the training facilities and programs for trainees at the Federal Law Enforcement Training Center. If you're in college and considering a federal law enforcement career, check out the internship opportunities described in this chapter.

If you're interested in a federal law enforcement career, you probably want to know what awaits you if you are accepted as a Treasury Enforcement Agent. The answer, as for any law enforcement position, is training—lots of training. You'll face classroom study in laws and procedures, physical training, and, of course, training in firearms and the other equipment you'll need to do your job. You might be surprised at some of the subjects you'll be studying—computer surveillance techniques, for instance. Read on to find out more about what awaits you as a federal enforcement agent trainee.

The Federal Law Enforcement Training Center (FLETC)

The Federal Law Enforcement Training Center, a bureau of the Department of Homeland Security, serves as an interagency training organization for over 80 federal agencies, including the four agencies with which this book deals—the U.S. Secret Service, Customs and Immigration Enforcement, the Internal Revenue Service, and the Bureau of Alcohol, Tobacco, Firearms and Explosives. The FLETC employs law enforcement experts; provides facilities, support services, and technical assistance; conducts law enforcement research and development; and shares

Prior to 1970, the quality of training received by federal law enforcement officers and agents varied greatly from agency to agency, and there was a lot of duplication of effort. Two government studies conducted in the late 1960s documented an urgent need for high-quality, cost-effective training, and so the Congress authorized funding for a center to provide such training: the FLETC.

law enforcement technology. The center primarily trains federal officers but also serves the state, local, and international law enforcement communities with training programs tailored to their special needs.

The Training Facilities

The FLETC is distributed over three main campuses. Besides these three campuses, the FLETC also maintains a liaison office near Washington, DC.

The Charleston Center

Situated at the former Charleston Naval Base in South Carolina, this facility is one of the three FLETC residential training centers. Maritime law enforcement training is one of its central features.

The Glynco Center

Glynco is the main campus, located on the southeastern coast of Georgia near Brunswick, between Savannah, Georgia, and Jacksonville, Florida. It occupies 1,500 acres of land and over 100 buildings, all devoted to the many and varied training courses offered by the FLETC.

The Artesia Center

This satellite center between Roswell and Carlsbad, New Mexico, supports programs for agencies located principally in the Southwest. Besides a variety of advanced and specialized programs for the FLETC's other participating organizations, the Artesia center houses the U.S. Bureau of Indian Affairs Indian Police Academy.

The Cheltenham Center

Located in Cheltenham, Maryland, 15 miles outside of Washington, DC, this training center is a nonresidential facility that primarily serves law enforcement officers in the DC area.

Training Programs

Basic Criminal Investigation Training Program

The FLETC offers law enforcement training programs of varying lengths, from basic training to advanced and specialized training, for its participating federal organizations. (Nonparticipating organizations may also attend these programs, on a space-available basis.)

As a trainee for the job of Treasury Enforcement Agent, you'll go through the Basic Criminal Investigation Training Program. Following are examples of the lessons taught in the basic program. The list is not exhaustive, but it will give you some idea of what kinds of subjects you'll be studying when you begin your training, no matter what agency you are hired into. In this basic program, you will receive several hours of instruction on each of the following subjects:

- Basic marksmanship
- Bombs and explosives
- Civil rights
- Computer training for investigation
- Contemporary terrorism
- Crime scene investigation
- Detention and arrest
- Drugs of abuse/narcotics lab

- Electronic communications
- Execution of a search warrant
- Federal courts and procedures
- Fingerprints
- Firearms policy
- Interviewing techniques
- Investigative report writing
- Judgment pistol shooting
- Nonlethal control techniques
- Obstruction of justice/false statements
- Personal protection
- Physical conditioning
- Rapid building entry and search techniques
- Search and seizure
- Sexual harassment and cultural diversity
- Sources of electronic information
- Sources of information (including use of informants)
- Techniques of surveillance

Advanced and Specialized Training

Depending on your assignment, you may also face specialized training at some point in your career. In addition to the basic programs, the FLETC develops and offers advanced and specialized training in subjects that are common to two or more of its participating organizations. Well over 100 different agency-specific programs are conducted at the FLETC, among which are programs devised by and for the four agencies that are the subjects of this book. The courses of study are decided on by the separate agencies—that is, the participating organizations design and help conduct advanced programs to meet their particular training requirements. These courses change somewhat from term to term. The center's resources, support services, and staff expertise assist the organizations in developing and conducting a wide variety of agency-specific training programs. Following are examples of subjects available at the FLETC that the agencies might choose to include in their programs:

- Arrest techniques
- Computer network investigations
- Counterterrorism
- Covert electronic surveillance
- Crisis management
- Critical incident response
- Cyber-counterterrorism
- Firearms training
- Infrastructure protection
- International banking and money laundering
- Land transportation antiterrorism
- Law enforcement control tactics
- Money laundering and asset forfeiture
- Physical security
- Seaport security
- Seized computer and evidence recovery
- Understanding human behavior
- Weapons of mass destruction
- White collar crime

Physical Training

During the training programs, trainees are required to complete the Physical Efficiency Battery (PEB). The PEB consists of five fitness items that are performed during a single physical fitness evaluation session. The PEB measures:

- Body fat (skinfold technique)
- Flexibility (sit and reach test)
- Speed and agility (Illinois agility test)
- Upper body strength (bench press)
- Aerobic capacity (1.5 mile run)

Thereafter, rigorous physical training is an integral part of the entire program.

Firearms Training

The firearms division of FLETC provides training in the safe handling and justifiable use of firearms. You may take instruction in safe handling and application of some of the following:

- Handguns
- Shotguns
- Submachine guns
- Semiautomatic rifles
- Scoped rifles

Firearms courses incorporate the latest instructional methods, techniques, and technology. Various instructional methodologies including conferences, lectures, role playing, demonstrations, discussions, and practical exercises are used. The topics covered in advanced courses include:

- Firearms safety rules and regulations
- Trauma management
- Basic marksmanship instruction (revolver)
- Target analysis
- Semiautomatic lecture/laboratory
- Advanced shotgun techniques
- Rifle lecture/laboratory
- Tactical speed shooting techniques
- Downed/disabled officer course
- Judgment pistol shooting
- Handgun/shotgun stress
- Instinctive reaction
- Advanced handgun/shotgun stress
- Dual assailant
- Submachine gun familiarization
- Ballistics
- Off-range safety
- Officer survival

Student Internship Program

The FLETC also has a college intern program offered three times yearly. Each session is 12 weeks in length. An intern participates in a 50/50 program. He or she is assigned to a supervisor in a FLETC division or to a supervisor with a participating agency for work assignments that take approximately half the intern's time. The other half of the intern's time is devoted to auditing classes and activities in one of the FLETC's training programs.

Benefits

Interns get real work, as well as access to the FLETC's training and recreational facilities. Interns also receive $31 per day (seven days per week) of taxable income to help defray the cost of meals, incidental expenses, and travel. Interns are required to live at the FLETC facility and are provided dormitory accommodations at no cost. Interns receive mandatory unifroms for training and physical conditioning.

Qualifications

You might expect that internships are offered to Criminal Justice majors. That's true, but intern opportunities are available to majors in Forensic Sciences, Psychology, or Computer Forensics as well. Students with other academic focuses may also be selected for the program if they demonstrate a strong interst in a federal law enforcement career. Seniors interested in applying must be currently enrolled, must have completed 135 quarter hours or 90 semester hours of a baccalaureate program, and must be in the upper third of their class academically.

Students enrolled in a graduate program may also apply. In either undergraduate or graduate programs, the internship must be completed as part of the student's academic requirements and done prior to graduation. Selection is highly competitive and is based upon grade point averages (major and overall), leadership and community participation, work experiences, professional experiences related to the applicant's major, a narrative essay, a nomination form, and a telephone interview.

How to Apply

To apply, intern applicants must:

- Complete a Form OF 612 (Application for Government Employment) or resume
- Complete an Intern Application and narrative essay
- Submit official college transcript(s)
- Have an appropriate college official complete an Intern Nomination form
- Show proof that the internship is required for completeing the degree

If you are interested in this program, you should send for an application package or information from:

Human Resources Division
FLETC
1131 Chapel Crossing Road
Building 46
Glynco, GA 31524
912-261-4162
www.fletc.gov/twd/college_intern_program.htm

For More Information

More information on FLETC training can be obtained by writing or calling the national office or the FLETC office associated with the agency you're applying with.

Senior Associate Director
FLETC
555 11th Street, NW
Suite 400
Washington, DC 20004
202-927-8940

FLETC Chief, Alcohol, Tobacco, Firearms and Explosives
National Academy, Trlr. 761
1131 Chapel Crossing Road
Glynco, GA 31524

FLETC Assistant Special Agent in Charge, U.S. Secret Service
Building TH 386B
1131 Chapel Crossing Road
Glynco, GA 31524

FLETC Director, U.S. Immigration and Customs Enforcement Academy
Building 68
1131 Chapel Crossing Road
Glynco, GA 31524

FLETC Director, Internal Revenue Service, National Criminal Investigation Training Academy
Building 69
1131 Chapel Crossing Road
Glynco, GA 31524

3 ▶ OFFICIAL SAMPLE QUESTIONS

CHAPTER SUMMARY
This chapter consists of official explanations and sample questions provided by the Department of the Treasury for the TEA exam.

The U.S. Office of Personnel Management describes the test as a "written abilities test." The test consists of five parts.

Part A consists of 25 Verbal Reasoning questions. You are allowed 50 minutes to complete these questions. It is to your advantage to answer all 25 questions, because there is no penalty for incorrect answers. If you are unsure of an answer, make the best choice that you can by guessing.

Part B consists of 20 Arithmetic Reasoning questions. You are allowed 50 minutes to complete these questions. It is to your advantage to answer all 20 questions, because there is no penalty for incorrect answers. If you are unsure of an answer, make the best choice that you can by guessing.

Part C consists of 30 Problems for Investigation. You are allowed 60 minutes to complete these problems. It is to your advantage to answer all 30 problems, because there is no penalty for incorrect answers. Use only the information given in the problem; do NOT use knowledge gained from any previous law enforcement experience you may have. If you are unsure of your answer, select the best choice that you can.

Parts D and E are described as an "Applicant Experience Questionnaire." It consists of 70 questions designed to highlight skills, achievements, and experience. It is to your advantage to answer all 70 questions.

Sample Questions for Test 546 and Test 548

This chapter provides samples of the types of questions found in Test 546 and Test 548. Each test is divided into three parts: Part A, Verbal Reasoning; Part B, Arithmetic Reasoning; and Part C, Problems for Investigation. The sample questions in this lesson are similar to the questions you will find in the actual tests in terms of difficulty and form.

Part A—Verbal Reasoning Questions

In each of these questions, you will be given a paragraph that contains all the information necessary to infer the correct answer. Use **only** the information provided in the paragraph. Do not speculate or make assumptions that go beyond this information. Also, assume that all information given in the paragraph is true, even if it conflicts with some fact known to you. Only one correct answer can be validly inferred from the information contained in the paragraph.

Pay special attention to negated verbs (for example, "are *not*") and negative prefixes (for example, "*in*complete" or "*dis*organized"). Also, pay special attention to quantifiers, such as "all," "none," and "some." For example, from a paragraph in which it is stated that "it is not true that all contracts are legal," one can validly infer that "some contracts are not legal," or that "some contracts are illegal," or that "some illegal things are contracts," but one **cannot** validly infer that "no contracts are legal" or that "some contracts are legal." Similarly, from a paragraph that states "all contracts are legal" and "all contracts are two-sided agreements," one can infer that "some two-sided agreements are legal," but one **cannot** validly infer that "all two-sided agreements are legal."

Bear in mind that, in some tests, universal quantifiers such as "all" and "none" often give away incorrect response choices. That is not the case in this test. Some correct answers will refer to "all" or "none" of the members of a group.

Be sure to distinguish between essential information and unessential, peripheral information. That is to say, in a real test question, the previous example ("all contracts are legal" and "all contracts are two-sided agreements") would appear in a longer, full-fledged paragraph. It would be up to you to separate the essential information from its context, and then to realize that a response choice that states "some two-sided agreements are legal" represents a valid inference and hence the correct answer.

Sample questions 1 and 2 are examples of the verbal reasoning questions on each test.

1. Impressions made by the ridges on the ends of the fingers and thumbs are useful means of identification, since no two persons have the same pattern of ridges. If finger patterns from fingerprints are not decipherable, then they cannot be classified by general shape and contour or by pattern type. If they cannot be classified by these characteristics, then it is impossible to identify the person to whom the fingerprints belong.

The paragraph best supports the statement that
a. if it is impossible to identify the person to whom fingerprints belong, then the fingerprints are not decipherable.
b. if finger patterns from fingerprints are not decipherable, then it is impossible to identify the person to whom the fingerprints belong.
c. if fingerprints are decipherable, then it is impossible to identify the person to whom they belong.
d. if fingerprints can be classified by general shape and contour or by pattern type, then they are not decipherable.
e. if it is possible to identify the person to whom fingerprints belong, then the fingerprints cannot be classified by general shape and contour or pattern.

The correct answer is choice **b**. The essential information from which the answer can be inferred is contained in the second and third sentences. These sentences state that "if finger patterns from fingerprints are not decipherable, then they cannot be classified by general shape and contour or by pattern type. If they cannot be classified by these characteristics, then it is impossible to identify the person to whom they belong." Since choice **b** refers to a condition in which finger patterns from fingerprints are not decipherable, we know that, in that circumstance, they cannot be classified by general shape and contour or by pattern type. From the paragraph, we can infer that since they cannot be classified by these characteristics, it is impossible to identify the person to whom the fingerprints belong.

Choice **a** cannot be inferred because the paragraph does not give information about all the circumstances under which it is impossible to identify the person to whom the fingerprints belong. It may be that the person is not identifiable for reasons other than the decipherability of the person's fingerprints.

Choice **c** is incorrect because the paragraph does not provide enough information to conclude whether it would be possible to identify the person to whom the fingerprints belong from the mere fact of the decipherability of the fingerprints.

Choice **d** is incorrect because it contradicts the information in the second sentence of the paragraph. From that sentence, it can be concluded that if fingerprints can be classified by general shape and contour or by pattern type, they are decipherable.

Choice **e** is incorrect for a similar reason; it contradicts the information presented in the third sentence of the paragraph.

2. Law enforcement agencies use scientific techniques to identify suspects or to establish guilt. One obvious application of such techniques is the examination of a crime scene. Some substances found at a crime scene yield valuable clues under microscopic examination. Clothing fibers, dirt particles, and even pollen grains may reveal important information to the careful investigator. Nothing can be overlooked because all substances found at a crime scene are potential sources of evidence.

The paragraph best supports the statement that
a. all substances that yield valuable clues under microscopic examination are substances found at a crime scene.
b. some potential sources of evidence are substances that yield valuable clues under microscopic examination.
c. some substances found at a crime scene are not potential sources of evidence.
d. no potential sources of evidence are substances found at a crime scene.
e. some substances that yield valuable clues under microscopic examination are not substances found at a crime scene.

The correct answer is choice **b**. The essential information from which the answer can be inferred is contained in the third and fifth sentences. The third sentence tells us that "some substances found at a crime scene yield valuable clues under microscopic examination." The fifth sentence explains that "all substances found at a crime scene are potential sources of evidence." Therefore, we can conclude that "some potential sources of evidence are substances that yield valuable clues under microscopic examination."

Choice **a** cannot be inferred because the paragraph does not support the statement that all substances that yield valuable clues are found exclusively at a crime scene. It may be that valuable clues could be found elsewhere.

Choices **c** and **d** are incorrect because they contradict the fifth sentence of the paragraph, which clearly states "all substances found at a crime scene are potential sources of evidence."

Choice **e** is incorrect because the paragraph provides no information about the value of substances found somewhere other than at the crime scene.

Part B—Arithmetic Reasoning Questions

In this part, you will have to solve problems formulated in both verbal and numeric form. You will have to analyze a paragraph in order to set up the problem, and then solve it. If the exact answer is not given as one of the response choices, you should select choice **e**, "none of these." Sample questions 3 and 4 are examples of the arithmetic reasoning questions in each test. The use of calculators will **NOT** be permitted during the actual testing; therefore, they should not be used to solve these sample questions.

3. A police department purchases badges at $16 each for all the graduates of the police training academy. The last training class graduated ten new officers. What is the total amount of money the department will spend on badges for these new officers?
   a. $70
   b. $116
   c. $160
   d. $180
   e. none of these

The correct answer is choice **c**. It can be obtained by computing the following:

$$16 \times 10 = 160$$

The badges are priced at $16 each. The department must purchase ten of them for the new officers. Multiplying the price of one badge ($16) by the number of graduates (10) gives the total price for all of the badges.

Choices **a**, **b**, and **d** are the results of erroneous computations.

4. An investigator rented a car for six days and was charged $450. The car rental company charged $35 per day plus $.30 per mile driven. How many miles did the investigator drive the car?
   a. 800
   b. 900
   c. 1,290
   d. 1,500
   e. none of these

The correct answer is choice **a**. It can be obtained by computing the following:

$$6(35) + .30x = 450$$

The investigator rented the car for six days at $35 per day, which is $210; $210 subtracted from the total charge of $450 leaves $240, the portion of the total charge that was expended for the miles driven. This amount divided by the charge per mile ($240 ÷ .30) gives the number of miles (800) driven by the investigator.

Choices **b**, **c**, and **d** are the results of erroneous computations.

Part C—Problems for Investigation

In this part, you will be presented with a paragraph and several related statements. Sample questions 5 through 9 are based on the following paragraph and statements. Read them carefully and then answer questions 5 through 9.

On October 30, the Belton First National Bank discovered that the $3,000 it had received that morning from the Greenville First National Bank was in counterfeit $10, $20, and $50 bills. The genuine $3,000 had been counted by Greenville First National Bank clerk Iris Stewart the preceding afternoon. The bills were packed in eight black leather satchels and stored in the bank vault overnight. Greenville First National clerk, Brian Caruthers, accompanied carriers James Clark and Howard O'Keefe to Belton in an armored truck. Belton First National clerk Cynthia Randall discovered the counterfeit bills when she examined the serial numbers of the bills.

During the course of the investigation, the following statements were made:

(1) Gerald Hathaway, clerk of the Greenville bank, told investigators that he had found the bank office open when he arrived at work on the morning of October 30. The only articles that appeared to be missing were eight black leather satchels of the type used to transport large sums of money.

(2) Jon Perkins, head teller of the Greenville bank, told investigators that he did not check the contents of the black leather satchels after locking them in the vault around 4:30 P.M. on October 29.

(3) Henry Green, janitor of the Greenville bank, said that he noticed Jon Perkins leaving the bank office around 5:30 P.M., one-half hour after the bank closed on October 29. He said that Perkins locked the door.

(4) A scrap of cloth, identical to the material of the carriers' uniforms, was found caught in the seal of one of the black leather satchels delivered to Belton.

(5) Brian Caruthers, clerk, said he saw James Clark and Howard O'Keefe talking in a secretive manner in the armored truck.

(6) Thomas Stillman, Greenville bank executive, identified the eight black leather satchels containing the counterfeit money, which arrived at the Belton First National Bank, as the eight satchels that had disappeared from the bank office. He had noticed a slight difference in the linings of the satchels.

(7) Virginia Fowler, bank accountant, noticed two $10 bills with the same serial numbers as the lost bills in a bank deposit from Ferdinand's Restaurant of Greenville.

(8) Vincent Johnson, manager of Ferdinand's Restaurant, told police that Iris Stewart frequently dined there with her boyfriend.

5. Which one of the following statements best indicates that satchels containing the counterfeit bills were substituted for satchels containing genuine bills while they were being transported from Greenville to Belton?
   a. Statement 1
   b. Statement 3
   c. Statement 4
   d. Statement 5
   e. Statement 7

6. Which one of the following statements best links the information given in Statement 1 with the substitution of the counterfeit bills?
   a. Statement 2
   b. Statement 3
   c. Statement 4
   d. Statement 5
   e. Statement 6

7. Which one of the following statements, along with Statement 7, best indicates that the substitution of the counterfeit bills casts suspicion on at least one employee of the Greenville bank?
   a. Statement 1
   b. Statement 2
   c. Statement 3
   d. Statement 5
   e. Statement 8

8. Which one of the following statements would least likely be used in proving a case?
a. Statement 1
b. Statement 3
c. Statement 4
d. Statement 5
e. Statement 7

9. Which one of the following statements best indicates that the substitution of the counterfeit bills could have taken place before the satchels left the Greenville bank?
a. Statement 1
b. Statement 2
c. Statement 3
d. Statement 4
e. Statement 7

Here are the answers for questions 5 through 9:

5. c.
6. e.
7. e.
8. d.
9. d.

4 ▶ THE LEARNINGEXPRESS TEST PREPARATION SYSTEM

CHAPTER SUMMARY

Taking the Treasury Enforcement Exam exam can be difficult. It demands a lot of preparation if you want to achieve a top score, and you need a good score if you want to be hired as a Treasury Enforcement Agent. The LearningExpress Test Preparation System, developed exclusively for LearningExpress by leading test experts, gives you the discipline and attitude you need to be successful.

Taking the TEA exam is no picnic, and neither is getting ready for it. Your future career as a Treasury Enforcement Agent depends on your getting a high score, but there are all sorts of pitfalls that can keep you from doing your best on this all-important exam. Here are some of the obstacles that can stand in the way of your success:

- Being unfamiliar with the format of the exam
- Being paralyzed by test anxiety
- Leaving your preparation to the last minute
- Not preparing at all!
- Not knowing vital test-taking skills: how to pace yourself through the exam, how to use the process of elimination, and when to guess
- Not being in tip-top mental and physical shape
- Being unprepared on test day by arriving late at the test site, skipping breakfast, or not dressing comfortably

What's the common denominator in all these test-taking pitfalls? One word: control.

Fortunately, the LearningExpress Test Preparation System helps puts you in control. In just nine easy-to-follow steps, you will learn everything you need to know to make sure that you are in charge of your preparation and your performance on the exam. You will have taken all the steps you need to take to get a high score on the TEA exam.

We estimate that working through the entire system will take you approximately three hours, though it's perfectly okay if you work faster or slower than the time estimates assume. If you can take a whole afternoon or evening, you can work through the whole LearningExpress Test Preparation System in one sitting. Otherwise, you can break it up, and do just one or two steps a day for the next several days. It's up to you—remember, you're in control.

Step 1. Get Information	50 minutes
Step 2. Conquer Test Anxiety	20 minutes
Step 3. Make a Plan	25 minutes
Step 4. Learn to Manage Your Time	10 minutes
Step 5. Learn to Use the Process of Elimination	20 minutes
Step 6. Know When to Guess	20 minutes
Step 7. Reach Your Peak Performance Zone	10 minutes
Step 8. Get Your Act Together	10 minutes
Step 9. Do It!	5 minutes
TOTAL	**3 HOURS**

Here's how the LearningExpress Test Preparation System works: Nine easy steps lead you through everything you need to know and do to get ready to master your exam. Each of the following steps includes both reading about the step and one or more activities. It's important that you do the activities along with the reading, or you won't be getting the full benefit of the system. Each step tells you approximately how much time that step will take you to complete.

Step 1: Get Information

Time to complete: 50 minutes
Activities: Use the following suggestions to find out about the content of your exam

Knowledge is power. The first step in the LearningExpress Test Preparation System is finding out everything you can about the TEA exam. Once you have your information, the next steps in the LearningExpress Test Preparation System will show you what to do about it.

Part A: Straight Talk about the TEA Exam

Why do you have to take this exam? The U.S. Office of Personnel Management describes the TEA exam as a "written abilities test," and for that reason, the test is extremely important. If an applicant cannot communicate in writing or readily understand written communications, then that applicant simply cannot handle the important duties inherent in positions with the Departments of the Treasury or Homeland Security. It's as simple as that. Fortunately, with the help of this book, you can vastly improve your communications skills.

Of course, there are all sorts of things a written exam like this can't test. So keep some perspective when you take this exam. Don't make the mistake of thinking that your score determines who you are or how smart you are or whether you'll make a good Treasury Enforcement Agent. However, how you do on the exam is still vitally important to you because your chances of being hired depend on your score. And that's why you're here—using the LearningExpress Test Preparation System to achieve control over your exam.

Part B: What's on the Test

If you haven't already done so, stop here and read the first lesson of this book, which gives you vital information on the TEA exam. The TEA exam is given at irregular times, so it is vitally important that you check with one of the information numbers in Lesson 1. Note that all openings have a *filing period* or *application window*, a specific time period during which applications will be accepted, and it is extremely important that you find out what that window is or you might have to wait for the next opportunity.

The TEA exam tests the skills reflected in the practice exams in this book:

- **Verbal Reasoning**: demonstrating skills in understanding the literal meaning of a written passage and making inferences from what you read

- **Arithmetic Reasoning**: reasoning through word problems and demonstrating basic math skills
- **Problems for Investigation**: demonstrating your ability to use both common sense and intuition as you analyze a problem, and your ability to maintain your objectivity until all the facts are in

Step 2: Conquer Test Anxiety

Time to complete: 20 minutes
Activity: Take the Test Stress Test

Having complete information about the exam is the first step in getting control of the exam. Next, you have to overcome one of the biggest obstacles to test success: test anxiety. Test anxiety can not only impair your performance on the exam itself but can even keep you from preparing. In Step 2, you'll learn stress management techniques that will help you succeed on your exam. Learn these strategies now, and practice them as you work through the exams in this book, so they'll be second nature to you by exam day.

Combating Test Anxiety

The first thing you need to know is that a little test anxiety is a good thing. Everyone gets nervous before a big exam—and if that nervousness motivates you to prepare thoroughly, so much the better. The key is to keep stress at a level that does not impair your peformance, but rather gives you a little extra edge—just the kind of edge you need to do well in an examination room.

On page 35 is the Test Stress Test. Stop here and answer the questions on that page, to find out whether your level of test anxiety is something you should worry about.

Stress Management before the Test

If you feel your level of anxiety getting the best of you in the weeks before the test, here is what you need to do to bring the level down again:

- **Get prepared.** There's nothing like knowing what to expect and being prepared for it to put you in control of test anxiety. That's why you're reading this book. Use it faithfully, and remind yourself that you're better prepared than most of the people taking the test.
- **Practice self-confidence.** A positive attitude is a great way to combat test anxiety. Say to yourself, "I'm prepared. I'm full of self-confidence. I'm going to ace this test. I know I can do it." Say it into a tape recorder and play it back once a day. If you hear it often enough, you'll believe it.
- **Fight negative messages.** Every time someone starts telling you how hard the exam is or how it's almost impossible to get a high score, respond by using your self-confidence messages listed above. If the someone with the negative messages is *you*, telling yourself *you don't do well on exams, you just can't do this,* don't listen. Turn on your tape recorder and listen to your self-confidence messages.
- **Visualize.** Imagine yourself boarding the plane that will take you to your first special agent assignment. Think of yourself coming home with your first paycheck as a Treasury Enforcement Agent and taking your family or friends out to celebrate. Visualizing success can help make it happen—and it reminds you of why you're working hard to prepare for the exam.
- **Exercise.** Physical activity helps calm your body down and focus your mind. Besides, being in good physical shape can actually help you do well on the exam. Go for a run, lift weights, go swimming—and do it regularly.

Stress Management on Test Day

There are several ways you can bring down your level of test anxiety on test day. They'll work best if you practice them in the weeks before the test, so you know which ones work best for you.

- **Deep breathing.** Take a deep breath while you count to five. Hold the deep breath for the count of one, then let it out on a count of five. Repeat several times.
- **Move your body.** Try rolling your head in a circle. Rotate your shoulders. Shake your hands from the wrist. Many people find these movements very relaxing.
- **Visualize again.** Think of the place where you are most relaxed: lying on the beach in the sun, walking through the park, or whatever. Now close your eyes and imagine you're actually there. If you practice in advance, you'll find that you need only a few seconds of this exercise to experience a significant increase in your sense of well-being.

When anxiety threatens to overwhelm you right there during the exam, there are still things you can do to manage the stress level:

- **Repeat your self-confidence messages.** You should have them memorized by now. Say them quietly to yourself, and believe them.
- **Visualize one more time.** This time, visualize yourself moving smoothly and quickly through the test, answering every question right and finishing just before time is up. Like most visualization techniques, this one works best if you've practiced it ahead of time.
- **Find an easy question.** Skim over the test until you find an easy question, and answer it. Getting even one circle filled in gets you into the test-taking groove.
- **Take a mental break.** Everyone loses concentration once in a while during a long test. It's normal,

Test Stress Test

You need to worry about test anxiety only if it is extreme enough to impair your performance. The following questionnaire will provide a diagnosis of your level of test anxiety. In the blank before each statement, write the number that most accurately describes your experience.

0 = Never   1 = Once or twice   2 = Sometimes   3 = Often

_____ I have gotten so nervous before an exam that I simply put down the books and didn't study for it.

_____ I have experienced disabling physical symptoms such as vomiting and severe headaches because I was nervous about an exam.

_____ I have simply not showed up for an exam because I was scared to take it.

_____ I have experienced dizziness and disorientation while taking an exam.

_____ I have had trouble filling in the little circles because my hands were shaking too hard.

_____ I have failed an exam because I was too nervous to complete it.

_____ **Total: Add up the numbers in the blanks above.**

Your Test Stress Score

Here are the steps you should take, depending on your score. If you scored:

- **Below 3,** your level of test anxiety is nothing to worry about; it's probably just enough to give you that little extra edge.
- **Between 3 and 6,** your test anxiety may be enough to impair your performance, and you should practice the stress management techniques listed in this section to try to bring your test anxiety down to manageable levels.
- **Above 6,** your level of test anxiety is a serious concern. In addition to practicing the stress management techniques listed in this section, you may want to seek additional, personal help. Call your local high school or community college and ask for the academic counselor. Tell the counselor that you have a level of test anxiety that sometimes keeps you from being able to take the exam. The counselor may be willing to help you or may suggest someone else you should talk to.

so you shouldn't worry about it. Instead, accept what has happened. Say to yourself, "Hey, I lost it there for a minute. My brain is taking a break." Put down your pencil, close your eyes, and do some deep breathing for a few seconds. Then you're ready to go back to work.

Try these techniques ahead of time so that they will be effective on exam day.

Step 3: Make a Plan

Time to complete: 25 minutes
Activity: Construct a study plan

Maybe the most important thing you can do to get control of yourself and your exam is to make a study plan. Too many people fail to prepare simply because they fail to plan. Spending hours on the day before the exam poring over sample test questions not only raises your level of test anxiety, but it also is simply no substitute for careful preparation and practice over time.

Don't fall into the cram trap. Take control of your preparation time by mapping out a study schedule. All the instructional material you will need to study for the TEA exam is in Lesson 3 ("Sample Questions") and Lessons 6 through 8, so a study schedule is built into the system. The best way to devise your study plan is to first do the diagnostic TEA exam in Lesson 5 of this book, and then base your plan on your scores in the individual sections, concentrating on the areas that give you the most trouble.

On the following pages are schedules of what you should do when, based on how much time you have before you take the exam.

Even more important than making a plan is making a commitment. You can't improve your reading, math, or problem-solving skills overnight. You have to set aside some time every day for study and practice. Try for at least 30 minutes a day. Thirty minutes daily will do you much more good than two hours on Saturday.

If you have months before the exam, you're lucky. Don't put off your study until the week before the exam. Start now. A few minutes a day, with half an hour or more on weekends, can make a big difference in your score—and in your chances of getting a Treasury Enforcement Agent job!

Schedule A: The Leisure Plan

If you have six months or more in which to prepare, you're lucky! Make the most of your time.

TIME	PREPARATION
Exam minus 6 months	Take the diagnostic TEA exam in Chapter 5 and skim the sample questions in Chapter 3 and instructional Chapters 6, 7, and 8. Based on your scores on the individual sections of the diagnostic exam, divide up the next six months into segments of time that you estimate each chapter will take. Be sure to schedule in more time on those skills that give you problems.
Exam minus 6 months to 2 months	Work steadily and calmly through each chapter, sticking to your schedule and being sure to do the practice exercises. Besides working through the chapters, be sure to read more during these months than you are accustomed to—novels, non-fiction books, magazines, newspapers; it is very important for the TEA exam that your reading skills be honed.
Exam minus 2 months	Take the first practice exam. Use your score to help you decide where to concentrate your efforts. Review the relevant instructional chapters and get the help of a friend or teacher.
Exam minus 2 weeks	Take the second practice test to see how much you've improved, and then, again, review the areas that give you the most trouble.
Exam minus 1 day	Relax. Do something unrelated to the exam. Eat a good meal and go to bed at your usual time.

Schedule B: The Just-Enough-Time Plan

If you have three to five months before the exam, that should be enough time to prepare for the written test. This schedule assumes four months; stretch it out or compress it if you have more or less time.

TIME	PREPARATION
Exam minus 4 months	Take the diagnostic TEA exam in Chapter 5 and skim the sample questions in Chapter 3 and instructional Chapters 6, 7, and 8. Based on your scores on the individual sections of the diagnostic exam, divide up the next four months into segments of time that you estimate each chapter will take. Be sure to schedule in more time on those skills that give you problems.
Exam minus 4 months to 1 month	Work steadily and calmly through each chapter, sticking to your schedule and being sure to do the practice exercises. Besides working through the chapters, schedule in more reading during these months than you are used to doing—novels, nonfiction books, magazines, newspapers; it is very important for the TEA exam that your reading skills be in top shape. If you fall behind in your schedule, remember that you're in control—it's your schedule. Don't undermine your efforts by thinking, "I'll never make it!" Just take a look at the schedule, see where you went awry, revise the schedule for the time you have left, and continue.
Exam minus 2 months	Take the first practice exam. Use your score to help you decide where to concentrate your efforts. Review the relevant instructional chapters and get the help of a friend or teacher.
Exam minus 2 weeks	Take the second practice test to see how much you've improved, and then, again, review the areas that give you the most trouble.
Exam minus 1 day	Relax. Do something unrelated to the exam. Eat a good meal and go to bed at your usual time.

Schedule C: More Study in Less Time

If you have one to three months before the exam, you still have enough time for some concentrated study that will help you improve your score. This schedule is built around a two-month timeframe. If you have only one month, spend an extra couple of hours a week to get all these steps in. If you have three months, take some of the steps from Schedule B and fit them in.

TIME	PREPARATION
Exam minus 2 months	Take the diagnostic TEA exam in Chapter 5 and skim the sample questions in Chapter 3 and instructional Chapters 6, 7, and 8. Based on your scores on the individual sections of the diagnostic exam, divide up the next month into segments of time that you estimate each lesson will take. Be sure to schedule in more time on those skills that give you problems.

TIME	PREPARATION
Exam minus 2 months to exam minus 1 month	Work quickly, but steadily and calmly, through each lesson, sticking to your schedule and being sure to do the practice exercises. Besides working through the instructional lessons, schedule in more reading than you usually do—novels, non-fiction books, magazines, newspapers; it is crucial for the TEA exam that your reading skills be their sharpest. If you fall behind in your schedule, remember that you are the one who devised the schedule, and you're in control. Look over your schedule, see where you got off track, revise the schedule for the time you have left, and forge ahead.
Exam minus 2 weeks	Take the first practice exam. Use your score to help you decide where to concentrate your efforts. Review the relevant instructional chapters and get the help of a friend or teacher.
Exam minus 1 week	Take the second practice test to see how much you've improved, and then, again, review the areas that give you the most trouble.
Exam minus 1 day	Relax. Do something unrelated to the exam. Eat a good meal and go to bed at your usual time.

Schedule D: The Short-Term Plan

If you have three weeks or less before the exam, you really have your work cut out for you. Carve an hour out of your day, *every day*, for study. This schedule assumes you have the whole three weeks to prepare; if you have less time, you'll have to compress the schedule accordingly.

TIME	PREPARATION
Exam minus 3 weeks	Take the diagnostic TEA exam in Chapter 5 and skim the sample questions in Chapter 3 and instructional Chapters 6, 7, and 8. Based on your score, choose one area to concentrate on this week: reading, math, or problems for investigation. Spend an hour a day working on that area.
Exam minus 2 weeks	First, skim over the instructional chapters on the areas you didn't study last week. Choose several exercises to do in the first three days of this week. For the rest of the days, go back to the one area you need the most work on, and review the chapter that was most difficult for you.
Exam minus 1 week	Take the first practice exam. Use your score to help you decide where to concentrate your efforts. Review the relevant chapter and get the help of a friend or teacher on those areas.
Exam minus 3 days	Take the second practice test to see how much you've improved, and then, again, review the areas that give you the most trouble.
Exam minus 1 day	Relax. Do something unrelated to the exam. Eat a good meal and go to bed at your usual time.

Step 4: Learn to Manage Your Time

Time to complete: 10 minutes to read, many hours of practice

Activities: Practice these strategies as you take the sample tests in this book

Steps 4, 5, and 6 of the LearningExpress Test Preparation System put you in charge of your exam by showing you test-taking strategies that work. Practice these strategies as you take the sample tests in this book, and then you'll be ready to use them on test day.

First, you'll take control of your time on the exam. The TEA exam (Parts A, B, and C) has a time limit of two hours 40 minutes, which may give you more than enough time to complete all the questions—or may not. It's a terrible feeling to hear the examiner say, "Five minutes left," when you're only three-quarters of the way through the test. Here are some tips to keep that from happening to *you*.

- **Follow directions.** If the directions are given orally, listen to them. If they're written on the exam booklet, read them carefully. Ask questions *before* the exam begins if there's anything you don't understand. In your exam booklet, write down the beginning time and the ending time of each part of the exam.
- **Pace yourself.** Glance at your watch every ten or 15 minutes, and compare the time to how far you've gotten in the exam. When one-quarter of the time has elapsed, you should be a quarter of the way through the exam, and so on. If you're falling behind, pick up the pace a bit.
- **Keep moving.** Don't get stuck on one question. If you don't know the answer, skip the question and move on. Circle the number of the question in your test booklet in case you have time to come back to it later.
- **Keep track of your place on the answer sheet.** If you skip a question, make sure you skip on the answer sheet, too. Check yourself every five to ten questions to make sure the question number and the answer sheet number are still the same.
- **Don't rush.** Although you should keep moving, rushing won't help. Try to keep calm and work methodically and quickly.

Step 5: Learn to Use the Process of Elimination

Time to complete: 20 minutes

Activity: Complete worksheet on Using the Process of Elimination

After time management, your next most important tool for taking control of your exam is using the process of elimination wisely. It's standard test-taking wisdom that you should always read all the answer choices before choosing your answer. This helps you find the right answer by eliminating wrong answer choices. And, sure enough, that standard wisdom applies to your exam, too.

Let's say you're facing a reading comprehension question that goes like this:

13. According to the passage above, "Biology uses a *binomial* system of classification." In the context of the passage, the word *binomial* most nearly means
  a. understanding the law.
  b. having two names.
  c. scientifically sound.
  d. having a double meaning.

If you happen to know what *binomial* means, of course, you don't need to use the process of elimination, but let's assume that you don't. Look over the answer choices. "Understanding the law" doesn't sound likely for something having to do with biology. So you eliminate choice **a**—and now you only have three answer choices to deal with. Mark an **X** next to choice **a** so you never have to read it again.

On to the other answer choices: If you know that the prefix *bi-* means *two,* as in *bicycle,* you'll flag choice **b** as a possible answer. Mark a check mark beside it, meaning "good answer, I might use this one."

Choice **c**, "scientifically sound," is a possibility. At least it's about science, not law. It could work here, though, when you think about it, having a "scientifically sound" classification system in a scientific field is kind of redundant. You remember the *bi* thing in *binomial,* and probably continue to like choice **b** better. But you're not sure, so you put a question mark next to choice **c**, meaning "well, maybe."

Now, choice **d**, "having a double meaning." You're still keeping in mind that *bi-* means *two,* so this one looks possible at first. But then you look again at the sentence the word belongs in, and you think, "Why would biology want a system of classification that has two meanings? That wouldn't work very well!" If you're really taken with the idea that *bi* means *two,* you might put a question mark here. But if you're feeling a little more confident, you'll put an **X**. You've already got a better answer picked out.

Now your question looks like this:

13. According to the passage above, "Biology uses a binomial system of classification." In the context of the passage, the word binomial most nearly means
  X **a.** understanding the law.
  ✔ **b.** having two names.
  ? **c.** scientifically sound.
  ? **d.** having a double meaning.

You've got just one check mark, for a good answer. If you're pressed for time, you should simply mark choice **b** on your answer sheet. If you've got the time to be extra careful, you could compare your check-mark answer to your question-mark answers to make sure that it's better. (It is: The *binomial* system in biology is the one that gives a two-part genus and species name like *homo sapiens.*)

It's good to have a system for marking good, bad, and maybe answers. We're recommending this one:

  X = bad
  ✔ = good
  ? = maybe

If you don't like these marks, devise your own system. Just make sure you do it long before test day—while you're working through the practice exams in this book—so you won't have to worry about it during the test.

Even when you think you're absolutely clueless about a question, you can often use process of elimination to get rid of one answer choice. If so, you're better prepared to make an educated guess, as you'll see in Step 6. More often, the process of elimination allows you to get down to only *two* possibly right answers. Then you're in a strong position to guess. And sometimes, even though you don't know the right answer, you find it simply by getting rid of the wrong ones, as you did in the example above.

Try using your powers of elimination on the questions in the Using the Process of Elimination worksheet on the next page. The answer explanations there show one possible way you might use the process to arrive at the right answer.

The process of elimination is your tool for the next step, which is knowing when to guess.

Step 6: Know When to Guess

Time to complete: 20 minutes
Activity: Complete worksheet on Your Guessing Ability
Armed with the process of elimination, you're ready to take control of one of the big questions in test-taking: Should I guess? The first and main answer is Yes. Unless an exam has a so-called "guessing penalty," you have nothing to lose and everything to gain from guessing.

Use the process of elimination to answer the following questions. (These questions are extra difficult to force you to use elimination.)

1. Ilsa is as old as Meghan will be in five years. The difference between Ed's age and Meghan's age is twice the difference between Ilsa's age and Meghan's age. Ed is 29. How old is Ilsa?
a. 4
b. 10
c. 19
d. 24

2. "All drivers of commercial vehicles must carry a valid commercial driver's license whenever operating a commercial vehicle." According to this sentence, which of the following people need NOT carry a commercial driver's license?
a. a truck driver idling his engine while waiting to be directed to a loading dock
b. a bus operator backing her bus out of the way of another bus in the bus lot
c. a taxi driver driving his personal car to the grocery store
d. a limousine driver taking the limousine to her home after dropping off her last passenger of the evening

3. Smoking tobacco has been linked to
a. increased risk of stroke and heart attack.
b. all forms of respiratory disease.
c. increasing mortality rates over the past ten years.
d. juvenile delinquency.

4. Which of the following words is spelled correctly?
a. incorrigible
b. outragous
c. domestickated
d. understandible

The more complicated answer depends on you—your personality and your "guessing intuition."

The TEA exam doesn't have a guessing penalty. The number of questions you answer correctly yields your score, and there's no penalty for wrong answers. So simply go ahead and guess. But try not to guess wildly unless you absolutely have to. Remember to read the question carefully. You may know more about the subject than you think. Use the process of elimination as outlined in Step 5.

"Yes," you might say, "but the whole idea of guessing makes me nervous. I'm not good at guessing."

Maybe, maybe not. Maybe you're not much of a risk-taker, so you don't like to guess. But remember, nothing bad can happen to you if you're wrong.

But maybe you really think you have lousy intuition. It seems like, when you have to guess, you *always* guess wrong! Test out your assumption about your guessing ability. Complete the Your Guessing Ability worksheet on page 43 to get an idea of how good or bad your intuition really is.

Remember, nothing can happen to you if you're wrong.

Answers

Here are the answers, as well as some suggestions as to how you might have used the process of elimination to find them.

1. d. You should have eliminated choice **a** off the bat. Ilsa can't be four years old if Meghan is going to be Ilsa's age in five years. The best way to eliminate other answer choices is to try plugging them in to the information given in the problem. For instance, for choice **b,** if Ilsa is ten, then Meghan must be five. The difference in their ages is five. The difference between Ed's age, 29, and Meghan's age, five, is 24. Is 24 two times five? No. Then choice **b** is wrong. You could eliminate choice **c** in the same way and be left with choice **d.**

2. c. Note the word *not* in the question, and go through the answers one by one. Is the truck driver in choice **a** "operating a commercial vehicle"? Yes, idling counts as "operating," so he needs to have a commercial driver's license. Likewise, the bus operator in choice **b** is operating a commercial vehicle; the question doesn't say the operator must be on the street. The limo driver in choice **d** is operating a commercial vehicle, even if it doesn't have a passenger in it. However, the cabbie in choice

c is *not* operating a commercial vehicle, but his own private car.

3. a. You could eliminate choice **b** simply because of the presence of the word *all.* Such absolutes hardly ever appear in correct answer choices. Choice **c** looks attractive until you think a little about what you know—aren't *fewer* people smoking these days, rather than more? So how could smoking be responsible for a higher mortality rate? (If you didn't know that *mortality rate* means the rate at which people die, you might keep this choice as a possibility, but you'd still be able to eliminate two answers and have only two to choose from.) And choice **d** is plain silly, so you could eliminate that one, too. And you're left with the correct choice, **a.**

4. a. How you used the process of elimination here depends on which words you recognized as being spelled incorrectly. If you knew that the correct spellings were *outrageous, domesticated,* and *understandable,* then you were home free. Surely you knew that at least one of those words was wrong!

Step 7: Reach Your Peak Performance Zone

Time to complete: 10 minutes to read; weeks to complete
Activity: Complete the Physical Preparation Checklist

To get ready for a challenge like a big exam, you have to take control of your physical, as well as your mental, state. Exercise, proper diet, and rest will ensure that your body works with, rather than against, your mind on test day, as well as during your preparation.

Exercise

If you don't already have a regular exercise program going, the time during which you're preparing for an exam is actually an excellent time to start one. And if you're already keeping fit—or trying to get that way—don't let the pressure of preparing for an exam fool you into quitting now. Exercise helps reduce stress by pumping wonderful good-feeling hormones called endorphins into your system. It also increases the oxygen supply throughout your body, including your brain, so you'll be at peak performance on test day.

The following are ten really hard questions. You're not supposed to know the answers. Rather, this is an assessment of your ability to guess when you don't have a clue. Read each question carefully, just as if you did expect to answer it. If you have any knowledge at all of the subject of the question, use that knowledge to help you eliminate wrong answer choices. Use this answer grid to fill in your answers to the questions.

ANSWER GRID

1. ⓐ ⓑ ⓒ ⓓ   **5.** ⓐ ⓑ ⓒ ⓓ   **9.** ⓐ ⓑ ⓒ ⓓ
2. ⓐ ⓑ ⓒ ⓓ   **6.** ⓐ ⓑ ⓒ ⓓ   **10.** ⓐ ⓑ ⓒ ⓓ
3. ⓐ ⓑ ⓒ ⓓ   **7.** ⓐ ⓑ ⓒ ⓓ
4. ⓐ ⓑ ⓒ ⓓ   **8.** ⓐ ⓑ ⓒ ⓓ

1. September 7 is Independence Day in
  a. India.
  b. Costa Rica.
  c. Brazil.
  d. Australia.

2. Which of the following is the formula for determining the momentum of an object?
  a. $p = mv$
  b. $F = ma$
  c. $P = IV$
  d. $E = mc^2$

3. Because of the expansion of the universe, the stars and other celestial bodies are all moving away from each other. This phenomenon is known as
  a. Newton's first law.
  b. the big bang.
  c. gravitational collapse.
  d. Hubble flow.

4. American author Gertrude Stein was born in
  a. 1713.
  b. 1830.
  c. 1874.
  d. 1901.

5. Which of the following is NOT one of the Five Classics attributed to Confucius?
  a. the *I Ching*
  b. the *Book of Holiness*
  c. the *Spring and Autumn Annals*
  d. the *Book of History*

6. The religious and philosophical doctrine that holds that the universe is constantly in a struggle between good and evil is known as
  a. Pelagianism.
  b. Manichaeanism.
  c. neo-Hegelianism.
  d. Epicureanism.

7. The third Chief Justice of the U.S. Supreme Court was
  a. John Blair.
  b. William Cushing.
  c. James Wilson.
  d. John Jay.

8. Which of the following is the poisonous portion of a daffodil?
  a. the bulb
  b. the leaves
  c. the stem
  d. the flowers

9. The winner of the Masters golf tournament in 1953 was
  a. Sam Snead.
  b. Cary Middlecoff.
  c. Arnold Palmer.
  d. Ben Hogan.

10. The state with the highest per capita personal income in 1980 was
  a. Alaska.
  b. Connecticut.
  c. New York.
  d. Texas.

Answers
Check your answers against the following correct answers.

1. c.	**5.** b.	**9.** d.
2. a.	**6.** b.	**10.** a.
3. d.	**7.** b.	
4. c.	**8.** a.	

How Did You Do?

You may have simply gotten lucky and actually known the answer to one or two questions. In addition, your guessing was more successful if you were able to use the process of elimination on any of the questions. Maybe you didn't know who the third Chief Justice was (question 7), but you knew that John Jay was the first. In that case, you would have eliminated choice **d** and therefore improved your odds of guessing right from one in four to one in three.

According to probability, you should get $2\frac{1}{2}$ answers correct, so getting either two or three right would be average. If you got four or more right, you may be a really terrific guesser. If you got one or none right, you may be a really bad guesser.

Keep in mind, though, that this is only a small sample. You should continue to keep track of your guessing ability as you work through the sample questions in this book. Circle the numbers of questions you guess on as you make your guess; or, if you don't have time while you take the practice tests, go back afterward and try to remember which questions you guessed at. Remember, on a test with five answer choices, your chances of getting a right answer is one in five. So keep a separate "guessing" score for each exam. How many questions did you guess on? How many did you get right? If the number you got right is at least one-fifth of the number of questions you guessed on, you are at least an average guesser, maybe better—and you should always go ahead and guess on the real exam. If the number you got right is significantly lower than one-fifth of the number you guessed on, maybe you're not such a good guesser. Since there's no guessing penalty you would, frankly, be safe in guessing anyway, but maybe you'd feel more comfortable if you guessed only selectively, when you can eliminate a wrong answer or at least have a good feeling about one of the answer choices.

A half hour of vigorous activity—enough to raise a sweat—every day should be your aim. If you're really pressed for time, every other day is okay. Choose an activity you like and get out there and do it. Jogging with a friend always makes the time go faster, or take a radio.

But don't overdo. You don't want to exhaust yourself. Moderation is the key.

Diet

What your body needs for peak performance is simply a balanced diet. Eat plenty of fruits and vegetables, along with protein and carbohydrates. Foods that are high in lecithin (an amino acid), such as fish and beans, are especially good "brain foods."

As you prepare for the exam, go easy on caffeine and nicotine, and eliminate alcohol from your system at least two weeks before the exam.

The night before the exam, you might "carbo-load" the way athletes do before a contest. Eat a big plate of spaghetti, rice and beans, or whatever your favorite carbohydrate is.

Rest

You probably know how much sleep you need every night to be at your best, even if you don't always get it. Make sure you do get that much sleep, though, for at least a week before the exam. Moderation is important here, too. Extra sleep will just make you groggy.

If you're not a morning person and your exam will be given in the morning, you should reset your internal clock so that your body doesn't think you're taking an exam at 3 A.M. You have to start this process well before the exam. The way it works is to get up half an hour earlier each morning, and then go to bed half an hour earlier that night. Don't try it the other way around; you'll just toss and turn if you go to bed early without having gotten up early. The next morning, get up another half an hour earlier, and so on. How long you will have to do this depends on how late you're used to getting up.

Step 8: Get Your Act Together

Time to complete: 10 minutes to read; time to complete will vary
Activity: Complete Final Preparations worksheet
You're in control of your mind and body; you're in charge of test anxiety, your preparation, and your test-taking strategies. Now it's time to take charge of external factors, like the testing site and the materials you need to take the exam.

Find Out Where the Test Is and Make a Trial Run

You'll know ahead of time when and where your exam is being held. But do you know how to get to the testing site? Do you know how long it will take to get there? If not, make a trial run, preferably on the same day of the week at the same time of day. Make note, on the Final Preparations worksheet, of the amount of time it will take you to get to the exam site. Plan on arriving 10–15 minutes early so you can get the lay of the land, use the bathroom, and calm down. Then figure out how early you will have to get up that morning, and make sure you get up that early every day for a week before the exam.

Gather Your Materials

The night before the exam, lay out the clothes you will wear and the materials you have to bring with you to the exam. Plan on dressing in layers; you won't have any control over the temperature of the examination room. Have a sweater or jacket you can take off if it's warm. Use the checklist on the Final Preparations worksheet to help you pull together what you'll need.

Don't Skip Breakfast

Even if you don't usually eat breakfast, do so on exam morning. A cup of coffee doesn't count. Don't do doughnuts or other sweet foods, either. A sugar high will leave you with a sugar low in the middle of the exam. A mix of protein and carbohydrates is best: Cereal with milk and just a little sugar, or eggs with toast, will do your body a world of good.

Physical Preparation Checklist

For the week before the test, write down 1) what physical exercise you engaged in and for how long and 2) what you ate for each meal. Remember, you're trying for at least half an hour of exercise every other day (preferably every day) and a balanced diet that's light on junk food.

Exam minus 7 days

Exercise: _____ for _____ minutes

Breakfast: _____

Lunch: _____

Dinner: _____

Snacks: _____

Exam minus 6 days

Exercise: _____ for _____ minutes

Breakfast: _____

Lunch: _____

Dinner: _____

Snacks: _____

Exam minus 5 days

Exercise: _____ for _____ minutes

Breakfast: _____

Lunch: _____

Dinner: _____

Snacks: _____

Exam minus 4 days

Exercise: _____ for _____ minutes

Breakfast: _____

Lunch: _____

Dinner: _____

Snacks: _____

Exam minus 3 days

Exercise: _____ for _____ minutes

Breakfast: _____

Lunch: _____

Dinner: _____

Snacks: _____

Exam minus 2 days

Exercise: _____ for _____ minutes

Breakfast: _____

Lunch: _____

Dinner: _____

Snacks: _____

Exam minus 1 day

Exercise: _____ for _____ minutes

Breakfast: _____

Lunch: _____

Dinner: _____

Snacks: _____

Step 9: Do It!

Time to complete: 5 minutes, plus test-taking time
Activity: Ace the TEA exam!

Fast forward to exam day. You're ready. You made a study plan and followed through. You practiced your test-taking strategies while working through this book. You're in control of your physical, mental, and emotional state. You know when and where to show up and what to bring with you. In other words, you're better prepared than most of the other people taking the TEA exam with you.

Just one more thing. When you're done with the TEA exam, you will have earned a reward. Plan a celebration for exam night. Call up your friends and family and plan a party, or have a nice dinner for two—give yourself something to look forward to.

And then do it. Go into the exam full of confidence, armed with test-taking strategies you've practiced. You're in control of yourself, your environment, and your performance on the exam. You're ready to succeed. Go in there and ace the exam, and look forward to your future career as a special agent.

Final Preparations

Getting to the Exam Site
Location of exam: _____

Date of exam: _____

Time of exam: _____

Do I know how to get to the exam site?   Yes ___   No ___   *If no, make a trial run.*

Time it will take to get to the exam site: _____

Things to Lay Out the Night before the Exam

Clothes I will wear   ___

Sweater/jacket   ___

Watch   ___

Admission card   ___

Photo ID   ___

Four No. 2 pencils   ___

_____   ___

_____   ___

5 ▶ DIAGNOSTIC TREASURY ENFORCEMENT AGENT EXAM

CHAPTER SUMMARY
This is the first of the three practice tests in this book based on the Treasury Enforcement Agent (TEA) exam. Use this test to see how you would do if you were to take the exam today.

This diagnostic practice exam is of the same type as the real Treasury Enforcement Agent exam you will be taking. Like the real exam, it is divided into three sections. Part A, the Verbal Reasoning portion, consists of 25 short reading passages, each accompanied by a multiple-choice question. Part B, the Arithmetic Reasoning portion, consists of 20 word or numeric problems, each accompanied by a multiple-choice question. Part C, the Problems for Investigation portion, consists of several short narratives that describe a criminal or possibly criminal event, each accompanied by a list of ten or 11 statements that were made while the event was being investigated, followed by several questions about the statements.

Each section of the exam is timed, but for now, as you take this first practice exam, do not worry too much about timing. Just take the test in as relaxed a manner as you can to find out which areas you are skilled in and which ones will need extra work.

The answer sheet you should use is on page 51. Then comes the exam itself, and after that is the answer key. Each answer on the test is explained in the answer key to help you find out why the correct answers are right and the incorrect answers wrong. The answer key is followed by a section on how to score your exam.

Part A: Verbal Reasoning

1. ⓐ ⓑ ⓒ ⓓ ⓔ
2. ⓐ ⓑ ⓒ ⓓ ⓔ
3. ⓐ ⓑ ⓒ ⓓ ⓔ
4. ⓐ ⓑ ⓒ ⓓ ⓔ
5. ⓐ ⓑ ⓒ ⓓ ⓔ
6. ⓐ ⓑ ⓒ ⓓ ⓔ
7. ⓐ ⓑ ⓒ ⓓ ⓔ
8. ⓐ ⓑ ⓒ ⓓ ⓔ
9. ⓐ ⓑ ⓒ ⓓ ⓔ

10. ⓐ ⓑ ⓒ ⓓ ⓔ
11. ⓐ ⓑ ⓒ ⓓ ⓔ
12. ⓐ ⓑ ⓒ ⓓ ⓔ
13. ⓐ ⓑ ⓒ ⓓ ⓔ
14. ⓐ ⓑ ⓒ ⓓ ⓔ
15. ⓐ ⓑ ⓒ ⓓ ⓔ
16. ⓐ ⓑ ⓒ ⓓ ⓔ
17. ⓐ ⓑ ⓒ ⓓ ⓔ
18. ⓐ ⓑ ⓒ ⓓ ⓔ

19. ⓐ ⓑ ⓒ ⓓ ⓔ
20. ⓐ ⓑ ⓒ ⓓ ⓔ
21. ⓐ ⓑ ⓒ ⓓ ⓔ
22. ⓐ ⓑ ⓒ ⓓ ⓔ
23. ⓐ ⓑ ⓒ ⓓ ⓔ
24. ⓐ ⓑ ⓒ ⓓ ⓔ
25. ⓐ ⓑ ⓒ ⓓ ⓔ

Part B: Arithmetic Reasoning

1. ⓐ ⓑ ⓒ ⓓ ⓔ
2. ⓐ ⓑ ⓒ ⓓ ⓔ
3. ⓐ ⓑ ⓒ ⓓ ⓔ
4. ⓐ ⓑ ⓒ ⓓ ⓔ
5. ⓐ ⓑ ⓒ ⓓ ⓔ
6. ⓐ ⓑ ⓒ ⓓ ⓔ
7. ⓐ ⓑ ⓒ ⓓ ⓔ

8. ⓐ ⓑ ⓒ ⓓ ⓔ
9. ⓐ ⓑ ⓒ ⓓ ⓔ
10. ⓐ ⓑ ⓒ ⓓ ⓔ
11. ⓐ ⓑ ⓒ ⓓ ⓔ
12. ⓐ ⓑ ⓒ ⓓ ⓔ
13. ⓐ ⓑ ⓒ ⓓ ⓔ
14. ⓐ ⓑ ⓒ ⓓ ⓔ

15. ⓐ ⓑ ⓒ ⓓ ⓔ
16. ⓐ ⓑ ⓒ ⓓ ⓔ
17. ⓐ ⓑ ⓒ ⓓ ⓔ
18. ⓐ ⓑ ⓒ ⓓ ⓔ
19. ⓐ ⓑ ⓒ ⓓ ⓔ
20. ⓐ ⓑ ⓒ ⓓ ⓔ

Part C: Problems for Investigation

1. ⓐ ⓑ ⓒ ⓓ ⓔ
2. ⓐ ⓑ ⓒ ⓓ ⓔ
3. ⓐ ⓑ ⓒ ⓓ ⓔ
4. ⓐ ⓑ ⓒ ⓓ ⓔ
5. ⓐ ⓑ ⓒ ⓓ ⓔ
6. ⓐ ⓑ ⓒ ⓓ ⓔ
7. ⓐ ⓑ ⓒ ⓓ ⓔ
8. ⓐ ⓑ ⓒ ⓓ ⓔ
9. ⓐ ⓑ ⓒ ⓓ ⓔ
10. ⓐ ⓑ ⓒ ⓓ ⓔ

11. ⓐ ⓑ ⓒ ⓓ ⓔ
12. ⓐ ⓑ ⓒ ⓓ ⓔ
13. ⓐ ⓑ ⓒ ⓓ ⓔ
14. ⓐ ⓑ ⓒ ⓓ ⓔ
15. ⓐ ⓑ ⓒ ⓓ ⓔ
16. ⓐ ⓑ ⓒ ⓓ ⓔ
17. ⓐ ⓑ ⓒ ⓓ ⓔ
18. ⓐ ⓑ ⓒ ⓓ ⓔ
19. ⓐ ⓑ ⓒ ⓓ ⓔ
20. ⓐ ⓑ ⓒ ⓓ ⓔ

21. ⓐ ⓑ ⓒ ⓓ ⓔ
22. ⓐ ⓑ ⓒ ⓓ ⓔ
23. ⓐ ⓑ ⓒ ⓓ ⓔ
24. ⓐ ⓑ ⓒ ⓓ ⓔ
25. ⓐ ⓑ ⓒ ⓓ ⓔ
26. ⓐ ⓑ ⓒ ⓓ ⓔ
27. ⓐ ⓑ ⓒ ⓓ ⓔ
28. ⓐ ⓑ ⓒ ⓓ ⓔ
29. ⓐ ⓑ ⓒ ⓓ ⓔ
30. ⓐ ⓑ ⓒ ⓓ ⓔ

Part A: Verbal Reasoning

Read each of the following reading passages carefully, and answer the question below it by choosing the best of the five possible answer choices.

In cities throughout the country, there is a new direction in local campaign coverage. Frequently in local elections, journalists are not giving voters enough information to understand the issues and evaluate the candidates. The local news media devotes too much time to scandal and not enough time to policy.

1. The paragraph best supports the statement that the local news media
   a. is not doing an adequate job when it comes to covering local campaigns.
   b. does not understand either campaign issues or politics.
   c. should learn how to cover politics by watching the national news media.
   d. spends more time covering criminals than it does covering politicians.
   e. has no interest in covering stories about local political events.

Improved vehicle mileage is easily attained by setting a few simple rules. Always make sure your tire pressure is within the recommended settings. Avoid fast starts at traffic lights or stop signs, and slowly accelerate to your desired speed. On a highway, pick a lane and try and maintain an even, steady speed. When driving in the city, choose a route with a minimal number of stop signs and traffic lights to avoid having to speed up and slow down.

2. The paragraph best supports the statement that
   a. a vehicle's tire pressure is always too low.
   b. traffic lights ruin a vehicle's mileage.
   c. lane changes on a highway will negate any gains from slower starts at traffic lights.
   d. your vehicle mileage can depend on your driving habits and tire condition.
   e. a more energy-efficient vehicle will save you money and time.

It is well known that the world urgently needs adequate distribution of food, so that everyone gets enough. Adequate distribution of medicine is just as urgent. Medical expertise and medical supplies need to be redistributed throughout the world so that people in emerging nations will have proper medical care.

3. The paragraph best supports the statement that
   a. the majority of the people in the world have never been seen by a doctor.
   b. food production in emerging nations has slowed during the past several years.
   c. most of the world's doctors are selfish about giving time and money to the poor.
   d. the medical-supply industry should step up production of its products.
   e. many people who live in emerging nations are not receiving proper medical care.

The criminal justice system needs to change. The system could be more just if it allowed victims the opportunity to confront the person who has harmed them. Also, mediation between victims and their offenders would give the offenders a chance to apologize for the harm they have done.

4. The paragraph best supports the statement that victims of a crime should
   a. learn to forgive their offenders.
   b. have the right to confront their offenders.
   c. learn the art of mediation.
   d. insist that their offenders be punished.
   e. have the right to impose a sentence on their offenders.

Desktop and laptop computers require routine maintenance. Dust buildup on internal components can cause them to overheat by not allowing the cooling system to work properly. A simple cleaning with compressed air can improve the cooling system's efficiency. Trained computer maintenance personnel should open and clean computers regularly.

5. The paragraph best supports the statement that
   a. large mainframe computers do not need maintenance.
   b. a computer's warranty will be void if maintenance is not performed.
   c. a computer will malfunction if it overheats.
   d. proper maintenance will result in a computer that runs more efficiently.
   e. a computer should be used in as clean an area as possible.

Specially trained dogs are sometimes used to aid law enforcement agents by detecting explosives and the residue left by explosives. One of ways that these trained dogs can help agents is by uncovering evidence after a blast. Preventing possible bomb threats is another goal of these canines. Because they are conditioned to recognize the odor of smokeless powder and other types of fillers in explosives, "bomb dogs" can also detect firearms and ammunition hidden in vehicles or containers—even in containers buried underground. No useful detection instrument—including specially trained canine teams—can be left unutilized in the effort to prevent and investigate bomb and firearm threats.

6. The paragraph best supports the statement that
   a. specially trained dogs are the best way to detect explosives that are buried underground.
   b. "bomb dogs" are in high demand in law enforcement agencies.
   c. bomb-detecting instruments are more effective in uncovering explosives than canine teams.
   d. bomb-detection dogs should be used in investigating explosives threats.
   e. all available instruments, including specially trained dogs, should be used to detect bombs.

Many consumers know that credit card fraud on the Internet is on the rise. But what they may not know is that it is safer to enter their credit card number online at a secured website than it is to hand over their card to a waiter at a restaurant. Consumers can protect themselves by measures such as never letting their credit card out of sight if possible and never giving out credit card information over the phone if they not did initiate the call. All consumers need more reliable information about the ways to prevent credit card fraud.

7. The paragraph best supports the statement that
   a. it is impossible for consumers to take steps to protect themselves from credit card fraud.
   b. if consumers hand their credit card over to a waiter in a restaurant, they are asking to be victims of credit card fraud.
   c. supplying credit card information to a secured website is comparatively less risky than some other scenarios involving credit cards.
   d. there are guaranteed ways of making sure you do not encounter credit card fraud.
   e. information about preventive strategies for avoiding credit card fraud would help only some consumers.

Risk factors for youth violence include a young person's history of early aggressive behavior and use of drugs, alcohol, or tobacco, among others. Exposure to violence and family conflict and a lack of parental involvement in a child's life are other risk factors. Protective factors—positive experiences that may buffer young people from risk—are also important in preventing youth violence. An example of a protective factor is social or school involvement. Currently, researchers have not devoted enough study to protective factors, which are as significant as risk factors in predicting and preventing youth violence.

8. The paragraph best supports the statement that
   a. some risk factors are better predictors of youth violence than others.
   b. only some protective factors can accurately predict youth violence.
   c. protective factors are not as important as risk factors in preventing youth violence.
   d. risk factors for youth violence deserve more research.
   e. protective factors for youth violence deserve more research.

A law enforcement officer must write clean and concise reports. He or she should place events and observations in chronological order to draw a clear picture of when and how events occurred. Avoid acronyms and slang terms, as future readers may not be aware of the meanings. Never include opinions or conjectures, but do include observations and facts. A well-written report will stand on its own and require little in the way of questioning or explanation of the information included.

9. The paragraph best supports the statement that
   a. report writing is a difficult task that must be completed.
   b. officers may put their opinions into a police report when it is necessary to emphasize the information.
   c. a report must contain as much police jargon as possible to ensure civilians do not obtain any information.
   d. a good police report will prevent the officer from having to testify in court.
   e. an officer must pay attention to certain rules and details in order to produce an effective and concise report.

Recent history has been about ideologies: communism versus capitalism, fascism versus democracy. But the end of the Cold War has resulted in many subtle challenges throughout the world. Today, global politics is being reconfigured along cultural lines. Political boundaries are increasingly redrawn along ethnic and religious lines.

10. The paragraph best supports the statement that since the Cold War
   a. in most countries religion and ethnicity are more important than capitalism.
   b. religion and ethnicity have become more important than political ideology.
   c. throughout the world, political boundaries should be redrawn.
   d. most countries have adopted a capitalistic economic system.
   e. fascism and communism do not exist in the major countries of the world.

One New York publisher has estimated that 50,000 to 60,000 people in the United States want an anthology that includes the complete works of William Shakespeare. And what accounts for this renewed interest in Shakespeare? As scholars point out, his psychological insights into both male and female characters are amazing even today.

11. The paragraph best supports the statement that
   a. Shakespeare's characters are more interesting than fictional characters today.
   b. people today are interested in Shakespeare's work because of the characters.
   c. academic scholars are putting together an anthology of Shakespeare's work.
   d. New Yorkers have a renewed interested in the work of Shakespeare.
   e. Shakespeare was a psychiatrist as well as a playwright.

One difficulty in investigating art fraud is the reluctance of art buyers and art dealers to give evidence that they were defrauded by a forgery. Because dealers and collectors often stake their success on the strength of their reputations and their knowledge of art, they do not want to admit that they have been duped by counterfeiters. They believe that this admission could negatively affect their business. If more people came forward, law enforcement agencies could make significant progress in investigating and curbing art fraud.

12. The paragraph best supports the statement that
   a. art fraud investigations would be greatly helped by evidence provided by art dealers and collectors.
   b. it is impossible to investigate art fraud without the evidence provided by art dealers and collectors.
   c. law enforcement agents must depend on the testimony of art dealers.
   d. art dealers are often collaborators with counterfeiters.
   e. art dealers have a lot to gain and not much to lose in reporting art fraud.

Rehabilitation is a constructive way to improve the criminal justice system. The system's current emphasis on imprisonment is a failure. Without rehabilitation before and after their discharge from prison, offenders will usually commit more crimes.

13. The paragraph best supports the statement that
   a. criminals should no longer be sent to prison, but rather to rehabilitation centers.
   b. without rehabilitation, criminals always commit more than one crime.
   c. most prisons today are too overcrowded for effective rehabilitation.
   d. if criminals are rehabilitated, the crime rate will go down.
   e. the criminal justice system is unfair to the victims of crime.

Today's workforce has a new set of social values. Ten years ago, a manager who was offered a promotion in a distant city would not have questioned the move. Today, a manager in that same situation might choose family happiness instead of career advancement.

14. The paragraph best supports the statement that
   a. most managers are not loyal to the corporations for which they work.
   b. businesses today do not understand their employees' needs.
   c. employees' social values have changed over the past ten years.
   d. career advancement is not important to today's business managers.
   e. companies should require their employees to accept promotions.

Generation Xers are those people born roughly between 1965 and 1981. As employees, Generation Xers tend to be more challenged when they can carry out tasks independently. This makes Generation Xers the most entrepreneurial generation in history.

15. The paragraph best supports the statement that Generation Xers
   a. work harder than people from other generations.
   b. have a tendency to be self-directed workers.
   c. have an interest in making history.
   d. tend to work in jobs that require risk-taking behavior.
   e. like to challenge their bosses' work attitudes.

The practice of setting lower college admissions standards for athletes than for other students is commonplace. Because many student athletes have limited math and verbal skills, they do not belong in college. If colleges stopped recruiting athletes with limited academic skills, this would send a clear message: Athletic ability does not guarantee college admission.

16. The paragraph best supports the statement that the author believes that
   a. football and basketball players do not study.
   b. colleges should not have athletic teams.
   c. college admissions standards for athletes are too low.
   d. athletes do not belong on college campuses.
   e. college admissions standards for non-athletes are too high.

In the United States, voter involvement in election politics has declined over the past several decades. This trend is likely to continue. However, changing the way campaigns are run could slow this decrease—even stop it. For example, making campaigns shorter could help. Even though it seems like long campaigns would allow voters to learn more about candidates, these lengthy exposures to candidates have the opposite effect. Most voters are not ready to closely consider candidates months before the election. Yet, by the time the election approaches, voters still do not pay attention to the contest—partly because they have been worn down by lengthy campaigns. They may even have forgotten the candidates' positions on important issues by the time Election Day arrives.

17. The paragraph best supports the statement that
   a. voter involvement is declining because most citizens have a cynical view of politics.
   b. to maintain current voter involvement, campaigns should be shortened.
   c. lengthy campaigns allow voters to carefully study candidates.
   d. to substantially increase voter involvement, campaigns should be shortened.
   e. voter education initiatives would help voters understand the issues of an election.

Critical reading is a demanding process. To read critically, you must slow down your reading and, with pencil in hand, perform specific operations on the text. Mark up the text with your reactions, conclusions, and questions. When you read, become an active participant.

18. The paragraph best supports the statement that
   a. critical reading is a slow, dull, but essential process.
   b. critical reading requires thoughtful and careful attention.
   c. readers should get in the habit of questioning the truth of what they read.
   d. the best critical reading happens at critical times in a person's life.
   e. critical reading should take place at the same time each day.

Proficiency in correctly using firearms requires constant practice. The repetitive drawing and firing of a handgun creates muscle memory that can be used to the shooter's advantage. A firm but comfortable grip as the weapon is withdrawn from the holster is essential in achieving control of the weapon. An inattentive or cavalier attitude toward firearm training can result in accidents.

19. The paragraph best supports the statement that
   a. shooting a firearm comes naturally to some shooters.
   b. a shooter's attitude is not important when he or she is practicing.
   c. practice with firearms can improve proficiency and safety.
   d. weapons safety can be achieved only by going to the firing range.
   e. building confidence by practicing is an added advantage in firearms training.

There are no effective boundaries when it comes to pollutants. Studies have shown that toxic insecticides that have been banned in many countries are riding the wind from countries where they remain legal. Compounds such as DDT and toxaphene have been found in remote places like the Yukon and other Arctic regions.

20. The paragraph best supports the statement that
   a. toxic insecticides such as DDT have not been banned throughout the world.
   b. more pollutants find their way into polar climates than they do into warmer areas.
   c. studies have proven that many countries have ignored their own antipollution laws.
   d. DDT and toxaphene are the two most toxic insecticides in the world.
   e. even a worldwide ban on toxic insecticides would not stop the spread of DDT pollution.

The Fourth Amendment to the Constitution protects citizens against unreasonable searches and seizures. No search of a person's home or personal effects may be conducted without a written search warrant issued on probable cause. This means that a neutral judge must approve the factual basis justifying a search before it can be conducted.

21. The paragraph best supports the statement that the police cannot search a person's home or private papers unless they have
   a. legal authorization.
   b. direct evidence of a crime.
   c. read the person his or her constitutional rights.
   d. a reasonable belief that a crime has occurred.
   e. requested that a judge be present.

During colonial times in America, juries were encouraged to ask questions of the parties in the courtroom. The jurors were, in fact, expected to investigate the facts of the case themselves. If jurors conducted an investigation today, we would throw out the case.

22. The paragraph best supports the statement that
   a. juries are less important today than they were in colonial times.
   b. jurors today are less interested in court cases than they were in colonial times.
   c. courtrooms today are more efficient than they were in colonial times.
   d. jurors in colonial times were more informed than jurors today.
   e. the jury system in America has changed since colonial times.

Mathematics allows us to expand our consciousness. Mathematics tells us about economic trends, patterns of disease, and the growth of populations. Math is good at exposing the truth, but it can also perpetuate misunderstandings and untruths. Figures have the power to mislead people.

23. The paragraph best supports the statement that
   a. the study of mathematics is dangerous.
   b. words are more truthful than figures.
   c. figures are sometimes used to deceive people
   d. the power of numbers is that they cannot lie.
   e. the study of mathematics is more important than other disciplines.

Human technology developed from the first stone tools about two and a half million years ago. At the beginning, the rate of development was slow. Hundreds of thousands of years passed without much change. Today, new technologies are reported daily on television and in newspapers.

24. The paragraph best supports the statement that
   a. stone tools were not really technology.
   b. stone tools were in use for two and a half million years.
   c. there is no way to know when stone tools first came into use.
   d. in today's world, new technologies are constantly being developed.
   e. none of the latest technologies are as significant as the development of stone tools.

Money laundering refers to the practice of disguising profits derived from criminal activities and making the proceeds look like they came from a legitimate source. For example, one way to launder illegal income is to move it out of the United States and then bring it back in a "clean" form, such as loan proceeds. Launderers are always on the lookout for new ways to launder funds. Countries with growing financial systems can be especially susceptible to launderers who look for systems with ineffective or weak regulations and countermeasures. Some say that countries with developing economies cannot be too picky about the funds they attract. But they need to be wary and selective before they allow organized crime to become entrenched.

25. The paragraph best supports the statement that
   a. countries with growing economies need to cannot be too selective about the money they attract.
   b. all countries with growing financial systems have ineffective regulations.
   c. countries with growing economies need to take preventive measures against money laundering.
   d. countries with established economies are not susceptible to money-laundering schemes.
   e. by targeting money laundering, investigators also target the underlying criminal activity.

Part B: Arithmetic Reasoning

Analyze the following paragraphs, set up the problem for each one, and choose the correct solution from choices **a**, **b**, **c**, and **d**. If none of these four choices is correct, choose choice **e**, "none of these."

1. If a state police car travels at the speed of 62 mph for 15 minutes, how far will it travel? (Distance = Rate × Time)
a. 9.3 miles
b. 10.5 miles
c. 15.5 miles
d. 16 miles
e. none of these

2. The cost of a list of supplies for a Treasury Department office is as follows: $19.98, $52.20, $12.64, and $7.79. What is the total cost?
a. $91.30
b. $92.61
c. $93.60
d. $93.61
e. none of these

3. In a given area of the United States, there were about 215 highway accidents associated with drinking alcohol in one year. Of these, 113 were caused by excessive speed. About what percent of the accidents were speed-related?
a. 47%
b. 49%
c. 51%
d. 53%
e. none of these

4. A law enforcement agency receives a report of a drunk driver on the roadway on August 3 at 10:42 P.M. and another similar report on August 4 at 1:19 A.M. How much time has elapsed between reports?
a. 1 hour 37 minutes
b. 2 hours 23 minutes
c. 2 hours 37 minutes
d. 3 hours 23 minutes
e. none of these

5. How many feet of tape will a law enforcement officer need to tie off a crime scene area that is 34 feet long and 20 feet wide?
a. 54
b. 68
c. 88
d. 98
e. none of these

6. A locked ammunition box is about $2\frac{1}{2}$ centimeters thick. Approximately how thick is this box in inches ? (1 cm = 0.39 inches)
a. $\frac{1}{4}$ inch
b. $\frac{1}{3}$ inch
c. $\frac{1}{2}$ inch
d. $\frac{3}{4}$ inch
e. none of these

7. An import company has imported 5,026 tons of high-grade metal. The import duties exempt the first 2,000 tons; any amount beyond that, up to an additional 5,000 tons, is charged a duty at a rate of $3.00 per ton. Any amount above the additional allowance is computed at $9.00 per ton. What is the amount owed in import duties on the imported metal?
a. $9,234.00
b. $15,078.00
c. $9,078.00
d. $15,234.00
e. none of these

8. Special Agent Tate earns $31,000 a year. If she receives a 4.5% salary increase, how much will she earn?
    a. $31,945
    b. $32,045
    c. $32,250
    d. $32,395
    e. none of these

9. What is the perimeter of a pentagon with three sides of 3 inches, and the remaining sides 5 inches long?
    a. 19 inches
    b. 15 inches
    c. 14 inches
    d. 12 inches
    e. none of these

10. If it takes four law enforcement officers 1 hour 45 minutes to perform a particular job, how long would it take one officer working at the same rate to perform the same task alone?
    a. 4.5 hours
    b. 5 hours
    c. 7 hours
    d. 7.5 hours
    e. none of these

11. There are 176 men and 24 women serving in a particular battalion. What percentage of the battalion's force is women?
    a. 12%
    b. 14%
    c. 16%
    d. 24%
    e. none of these

12. When a burglar alarm system is installed in a home that is under construction, the system costs about 1.5% of the total building cost. The cost of the same system installed after the home is built is about 4% of the total building cost. How much would a homeowner save by installing an alarm system in a $150,000 home while the home is still under construction?
    a. $3,750
    b. $600
    c. $2,250
    d. $6,000
    e. none of these

13. The ratio of men to women in the room is 4 to 5. If there are 18 people in the room, how many are men?
    a. 9
    b. 8
    c. 10
    d. 7
    e. none of these

14. A safety box has three layers of metal, each with a different width. If one layer is $\frac{1}{8}$ inch thick, a second layer is $\frac{1}{6}$ inch thick, and the total thickness is $\frac{3}{4}$ inch thick, what is the width of the third layer?
    a. $\frac{5}{12}$
    b. $\frac{11}{24}$
    c. $\frac{7}{18}$
    d. $\frac{1}{2}$
    e. none of these

15. A person can be scalded by hot water at a temperature of about 122° F. What is the lowest temperature Centigrade a person could be scalded? $C = \frac{5}{9}(F - 32)$
    a. 57.5° C
    b. 55° C
    c. 53° C
    d. 52.5° C
    e. none of these

16. Studies have shown that automatic sprinkler systems save about $5,700 in damages per fire in stores and offices. If a particular community has on average 14 store and office fires every year, about how much money is saved each year if these buildings have sprinkler systems?
a. $28,500
b. $79,800
c. $81,800
d. $87,800
e. none of these

17. Which of these sets of angle measures form a right triangle?
a. 45°, 50°, 85°
b. 40°, 40°, 100°
c. 20°, 30°, 130°
d. 40°, 50°, 90°
e. none of these

18. All of the rooms on the top floor of a government building are rectangular, with 8-foot ceilings. One room is 9 feet wide by 11 feet long. What is the combined area of the four walls, including doors and windows?
a. 99 square feet
b. 160 square feet
c. 320 square feet
d. 370 square feet
e. none of these

19. A driver making a cross-country round trip calculated that he will need 252 gallons of fuel to complete the trip. His fuel tank holds 19 gallons of fuel. Assuming he started with a full tank, how many times must he refuel in order to complete the trip?
a. 11
b. 14
c. 19
d. 8
e. none of these

20. Solve for x in the following equation:
$\frac{1}{3}x + 3 = 8$
a. 33
b. 15
c. 11
d. 3
e. none of these

Part C: Problems for Investigation

Carefully read each of the following paragraphs and the statements that come after it, and then answer the questions by choosing the best of the five possible answer choices.

First Bank has recently had a problem with teller drawers coming up short. Banks anticipate a certain amount of this kind of loss, so bank officials were not overly concerned until they began to notice a pattern. Every two or three days, for a period of six months, the cash at teller station 3 would be short; occasionally, another drawer would be short. Vice President Ralph Jensen reported the pattern and authorities were called. There are a total of twelve teller stations, but it is rare that all twelve are open at once. The number of stations that are open depends on the number of tellers working and the amount of business being transacted.

During the course of the investigation, the following statements were made.

1. Vice President Jensen stated that he personally tallied the drawer totals at the end of each business day; on days when he did not work, the tallies were done by Vice President Enrique Cruz.

2. Gloria Dennis, the teller supervisor, said that she usually opened teller stations in order—that is, station 1 would be opened first, station 2 second, and so on. Each teller is assigned to a station for the shift, but they cover for each other on breaks.

3. Dennis also stated that there is an average of five stations open at any given time, but sometimes, as few as two stations are open.

4. Teller Dave Feller said that the tellers came and went from work at staggered times and that more than half of the tellers worked only part time.

5. Teller Marilyn Nguyen said that Felicia Ralston, another teller, had recently gotten divorced and complained that her ex-husband was not paying child support.

6. Vice President Cruz stated that the tallies had never been short on the days he did them.

7. Teller Felicia Ralston said that recently, a new customer, John Mitchell, had been coming in every few days, and often, he only wanted change for a large bill. Ralston thought he might be a drug dealer.

8. Teller Mike Richards said that, although tellers were not assigned to particular stations all the time, each teller had a favorite station and Gloria normally let them work at those stations. Richards said that both Ralston and Nguyen liked station 3.

9. Head of Personnel Heidi Sargent checked the records and said that tellers Nguyen, Ralston, Richards, Ford, Beloit, and Rawlings were all working on days when station 3 came up short. In addition, Gloria Dennis and Ralph Jensen worked all of those days. Teller Feller worked all but two of those days.

10. Teller Sarah Beloit said that she saw Vice President Jensen and Teller Richards having lunch together once or twice a week for the last six months.

1. Which of the following statements could be
   attempts by one teller to divert suspicion to
   another teller?
   a. Statements 1 and 4
   b. Statements 3 and 6
   c. Statements 7 and 10
   d. Statements 1 and 6
   e. Statements 5 and 8

2. Which of the following statements cast suspicion
   on Ralph Jensen?
   a. Statements 6 and 10
   b. Statements 1 and 6
   c. Statements 1 and 9
   d. Statements 6 and 9
   e. Statements 9 and 10

3. Which of the following statements indicates that
   the drawer shortage might not be a case of
   employee theft?
   a. Statement 7
   b. Statement 9
   c. Statement 3
   d. Statement 5
   e. Statement 1

4. Which of the following statements is hearsay?
   a. Statement 10
   b. Statement 8
   c. Statement 7
   d. Statement 5
   e. Statement 6

5. Which of the following statements may offer a
   motive for the theft?
   a. Statement 4
   b. Statement 6
   c. Statement 5
   d. Statement 7
   e. Statement 10

6. Which of the following statements could lead to
   the conclusion that there is more than one thief?
   a. Statement 7
   b. Statement 5
   c. Statement 8
   d. Statement 9
   e. Statement 10

7. Which of the following statements provides the
   strongest alibi?
   a. Statement 7
   b. Statement 3
   c. Statement 5
   d. Statement 9
   e. Statement 1

In the past five years, the U.S. Postal Service has received an increasing number of complaints from people who say they sent money in a greeting card that was not received by the recipient. Instead, the cards arrived, sealed in their envelopes, but empty. The U.S. Postal Service maintains a distribution center at the airport, where the mail from six states is sorted and routed. A majority of the complaints of missing money involved cards going either to or from those six states. An investigation of the distribution center begins.

During the course of the investigation, the following statements were made.

1. Minnie Anders, regional supervisor for the six states, says that, since she took over this job, efficiency at the distribution center has increased.

2. Burt Lentz, supervisor of the distribution center, says that most of the mail sorting is done by machine.

3. Juana Pena, a distribution center employee, says that airport baggage handlers load and unload the mailbags from the airplanes.

4. William Moi, another employee, says that he heard that Burt Lentz was recently charged with domestic violence.

5. Megan Jensen, distribution center employee, says that one of her coworkers, Paul Arthur, recently bought a new Corvette and a boat.

6. Paul Arthur says that his grandmother died last year and left him some money, but that Megan Jensen was recently sued by her ex-husband because she was not paying child support.

7. Juana Pena says that William Moi has been taking several unauthorized breaks during his shift.

8. Burt Lentz says that sometimes mailbags come open while they are being transported. This happens about three times a month.

9. Juana Pena says that William Moi and Burt Lentz do not get along, and once, they exchanged blows on the loading dock.

10. Boris Michaels, supervisor of building maintenance, says that occasionally, the maintenance crew finds small bits of paper on the floor in the men's room, as though someone had been tearing open envelopes in there.

8. Which statement is least likely to further the investigation?
   a. Statement 1
   b. Statement 3
   c. Statement 5
   d. Statement 6
   e. Statement 7

9. Which statement along with Statement 9 indicates Burt Lentz has a history of violent behavior?
   a. Statement 2
   b. Statement 4
   c. Statement 8
   d. Statement 10
   e. Statement 6

10. Which two statements are purely circumstantial evidence?
   a. Statements 5 and 8
   b. Statements 3 and 6
   c. Statements 3 and 8
   d. Statements 5 and 6
   e. Statements 6 and 8

11. Which statement along with Statement 10 casts suspicion on William Moi?
   a. Statement 6
   b. Statement 4
   c. Statement 9
   d. Statement 8
   e. Statement 7

12. Which two statements indicate the theft is being committed by someone who is NOT employed by the U.S. Postal Service?
   a. Statements 1 and 3
   b. Statements 3 and 8
   c. Statements 2 and 10
   d. Statements 8 and 9
   e. Statements 1 and 9

13. Which statement is most helpful to authorities investigating this case?
   a. Statement 8
   b. Statement 5
   c. Statement 10
   d. Statement 3
   e. Statement 4

14. Which statement indicates a motive for the theft?
- **a.** Statement 7
- **b.** Statement 9
- **c.** Statement 1
- **d.** Statement 5
- **e.** Statement 10

15. Which statement is an attempt to establish innocence?
- **a.** Statement 1
- **b.** Statement 3
- **c.** Statement 4
- **d.** Statement 5
- **e.** Statement 6

On September 30, truck number seven of the A-1 Armored Car Company failed to return to the garage at the end of the day. The truck was staffed by driver Ned Wallace and guards May Cross and Philip Marshall. The dispatcher, Judy Raymond, called the truck's last scheduled pickup, Miners National Bank, and was told the deposits had been retrieved as usual. She then contacted the Federal Reserve Bank and discovered that truck number seven never arrived to make the deposit. Raymond, fearing a traffic accident, contacted local police. A short time later, the police notified Raymond that truck number seven had been located, empty and apparently abandoned, on Route 15. Raymond notified her boss, the company's owner, Jesse Stripe.

During the course of the investigation, the following statements were made.

1. Jesse Stripe said that all drivers and guards were bonded and many were formerly in the military.

2. Judy Raymond said that Wallace and Cross had both been employed by A-1 for more than ten years. Marshall was a new employee.

3. Alice Hoover, Stripe's administrative assistant, said that Wallace had asked for a pay advance last week. She also said it is against company policy to give advances.

4. Judy Raymond said that her assistant, Dave Lloyd, was in charge of assigning drivers and guards to particular trucks and routes.

5. Jesse Stripe said that he hired Marshall on Cross's recommendation.

6. Dave Lloyd said that it is company policy that personnel be randomly rotated among the company's 25 trucks. It was rare, but not impossible, for the same two or three employees to work together more than once or twice a month.

7. Guard Tito Juarez said that Ned Wallace owed him $2,000 from a friendly poker game played last week.

8. Driver Herb Moss said he heard Judy Raymond tell Dave Lloyd to assign Marshall and Cross to the same truck that morning. It was the fifth time that month that Moss saw them working together.

9. Guard Maize Schwartz said she didn't like working with Ned Wallace as he was always talking about government conspiracies.

10. Alice Hoover said that, according to personnel records, May Cross and Judy Raymond attended the University of Pennsylvania at the same time.

16. Which statement is hearsay?
- **a.** Statement 8
- **b.** Statement 6
- **c.** Statement 4
- **d.** Statement 2
- **e.** Statement 9

17. Which two statements indicate a conspiracy involving May Cross and Philip Marshall?
a. Statements 2 and 9
b. Statements 1 and 5
c. Statements 5 and 8
d. Statements 6 and 7
e. Statements 8 and 10

18. Which two statements indicate a conspiracy involving May Cross and Judy Raymond?
a. Statements 2 and 4
b. Statements 8 and 10
c. Statements 6 and 9
d. Statements 1 and 5
e. Statements 5 and 8

19. Which two statements indicate a motive for Ned Wallace?
a. Statements 2 and 9
b. Statements 1 and 8
c. Statements 4 and 6
d. Statements 3 and 7
e. Statements 5 and 10

20. Which statement is least damaging to May Cross?
a. Statement 5
b. Statement 10
c. Statement 2
d. Statement 8
e. Statement 3

21. Which statement is least helpful in solving the case?
a. Statement 5
b. Statement 6
c. Statement 4
d. Statement 1
e. Statement 9

You are an ICE agent assigned to a financial fraud task force comprised of FBI, IRS, DEA, and state and local police agencies. You are assigned as a team leader to conduct a search warrant at the home of Shaun Reedy, owner of an investment and consulting firm suspected of tax fraud. The company owned by Shaun Reedy lists John Dalton as a non-voting partner. A member of your search team is a computer forensics examiner from the San Diego Regional Computer Forensics Lab (RCFL), who will assist in collecting digital evidence.

During the course of the investigation, the following statements were made.

1. While at the home of Shaun Reedy, Linda Reedy, his wife, stated that she was certain Shaun was cheating on her, as a friend of hers saw Shaun with a woman in his car. She stated she was going to divorce Shaun and would be willing to testify against him.

2. IRS agent John Tompkins said he had a statement from another suspect in the case that stated Shaun Reedy was the one who kept all of the false financial records on a memory card that he would access on his work computer.

3. An importer, John Dalton, called the FBI offices and filed a complaint that Shaun Reedy had defrauded him of over $150,000, which Dalton said he invested in Reedy's company.

4. FBI agent Ignacio Montoya stated he interviewed Lisa Langstone at the office of Shaun Reedy. She stated she was the executive assistant to Reedy. Langstone said in a written statement that she was the account manager for Reedy and would write checks and transfer funds under his instructions. Langstone stated she knew how to use the bookkeeping software and had trained Shaun Reedy at his request.

5. A computer technician from a local IT service company stated that he had set up the computer systems at Shaun Reedy's office, and showed Shaun Reedy how to use a memory stick in the computer to back up and save files.

6. A follow-up interview with Linda Reedy disclosed that before she married Shaun Reedy, she had worked for John Dalton for two years as an importer of stone tiles and ceramic pottery. She stated her maiden name was Linda Barton. Linda Reedy stated she did not know anyone named Lisa Langstone.

7. Border Inspector Campbell said that a check of the border crossing information disclosed that Shaun Reedy had driven his car across the border from Mexico 48 times in the last 90 days. The vehicle had a passenger by the name of Lisa Langstone.

8. A records check of Lisa Langstone by DEA agent David Mason disclosed that she was arrested for narcotics smuggling and money laundering as Lisa Barton seven years ago, with an accomplice of Linda Barton, her sister. They both spent three years in jail. The printout was included in a report.

9. The RCFL examiner gave a report that stated several files from a memory stick found in a digital camera seized at the home of Shaun Reedy were bookkeeping files and spreadsheets. The examiner stated that bookkeeping software was installed on Shaun Reedy's home computer, and the software files indicated it was used almost daily.

10. Javier Sandoval stated that he was a fishing boat captain in Mexico and that Shaun Reedy would charter his boat for day trips frequently. The trips never lasted more than four or five hours, and the number of guests he would bring would vary.

22. Which statements indicate that Shaun Reedy frequently travels to Mexico and meets with others unknown to the investigators?
a. Statements 7 and 10
b. Statements 4 and 10
c. Statements 8 and 9
d. Statements 7 and 8
e. none of these

23. Which statement may indicate a motive for Linda Reedy to lie?
a. Statement 1
b. Statement 7
c. Statement 8
d. Statement 9
e. none of these

24. In addition to statement 4, what other statements indicate Lisa Langstone could be involved in the case more than as an employee of Shaun Reedy?
a. Statements 8 and 9
b. Statements 7 and 8
c. Statements 6 and 7
d. Statements 7 and 10
e. none of these

25. Which statement has little value to the investigation?
a. Statement 10
b. Statement 8
c. Statement 1
d. Statement 4
e. none of these

26. Which statements indicate that Shaun Reedy may have been acting alone in the fraud?
 a. Statements 2, 5, and 9
 b. Statements 2, 6, and 8
 c. Statements 7, 8, and 10
 d. Statements 1, 7, and 10
 e. none of these

27. Which statement indicates Shaun Reedy was attempting to cover up his bookkeeping files?
 a. Statement 5
 b. Statement 6
 c. Statement 8
 d. Statement 9
 e. none of these

28. Which statement would indicate that both Lisa Langstone and Linda Reedy may have reasons to lie to the investigators?
 a. Statement 1
 b. Statement 8
 c. Statement 9
 d. Statement 10
 e. none of these

29. Which statements indicate that John Dalton may be a victim?
 a. Statements 3 and 9
 b. Statements 3 and 6
 c. Statements 4 and 6
 d. Statements 3 and 4
 e. none of these

30. Which two statements corroborate each other?
 a. Statements 1 and 4
 b. Statements 2 and 5
 c. Statements 5 and 10
 d. Statements 6 and 8
 e. none of these

Answers

Part A: Verbal Reasoning

1. a. The answer is implied by the statement that journalists are not giving voters enough information to understand issues and evaluate candidates. Choice **b** is incorrect because the paragraph does not say that the journalists do not understand the issues, only that they are withholding the information. Choices **c** and **d** are not in the passage. Choice **e** is incorrect because there is no indication that the journalists do not cover stories about political events.

2. d. Several factors state that the operator of a vehicle can control the vehicle through operation and maintenance, improving vehicle mileage. Choices **a** and **c** are incorrect as they are just single factors among many. Choice **b** is a broad statement, and the paragraph does indicate how to avoid or lessen this possible problem. Choice **e** has not been addressed in this paragraph.

3. e. This answer is implied by the statement that redistribution is needed so that people in emerging nations can have proper medical care. Choices **a**, **b**, and **c** are not mentioned in the passage. Choice **d** is also incorrect—the passage indicates that the distribution of medicine (not its production) is inadequate.

4. b. This answer is clearly stated in the first sentence of the paragraph. There is no support in the passage for choices **a**, **d**, or **e**. As for choice **c**, although mediation is mentioned, the statement does not indicate that victims should be the mediators.

5. d. This passage indicates that periodic maintenance is necessary for the computer to run optimally. Choices **a**, **b**, and **e** were not addressed in this passage, but some of them could be inferred. Choice **c** is implied, but not specifically addressed in this instance.

6. d. The essential information that supports this response is located in the last sentence of the paragraph. The negative terms of the sentence can be restated in positive terms in this way: "All useful detection instruments—including trained dog teams—should be used." Choice **a** is not supported by the paragraph: Although the paragraph claims that bomb dogs are useful in detecting explosives, it does not indicate that dog teams are the best form of detection. Choices **b** and **c** are also incorrect because the paragraph does not supply enough information to make these conclusions. Choice **e** sounds similar to the concluding sentence in the paragraph, but includes a key difference. Whereas the paragraph states that "no useful detection instrument" should be unused, choice **e** claims that all available instruments, regardless of their effectiveness, should be used.

7. c. Choice **c** is supported by the second sentence in the paragraph. The paragraph offers at least one other scenario involving credit cards (giving a card to a waiter) that is more risky than shopping online with a credit card at a secured website. Choice **a** is incorrect because the paragraph contradicts this statement. Choice **b** is too strong a statement to be correct—the paragraph claims that such behavior puts consumers at risk, not that they are "asking to be a victim of credit card fraud." The term "guaranteed" used in choice **d** is too absolute to be supported by the paragraph. Choice **e** is incorrect because it claims that "only some consumers" would be helped by information about credit card fraud, whereas the paragraph states that "all consumers" would be helped.

8. e. The last sentence in the paragraph gives the essential information. Choice **a** is outside the scope of the passage: The paragraph does not compare the value of different risk factors. Choice **b** is not supported by the paragraph, and choices **c** and **d** are directly contradicted by the information in the paragraph.

9. e. A well-written report is an easy task if some simple principles are followed. Choice **a** is not addressed and is therefore an incorrect answer. Choices **b** and **c** are incorrect because they were not addressed in the paragraph. Choice **d**, while implied, is not entirely correct.

10. b. The paragraph clearly states that while political ideologies were important before the cold war, after the Cold War, ethnic and religious boundaries became more important than political ones. The paragraph offers no support for choice **a**. Although the writer states that boundaries are being redrawn, he or she does not say that they should be (choice **c**). Choice **d** has no relation to the passage. Choice **e** is incorrect because the paragraph does not discuss the current existence of communism or fascism.

11. b. The last sentence in the paragraph clearly gives support for the idea that the interest in Shakespeare is due to the development of his characters. Choice **a** is incorrect because the writer never makes this type of comparison. Choice **c** is incorrect because even though scholars are mentioned in the paragraph, there is no indication that the scholars are compiling the anthology. Choice **d** is incorrect because there is no support to show that most New Yorkers are interested in this work. There is no support for choice **e** either.

12. a. Choice **a** is backed up by the statement in the last sentence of the paragraph that investigators could make "significant progress" if more individuals reported art fraud. Choices **b** and **c** are incorrect because they make absolute claims (note the terms "impossible" and "must depend," respectively) that are not supported by the paragraph. Choice **d** is not inferred by the paragraph. Choice **e** is contradicted in the paragraph, which states that dealers and buyers perceive that they do have a lot to lose—reputation and business—by reporting art fraud.

13. d. A very strong inference can be made to support this statement. The writer stresses that without rehabilitation, there will be more crime, so it is reasonable to infer that crime will go down with rehabilitation. Choice **a** is wrong because the writer clearly states that rehabilitation should occur before and after prison. Although the writer states that offenders without rehabilitation usually commit more crimes, he or she does not say that criminals always commit more crimes (choice **b**). Choice **c** is not in the paragraph. Although some people may believe that choice **e** is true, this is not mentioned in the paragraph.

14. c. A change in employee social values over the past ten years is implied in the whole paragraph, but particularly in the first sentence. Choice **a** is incorrect because the loyalty of the managers to their corporations is never discussed. There is no support for choice **b**. In choice **d**, perhaps career advancement is less important than it once was, but the paragraph does not indicate that advancement in unimportant to managers. Choice **e** is an opinion that is not supported.

15. b. The support for choice **b** is given in the second sentence of the paragraph. Generation Xers like to work independently, which means they are self-directed. No support is given for either choice **a** or choice **c**. Choice **d** is not related to the paragraph. Although the paragraph mentions that Generation Xers like to be challenged, it does not say they like the challenge their bosses' attitudes; therefore, choice **e** can be ruled out.

16. c. The first sentence states that it is commonplace for college to set low admissions standards for athletes. The second sentence implies that the author believes that since the standards are low, some athletes should not be in college. Although it may follow that if athletes do not study, they will have limited skills, there is not enough support in the paragraph to support choice **a**. There is no support for choices **b** or **d**. Neither is there any indication that the author believes that admissions standards for nonathletes are too high (choice **e**).

17. b. The support for choice **b** is in the third and fourth sentences of the passage. Choices **a** and **e** bring up issues—voters' cynical view of politics and voter education initiatives—that are not discussed in the paragraph and are therefore outside of its scope. Choice **c** is contradicted by the fifth sentence of the paragraph that states that "even though it seems like long campaigns would allow voters to learn more about candidates, these lengthy exposures to candidates have the opposite effect." The claim made in choice **d** that short campaigns would "substantially increase" voter involvement is too strong to be supported by the paragraph.

18. b. This answer is implied by the whole paragraph. The author stresses the need to read critically by performing thoughtful and careful operations on the text. Choice **a** is incorrect because the author never says that reading is dull. Choices **c**, **d**, and **e** are not supported by the paragraph.

19. c. The passage explains that practice is required to achieve proficiency. Choices **a**, **b**, and **d** were not specifically addressed in the passage and are dispelled by the statements. Choice **e**, while implied by the passage, is not specifically addressed.

20. a. The support for this choice is in the second sentence, which states that in some countries, toxic insecticides are still legal. Choice **b** is incorrect because even though polar regions are mentioned in the paragraph, there is no support for the idea that warmer regions are not just as affected. There is no support for choice **c**. Choice **d** can be ruled out because there is nothing to indicate that DDT and toxaphene are the most toxic. Choice **e** is illogical.

21. a. The second and third sentences combine to give support to choice **a**. The statement stresses that there must be a judge's approval (i.e., legal authorization) before a search can be conducted. Choices **b** and **d** are incorrect because it is not enough for the police to have direct evidence or a reasonable belief—a judge must authorize the search for it to be legal. Choices **c** and **e** are not mentioned in the passage.

22. e. The paragraph focuses on the idea that the jury system is different from what it was in colonial times. There is no support given for choices **a**, **b**, or **c**. Choice **d** is incorrect because even though jurors in colonial times were expected to investigate and ask questions, this does not necessarily mean that they were more informed than today's jurors.

23. c. This answer is clearly stated in the last sentence of the paragraph. Choice **a** can be ruled out because there is no support to show that studying math is dangerous. Words are not mentioned in the passage, which rules out choice **b**. Choice **d** is a contradiction to the information in the passage. There is no support for choice **e**.

24. d. The last sentence states that new technologies are reported daily, and this implies that new technologies are being constantly developed. There is no support for choice **a**. With regard to choice **b**, stone tools were first used two and a half million years ago, but they were not necessarily in use all that time. Choice **c** is clearly incorrect since the paragraph states when stone tools first came into use. Although some may agree that choice **e** is true, the author of the paragraph does not give support for this opinion.

25. c. The essential information that supports choice **c** is located in the fifth sentence of the paragraph. Choice **a**, on the other hand, is contradicted by the content of the fifth sentence of the paragraph. Choice **b** is incorrect because the term "all" is too absolute to be supported by the paragraph. Although the paragraph states that growing economies are "especially susceptible" to money laundering, it does not infer the reverse that established economies are not susceptible. Thus, choice **d** is incorrect. Although the statement in choice **e** may be true, the paragraph does not discuss the goal of money-laundering investigations.

Part B: Arithmetic Reasoning

1. c. Solving this problem requires converting 15 minutes to 0.25 hour, which is the time, then using the formula: 62 mph multiplied by 0.25 hour is 15.5 miles.

2. b. Add all the numbers together to solve this problem and arrive at the answer, $92.61.

3. d. Division is used to arrive at a decimal, which can then be rounded to the nearest hundredth and converted to a percentage: 113 divided by 215 is 0.5255. 0.5255 rounded to the nearest hundredth is 0.53, or 53%.

4. c. Subtraction and addition will solve this problem. From 10:42 to 12:42, two hours have elapsed. From 12:42 to 1:00, another 18 minutes has elapsed (60 minus 42 is 18). Then from 1:00 to 1:19, there is another 19 minutes, for a total of 2 hours 37 minutes.

5. e. There are two sides 34 feet long and two sides 20 feet long. Using the formula $P = 2L + 2W$ will solve this problem. Therefore, you should multiply 34 times 2 and 20 times 2, and then add the results: 68 plus 40 is 108.

6. e. The problem is solved by first converting a fraction to a decimal, then multiplying: 2.5 times 0.39 is 0.975, which is rounded to 1 inch.

7. c. The first 2,000 tons are exempt, leaving 3,026 tons. Since the $3.00 rate is for an *additional* 5,000 tons, the $9.00 rate is never reached: 3,026 × $3.00 = $9,078.00.

8. d. There are three steps involved in solving this problem. First, convert 4.5% to a decimal: 0.045. Multiply that by $31,000 to find out how much the salary increases. Finally, add the result

($1,395) to the original salary of $31,000 to find out the new salary, $32,395.

9. a. The sum of the sides equals the perimeter: (3 sides × 3 inches) + (2 sides × 5 inches) = 19 inches.

10. c. To solve the problem you have to first convert the total time to minutes (for the correct choice, c, this is 105 minutes), then multiply by 4 (420 minutes), then convert the answer back to hours by dividing by 60 minutes to arrive at the final answer, which is 7 hours. Or you can multiply $1\frac{3}{4}$ hours by 4 to arrive at the same answer.

11. a. Add the number of men and women to get the total number: 200. The number of women, 24, is 12% of 200.

12. a. First, you must subtract the percentage of the installation cost during construction (1.5%) from the percentage of the installation cost after construction (4%). To do this, begin by converting the percentages into decimals: 4% equals 0.04; 1.5% equals 0.015. Now subtract: 0.04 minus 0.015 equals 0.025. This is the percentage of the total cost that the homeowner will save. Multiply this by the total cost of the home to find the dollar amount: 0.025 times $150,000 is $3,750.

13. b. This problem can be done with an equation $4x + 5x = 18$. When solved, $x = 2$. Multiply 4 by 2 to find that there are 8 men.

14. b. To solve the problem, you must first find the common denominator, in this instance, 24. Then the fractions must be converted: $\frac{1}{8}$ equals $\frac{3}{24}$; $\frac{1}{6}$ equals $\frac{4}{24}$; $\frac{3}{4}$ equals $\frac{18}{24}$. Add the values for first and second layers together: $\frac{3}{24}$ plus $\frac{4}{24}$ is $\frac{7}{24}$, then subtract the sum from the total thickness ($\frac{18}{24}$): $\frac{18}{24}$ minus $\frac{7}{24}$ is $\frac{11}{24}$.

15. e. First, convert Fahrenheit to Centigrade using the formula given: $C = \frac{5}{9}(122 - 32)$; that is, C is equal to $\frac{5}{9}(90)$, so $C = 50$.

16. b. To solve this problem, multiply the amount saved per fire, $5,700, by the average number of fires: 5,700 times 14 is 79,800.

17. d. This is the only choice that includes a 90° angle.

18. c. Each 9-foot wall has an area of 9 × 8 or 72 square feet. There are two such walls, so those two walls combined have an area of 72 × 2 or 144 square feet. Each 11-foot wall has an area of 11 × 8 or 88 square feet, and again, there are two such walls: 88 × 2 = 176. Finally, add 144 and 176 to get 320 square feet.

19. e. The amount of 252 gallons is reduced by 19, leaving 233 gallons. 233 divided by 19 is 12.2, rounded up to 13 refills, which is not one of the choices.

20. b. $\frac{1}{3}x + 3 = 8$. In order to solve the equation, all numbers need to be on one side and all x values on the other. Therefore, $\frac{1}{3}x = 5$; $x = 15$.

Part C: Problems for Investigation

1. e. Statements 5 and 8 contain information provided by tellers that indicates motive or opportunity for other tellers to have embezzled the money.

2. b. The fact that only Jensen and Cruz ever tally the drawer totals, coupled with the fact that the drawers were never short when Cruz performed the tally, casts suspicion on Jensen.

3. a. Statement 7 presents the possibility that a bank customer is taking the money, possibly by way of a change scam.

4. d. Statement 5 is a statement made without personal knowledge, simply repeating what others said.

5. c. Statement 5 indicates an employee is having financial problems and that is a motive for theft. Even though a statement is hearsay, it can still be helpful to an investigation.

6. e. Statement 10 notes that a person who is a suspect, Jensen, is meeting regularly with a person who has access to the teller drawers, Teller Richards. This may indicate that the two are involved in the theft together.

7. d. Statement 9 lists the tellers that worked on days the drawers were short. Any teller who worked none or only some of those days would have a strong alibi.

8. a. The information in Statement 1 has no bearing on the case.

9. b. Statement 4 recounts information that Burt Lentz has acted violently toward someone in his home.

10. d. Statements 5 and 6. Circumstantial evidence is evidence from which the presence of a principle fact of the case can be inferred. From information about the purchase of expensive items and the need for money, one can infer a motive for theft.

11. e. Statement 7 indicates Moi is taking many unscheduled breaks; added to the information that maintenance workers have found evidence in the men's room, this statement casts suspicion on Moi as the thief.

12. b. Statements 3 and 8 indicate that nonpostal employees handle mailbags that on occasion come open. This provides an opportunity for a nonemployee to commit the theft.

13. c. Statement 10 is the only statement that provides possible direct evidence of someone tampering with envelopes.

14. d. Of these choices, only Statement 5 provides a motive, by indicating that an employee is spending large amounts of money.

15. e. Statement 6 provides both an explanation for Arthur's recent spending habits and gossip about another employee needing money. These may both be true, or they may be an attempt to divert investigators' attention.

16. a. Statement 8 is a statement made without personal knowledge, simply repeating what others said.

17. c. Statements 5 and 8 both provide information linking Cross and Marshall. In addition, both contain information that may indicate a plan to commit a crime.

18. b. Statements 8 and 10 indicate that Raymond and Cross may have known one another prior to this employment and that Raymond is willing to direct her subordinate as to his assignment of Cross.

19. d. Statements 3 and 7 both indicate that Wallace is in need of money, providing a motive for theft.

20. c. Statement 2 simply indicates the length of Cross's employment; there is nothing suspicious about that by itself.

21. e. Statement 9 recounts information that, even if true, provides only a tenuous motive for theft.

22. a. Both statements contain information that Shaun Reedy has traveled into Mexico, and statement 10 indicates that he has met with otherwise unidentified persons.

23. c. This statement indicates that Linda Reedy may have a criminal past and be related to a person named in the investigation. Further investigation into the situation may result in discovery of information that she does want her true identity to be revealed.

24. b. These statements indicate not only that Lisa Langstone has a criminal past, but also that she manages financial documents and travels with Shaun Reedy.

25. c. This statement is not proven and does not pertain to the investigation.

26. a. These statements indicate that Shaun Reedy had the technical knowledge and ability to maintain financial records on his home computer, as well as the ability to move data from the office to his home computer via the memory stick in his camera.

27. d. The statement shows that an attempt was made to make the memory stick seem like part of the camera in order to conceal it. The suspect probably did not expect authorities to look on a camera's memory for financial records.

28. b. This statement would indicate that the two women were related, and both had previously committed financial crimes as well as serving time in jail for those crimes.

29. b. This statement shows that John Dalton may have trusted Linda Reedy as a former employee of his, and that he may have been bilked out of $150,000 by investing in a company run by her now-husband Shaun Reedy.

30. d. Statement 6 has Linda Reedy admitting that her maiden name was Linda Barton, and statement 8 shows that she has a criminal past under that name.

Scoring

Because it is necessary for you to do well on all three sections of the TEA exam—Verbal Reasoning, Arithmetic Reasoning, and Problems for Investigation—you should figure your score on each section separately. All three sections can be scored in the same way. First, find the number of questions you got right in each section. Questions you skipped or got wrong don't count; just add up how many questions you got right in each section. Then divide by the number of questions in that section: 25 for Verbal Reasoning, 20 for Arithmetic Reasoning, and 30 for Problems for Investigation. If you get approximately 70% of the answers right on each section, you will pass the test. The tables on the following page will help you check your math by giving you percentage equivalents for some possible scores on each section.

What's much more important than your scores, for now, is how you did on each of the basic skills tested by the exam. You need to diagnose your strengths and weaknesses so that you can concentrate your efforts as you prepare for the exam.

Use your percentage scores in conjunction with the LearningExpress Test Preparation System in Lesson 4 of this book to help you devise a study plan. Then turn to the TEA sample questions in Lesson 3 and instructional Lessons 6, 7, and 8, which cover each of the basic skills tested on the TEA exam. You should plan to spend more time on the lessons that correspond to the questions you found hardest and less time on the lessons that correspond to areas in which you did well. After your study, try your hand at the other two practice exams in this book to see how much you've improved.

VERBAL REASONING	
NUMBER OF QUESTIONS RIGHT	APPROXIMATE PERCENTAGE
25	100%
23	92%
21	84%
19	76%
18	72%
16	64%
14	56%
13	52%

ARITHMETIC REASONING	
NUMBER OF QUESTIONS RIGHT	APPROXIMATE PERCENTAGE
20	100%
18	90%
17	85%
15	75%
14	70%
12	60%
11	55%
10	50%

PROBLEMS FOR INVESTIGATION	
NUMBER OF QUESTIONS RIGHT	APPROXIMATE PERCENTAGE
30	100%
27	90%
24	80%
23	75%
21	70%
20	65%
17	57%
15	50%

6 ▶ VERBAL REASONING

CHAPTER SUMMARY
The information, exercises, and tips included in this chapter are designed to help you improve your comprehension of written passages so that you can increase your test score on the Verbal Reasoning portion of the TEA exam.

Reading and reasoning from what you read are vital skills in almost any profession, and the job of Treasury Enforcement Agent is no exception. As soon as you begin your job, you will be expected to understand complex written material about the law and about regulations and policies pertaining to your position. Verbal reasoning is really just another name for reading comprehension.

The format of the Verbal Reasoning section of the TEA exam is multiple choice. Each question is based on a reading passage that is about a paragraph long. The format is similar to that found in many of the standardized tests you have most likely seen in school, so it will no doubt seem familiar to you. In fact, most types of standardized test questions test your reading skills—after all, if you can't read the question, you can't answer it!

Types of Reading Comprehension Questions

As noted, you have probably encountered reading comprehension questions before, where you are given a passage to read and then have to answer multiple-choice questions about it. This kind of question has two advantages for you as a test taker:

1. You don't have to know anything about the topic of the passage because
2. You're being tested only on the information the passage provides.

But the disadvantage is that you have to know where and how to find that information quickly in an unfamiliar text. This makes it easy to fall for one of the wrong answer choices, especially since they're designed to mislead you.

The best way to do well on this passage/question format is to be very familiar with the kinds of questions that are typically asked on the test. Questions most frequently ask you to:

1. Identify a specific **fact or detail** in the passage
2. Note the **main idea** of the passage
3. Make an **inference** based on the passage
4. Define a **vocabulary** word from the passage

In order for you to do well on a reading comprehension test, you need to know exactly what each of these questions is asking. **Facts and details** are the specific pieces of information that support the passage's main idea. The main idea is the thought, opinion, or attitude that governs the whole passage. Generally speaking, facts and details are indisputable—things that don't need to be proven, like statistics (18 million people) or descriptions (a green overcoat). Let's say, for example, you read a sentence that says, "After the department's reorganization, workers were 50% more productive." A sentence like this, which gives you the fact that 50% of workers were more productive, might

support a **main idea** that says, "Every department should be reorganized." Notice that this main idea is not something indisputable; it is an opinion. The writer thinks all departments should be reorganized, and because this is an opinion (and not everyone shares it), the writer needs to support that opinion with facts and details.

An **inference**, on the other hand, is a conclusion that can be drawn based on fact or evidence. For example, you can infer—based on the fact that workers became 50% more productive after the reorganization, which is a dramatic change—that the department had not been efficiently organized. The fact sentence, "After the department's reorganization, workers were 50% more productive," also implies that the reorganization of the department was the reason workers became more productive. There may, of course, have been other reasons, but we can infer only one from this sentence.

As you might expect, **vocabulary** questions ask you to determine the meaning of particular words. Often, if you've read carefully, you can determine the meaning of such words from their context, that is, how the word is used in the sentence or paragraph.

Practice Passage 1: Using the Four Question Types

The following is a sample test passage, followed by four questions. Read the passage carefully, and then answer the questions, based on your reading of the text, by circling your choice. Then refer to the previous list and note under your answer which type of question has been asked. Correct answers appear immediately after the questions.

Forensic science has been utilized as a crime-solving aid for many years. Forensics is applying proven science and technology in order to process items of evidence, to prove or disprove a point of law, in a court of law. With the advent of popular television shows and the streamlining of the forensic procedures depicted in these shows, many people have a misconception of forensic sciences and its practices.

Sir Francis Galton published a book in 1892 titled *Finger Prints*. In 1915, the organization now known as the International Association for Identification (IAI) was founded. Since that time, law enforcement has needed a continuous advancement in forensic science to assist in the solving of crimes.

1. The phrase "applying proven science and technology in order to process items of evidence, to prove or disprove a point of law, in a court of law" suggests that
   a. forensic sciences must be tested and updated as technology and science advance.
   b. a forensic scientist can prove theories only in a court of law.
   c. only a member of IAI can testify about forensic science.
   d. unproven scientific methods can be used if they prove your point.

   Question type _____

2. In what year was the International Association for Identification founded?
   a. 1892
   b. 1915
   c. 1789
   d. 1776

   Question type _____

3. The best title for this passage would be
   a. "Forensics as Entertainment."
   b. "The Forensic Advancement."
   c. "Forensic Science: An Evolving Tool for Law Enforcement."
   d. "Forensic Fingerprint Identification."

   Question type _____

4. The use of the word *advent* in the third sentence most nearly means
   a. advice.
   b. observation.
   c. applying.
   d. emerging.

   Question type _____

Answers and Explanations for Practice Passage 1

Don't just look at the right answers and move on. The explanations are the most important part, so read them carefully. Use these explanations to help you understand how to tackle each kind of question the next time you come across it.

1. **a.** Question type: Inference. The term *proven* in the quoted phrase suggests that scientific procedures must be scientifically valid before evidence can be tested, and conclusive results yield valid information.

2. **b.** Question type: Fact or detail. The passage states that the organization now known as the International Association for Identification was founded in 1915. Don't be confused by the date of a published book referenced in the passage as an example of the longevity of fingerprint knowledge.

3. **c.** Question type: Main idea. The title encompasses the whole of the article and states what may not be explicitly stated in the article itself. Noting that forensic science is utilized in television shows indicates how much it has impacted today's society and the point of view that forensics can be misconstrued as the final say, rather than a tool used by law enforcement.

4. **a.** Question type: Vocabulary. The word *advent* is used to describe recent television shows that focus on the use of forensic sciences. This shows that it is used as an emerging or new focus of entertainment subject matter.

Practice Passage 2

Following is a second sample passage followed by four questions, again testing each of the four question types. As you did with Practice Passage 1, read this passage carefully and answer the questions based on it, circling your choice and noting under your answer which type of question has been asked. As before, the answers immediately follow the questions.

There are many ways to go about preventing accidents on the job. The National Safety Council, for example, states that accident prevention depends on the three E's—engineering, education, and enforcement: (1) The job should be *engineered* for safety. For example, if a factory employee is using a machine with a blade that descends automatically, the machine should be equipped with a safety device that necessitates the worker using both hands, well out of range of the blade, in order to operate it. (2) Employees should be *educated* in safe procedures. The worker in this example should be carefully instructed and observed using the cutting machine before being allowed to operate it without supervision. (3) Safety rules should be *enforced*. If a worker is found disabling the machine's safety device so that the work can be done more quickly, that worker should be reprimanded or even fired. The implication is that accident prevention boils down to two basic activities: reducing unsafe conditions and reducing unsafe acts.

1. The paragraph suggests that
   a. jobs should be made safe for engineers.
   b. employees who follow safe procedures are smarter than those who don't.
   c. the National Safety Council enforces safety rules on the job.
   d. safety on the job is a team effort between employer and employee.

   Question type _____

2. Which of the following is an example of one of the "E's" recommended by the National Safety Council?
   a. working to prevent on-the-job accidents
   b. equipping a cutting machine with a safety device
   c. failing to equip a cutting machine with a safety device
   d. allowing a worker to do dangerous jobs without adequate supervision

   Question type _____

3. The word *enforced* as used in the section of passage after point (3) most nearly means that the safety rules are
   a. suggested.
   b. imposed.
   c. requested.
   d. rescinded.

   Question type _____

4. The passage best supports the statement that
   a. accident prevention depends on being well-informed and courteous.
   b. unsafe conditions should be reported to the National Safety Council.
   c. well-engineered products are safer.
   d. unsafe conditions and unsafe acts cause most accidents.

   Question type _____

Answers and Explanations for Practice Passage 2

1. d. Question type: Inference, as can be seen in the phrase *The paragraph suggests.* Choice **d** can be inferred from the passage (although it is not directly stated in it) if you carefully read the last sentence. The employer is presumably responsible for not having *unsafe conditions*, the employee for not committing *unsafe acts.* Choices **a** and **b** may be true, but they are not suggested by the passage. Choice **c** is completely false. The National Safety Council is mentioned in the passage, but nowhere is it stated that the NSC enforces safety rules on the job.

2. b. Question type: Fact or detail. The three "E's" are the NSC's safety recommendations, one of which is described in choice **b**. Choice **a** is a generalization based on the three "E's." Choices **c** and **d** are violations of the safety recommendations.

3. b. Question type: Vocabulary. The word has several similar meanings. Choices **a**, **c**, and **d** do not have the same meaning and, when substituted for *enforced*, change the meaning of the sentence completely. Choices **a** and **c** merely suggest that the safety requirements be utilized, and choice **d** completely reverses the meaning of the passage.

4. d. Question type: Main idea. In this passage, the main idea is contained in the last sentence, which implies that *unsafe conditions and unsafe acts* cause most accidents. Incidentally, the main idea can often (although not always) be found at the end of a passage. Choices **a** and **c** may be true but are not addressed in the passage. Choice **b**, *unsafe conditions should be reported to the National Safety Council*, is incorrect because, while the National Safety Council is mentioned in the passage, nothing is said about the reporting of unsafe conditions.

Notice that some of these questions begin with the phrase "The paragraph best supports the statement that . . ." Your TEA exam questions will probably be worded that way, but they will still all fall into the four main question types.

Detail and Main Idea Questions

Main idea questions and fact or detail questions both ask you for information that's right there in the passage. All you have to do is find it.

Detail or Fact Questions

In detail or fact questions, you have to identify a specific item of information from the test. This is usually the simplest kind of question. You just have to be able to separate important information from less important information. However, the choices may often be very similar, so you must be careful not to get confused.

Be sure you read the passage and questions carefully. In fact, it is usually a good idea to read the questions first, *before* you even read the passage, so you'll know what details to look out for.

Main Idea Questions

The main idea of a passage, like that of a paragraph or a book, is what the passage is *mostly* about. The main idea is like an umbrella that covers all of the ideas and details in the passage, so it is usually something general, not specific. For example, in Practice Passage 1, question 3 asked you what title would be best for the passage, and the correct answer was "The Age of Community Policing: Past and Future." This is the best answer because it presents an overview of the information given in the passage.

Sometimes, the main idea is stated clearly, often in the first or last sentence of the passage. The sentence that expresses the main idea is often referred to as the **topic sentence.**

At other times, the main idea is not stated in a topic sentence but is *implied* in the overall passage, and you'll need to determine the main idea by inference. Because there may be much information in the passage, the trick is to understand what all that information adds up to—the gist of what the author wants you to know. Often, some of the wrong answers on main idea questions are specific facts or details from the passage. A good way to test yourself is to ask, "Can this answer serve as a *net* to hold the whole passage together?" If not, chances are you've chosen a fact or detail, not a main idea.

Practice Passage 3: Detail and Main Idea Questions

Practice answering main idea and detail questions by working on the questions that follow this passage. Circle the answers to the questions, and then check your answers against the key that appears immediately after the questions.

There are three different kinds of burns: first degree, second degree, and third degree. It is important to be able to recognize these types of burns so that burn victims are given proper medical treatment. First-degree burns cause the skin to turn red but do not cause blistering. First-degree burns do not require medical treatment other than cooling of the skin with ice or cold water. Second-degree burns blister the skin and should be immersed in warm water and then wrapped in a sterile bandage. Third-degree burns char the skin and turn it black, or burn so deeply that the skin shows white. All third-degree burns should receive immediate hospital care.

1. Which of the following would be the best title for this passage?
    a. Dealing with Third-Degree Burns
    b. How to Recognize and Treat Different Burns
    c. Burn Categories
    d. Preventing Infection in Burns

2. Second-degree burns should be treated with
    a. ice.
    b. nothing.
    c. cold water.
    d. warm water.

3. First-degree burns turn the skin
    a. red.
    b. blue.
    c. black.
    d. white.

4. Which of the following best expresses the main idea of the passage?
    a. There are three different types of burns.
    b. Always have cold compresses on hand.
    c. Different burns require different types of treatment.
    d. Ice is good for treating burns.

Answers and Explanations for Practice Passage 3

1. **b.** Question type: Main idea, because it asks you to choose a title for the passage. This main idea is expressed in the second sentence, the topic sentence: "It is important to be able to recognize these types of burns so that burn victims are given proper treatment." Choice **b** expresses this idea and is the only title that encompasses all of the ideas expressed in the passage. Choice **a** is too limited; it deals only with one of the kinds of burns discussed in the passage. Likewise, choices **c** and **d** are too limited. Choice **c** covers types of burns but not their treatment, and choice **d** deals only with preventing infection.

2. **d.** Question type: Fact or detail. The answer is clearly expressed in the sentence, "Second-degree burns . . . should be immersed in warm water and then wrapped in a sterile bandage." It's easy to choose a wrong answer here because all of the answer choices are mentioned in the passage. You need to read carefully to be sure you match the right burn to the right treatment.

3. a. Question type: Fact or detail. The passage says that first-degree burns "cause the skin to turn red." Again, it's important to read carefully because all of the answer choices (except choice **b**, which can be eliminated immediately) are listed elsewhere in the passage.

4. c. Question type: Main idea. Choice **c** is the only answer that encompasses the whole passage. Choices **b** and **d** are limited to particular burns or treatments, and choice **a** discusses only burns, not their treatment. In addition, the second sentence tells us that "It is important to be able to recognize these types of burns so that burn victims are given proper medical treatment."

Practice Passage 4: Detail and Main Idea Questions

Again, circle the answers to the main idea and detail questions that follow this passage, and check your answers against the key that appears immediately afterward.

Two government studies conducted in the late 1960s documented an urgent need for high quality, cost-effective law enforcement training through the institution of a cadre of professional instructors, modern training facilities, and standardized course content. Responding to these studies, Congress authorized funding for the planning and construction of a consolidated Federal Law Enforcement Training Center (FLETC). In the early 1970s, the FLETC was established as a bureau of the Treasury Department and began training operations in temporary facilities in Washington, DC. Now a bureau of the Department of Homeland Security, FLETC has been the nation's leading organization for state-of-the-art federal law enforcement training for over 30 years.

1. The paragraph best supports the statement that training operations of the FLETC began
  a. in the late 1960s.
  b. in the early 1970s.
  c. during the Watergate scandal.
  d. immediately following the two government studies documenting need.

2. The best title for this passage is
  a. "Urgent Training Needs of the Treasury Department."
  b. "Establishment of the FLETC."
  c. "Government Studies and Their Outcome."
  d. "FLETC's Training Operations."

3. The FLETC was established as a direct result of
  a. demand by law enforcement agencies.
  b. demand by the Treasury Department.
  c. an order by the president of the United States.
  d. two government studies.

4. Funding for the FLETC was authorized by
  a. the Treasury Department.
  b. Congress.
  c. professional instructors.
  d. the president.

Answers and Explanations for Practice Passage 4

1. b. Question type: Detail. The third sentence of the passage states that the FLETC was established in 1970, so the *best* answer is choice **b**. Be careful to read closely or you might mistakenly choose choice **a**, since the 1960s are also mentioned in the passage. Choice **c** is also misleading, because you may know that Watergate occurred in the early 1970s. Remember that you should answer questions only on the basis of what is actually in the passage, not on your outside knowledge. Choice **d** is not in the passage and can be immediately eliminated.

2. b. Question type: Main idea. Choice **b** is the best choice because most of the passage is about *establishment of the FLETC*. Choice **a** is not the best choice because it is only partially correct. Choice **c** is too general. Choice **d** is not discussed in the passage.

3. d. Question type: Detail. This question is answered in the first sentence. The other choices are not in the passage.

4. b. Question type: Fact. This could confuse you if it is not read carefully. All of the answers except choice **d** are mentioned in the passage, but only choice **b** answers the question that is asked.

Inference and Vocabulary Questions

Questions that ask you about the meaning of vocabulary words in the passage and those that ask what the passage *suggests* or *implies* (inference questions) are different from detail or main idea questions. In vocabulary and inference questions, you usually have to pull ideas from the passage, sometimes from more than one place in the passage.

Inference Questions

Inference questions can be the most difficult to answer because they require you to draw meaning from the text when that meaning is implied rather than directly stated. Inferences are conclusions that we draw based on the clues the writer has given us. When you draw inferences, you have to be something of a detective, looking for such clues as word choice, tone, and specific details that suggest a certain conclusion, attitude, or point of view. You have to read between the lines in order to make a judgment about what an author was implying in the passage.

A good way to test whether you've drawn an acceptable inference is to ask, "What evidence do I have for this inference?" If you can't find any, you probably have the wrong answer. You need to be sure that

your inference is logical and that it is based on something that is suggested or implied in the passage itself—not by what you or others might think. Like a good detective, you need to base your conclusions on evidence—facts, details, and other information—not on random hunches or guesses.

Vocabulary Questions

Questions designed to test vocabulary are really trying to measure how well you can figure out the meaning of an unfamiliar word from its context. *Context* refers to the words and ideas surrounding a vocabulary word. If the context is clear enough, you should be able to substitute a nonsense word for the one being sought, and you would still make the right choice because you could determine meaning strictly from the sense of the sentence. For example, you should be able to determine the meaning of the following italicized nonsense word based on its context:

> The speaker noted that it gave him great *terivinix* to announce the winner of the Outstanding Leadership Award.

In this sentence, *terivinix* most likely means

- **a.** pain.
- **b.** sympathy.
- **c.** pleasure.
- **d.** anxiety.

Clearly, the context of an award makes choice **c**, *pleasure,* the best answer. Awards don't usually bring pain, sympathy, or anxiety.

When confronted with an unfamiliar word, try substituting a nonsense word and see if the context gives you the clue. If you're familiar with prefixes, suffixes, and word roots, you can also use this knowledge to help you determine the meaning of an unfamiliar word.

You should be careful not to guess at the answer to a vocabulary question based on how you may have seen the word used before or what you *think* it means. Many words have more than one possible meaning, depending on the context in which they're used, and a word you've seen used one way may mean something else in a test passage. Also, if you don't look at the context carefully, you may make the mistake of confusing the vocabulary word with a similar word. For example, the vocabulary word may be *taut* (meaning "tight"), but if you read too quickly or don't check the context, you might think the word is *tout* (meaning "publicize" or "praise") or *taunt* (meaning "tease"). Always make sure you read carefully and that what you think the word means fits into the context of the passage you're being tested on.

Practice Passage 5: Inference and Vocabulary Questions

The questions that follow this passage are strictly vocabulary and inference questions. Circle the answers to the questions, and then check your answers against the key that appears immediately after the questions.

Dealing with irritable patients is a challenge for healthcare workers. It is critical not to lose your patience. When handling irate patients, remember that they are not angry at you; they are projecting their anger *onto* you. If you respond with irritability, you will increase their hostility. The best thing to do is to remain calm and ignore any imprecations patients may hurl your way. Often, patients will try to anger you just to get some reaction out of you. If you react with anger, they win by getting your attention, but you both lose because the patient is less likely to get proper care.

1. The word irate as it is used in the passage most nearly means
   a. irregular, odd.
   b. happy, cheerful.
   c. ill-tempered, angry.
   d. sloppy, lazy.

2. The passage suggests that healthcare workers
   a. easily lose control of their emotions.
   b. are better off not talking to their patients.
   c. must be careful in dealing with irate patients because the patients may sue the hospital.
   d. may provide inadequate treatment if they become angry at patients.

3. An *imprecation* is most likely
   a. an object.
   b. a curse.
   c. a joke.
   d. a medication.

4. Which of the following best expresses the writer's views about irate patients?
   a. Irate patients usually just want some attention.
   b. Irate patients are always in pain.
   c. Irate patients should be made to wait for treatment.
   d. Managing irate patients is the key to a successful career.

Answers and Explanations for Practice Passage 5

1. c. Question type: Vocabulary. *Irate* means "ill-tempered, angry." It should be clear that choice **b**, *happy, cheerful*, is not the answer; dealing with happy patients is normally not "a challenge." Patients who are choice **a**, *irregular, odd*, or choice **d**, *sloppy, lazy*, may be a challenge in their own way, but they aren't likely to rouse a healthcare worker to anger. In addition, the passage explains that irate patients are not "*angry* at you," and *irate* is used as a synonym for *irritable*, which describes the patients under discussion in the first sentence.

2. d. Question type: Inference. The phrase "the passage *suggests*" might have told you. The idea that angry healthcare workers might give inadequate treatment is implied by the passage as a whole, which seems to be an attempt to prevent angry reactions to irate patients. Furthermore, the last sentence makes this inference possible: "If you react with anger . . . you both lose because the patient is less likely to get proper care." Choice **c** is not correct, because there is no mention of suits anywhere in this passage. Likewise, choice **b** is incorrect; the passage does suggest ignoring patients' insults, but nowhere does it recommend not talking to patients—it simply recommends not talking angrily. And while it may be true that some healthcare workers may lose control of their emotions, the passage does not provide any facts or details to support choice **a**, that they "*easily* lose control." Watch out for key works like *easily* that may distort the intent of the passage.

3. b. If you didn't know what an imprecation is, the context should reveal that it's something you can ignore, so neither choice **a**, an *object*, nor choice **d**, a *medication*, is a likely answer. Furthermore, choice **c** is not likely either, since an irate patient is not likely to be making jokes.

4. a. The writer seems to believe that some irate patients just want attention, as is suggested when the writer says, "Often patients will try to anger you just to get some reaction out of you. If you react with anger, they win *by getting your attention*." It should be clear that choice **b** cannot be the answer, because it includes an absolute: "Irate patients are *always* in pain." Perhaps *some* of the patients are often in pain, but an absolute like *always* is almost always wrong. Besides, this passage refers to patients who may be irate in the hospital, but we have no indication of what

these patients are like at other times. Choice **c** is also incorrect because the purpose of the passage is to ensure that patients receive "proper care" and that irate patients are not discriminated against because of their behavior. Thus, "irate patients should be made to wait for treatment" is not a logical answer. Finally, choice **d** cannot be correct because, although it may be true, there is no discussion of career advancement in the passage.

Review: Putting It All Together

A good way to solidify what you've learned about reading comprehension questions is for *you* to write the questions. Here's a passage, followed by space for you to write your own questions. Write one question of each of the four types: fact or detail, main idea, inference, and vocabulary.

The "broken window" theory was originally developed to explain how minor acts of vandalism or disrespect can quickly escalate to crimes and attitudes that break down the entire social fabric of an area. It is a theory that can easily be applied to any situation in society. The theory contends that if a broken window in an abandoned building is not replaced quickly, soon all the windows will be broken. In other words, a small violation, if condoned, leads others to commit similar or greater violations. Thus, after all the windows have been broken, the building is likely to be looted and perhaps even burned down. According to this theory, violations increase exponentially. Thus, if disrespect to a superior is tolerated, others will be tempted to be disrespectful as well. A management crisis could erupt literally overnight. For example, if one individual begins to disregard proper procedure by neglecting to keep up administrative reports, and this individual is not reprimanded, others will follow

When non-native speakers of English have trouble with reading comprehension tests, it's often because they lack the cultural, linguistic, and historical frame of reference that native speakers enjoy. People who have not lived in or been educated in the United States often don't have the background information that comes from reading American newspapers, magazines, and textbooks.

A second problem for non-native English speakers is the difficulty in recognizing vocabulary and idioms (expressions like "chewing the fat") that assist comprehension. In order to read with good understanding, it's important to have an immediate grasp of as many words as possible in the text. Test takers need to be able to recognize vocabulary and idioms immediately so that the ideas those words express are clear.

The Long View

Read newspapers, magazines, and other periodicals that deal with current events and matters of local, state, and national importance. Pay special attention to articles related to the career you want to pursue.

Be alert to new or unfamiliar vocabulary or terms that occur frequently in the popular press. Use a high-lighter pen to mark new or unfamiliar words as you read. Keep a list of those words and their definitions. Review them for 15 minutes each day. Although at first you may find yourself looking up a lot of words, don't be frustrated—you'll look up fewer and fewer as your vocabulary expands.

During the Test

When you are taking the test, make a picture in your mind of the situation being described in the passage. Ask yourself, "What did the writer most want me to think about this subject?"

Locate and underline the topic sentence that carries the main idea of the passage. Remember that the topic sentence—if there is one—may not always be the first sentence. If there doesn't seem to be one, try to determine what idea summarizes the whole passage.

---

suit by committing similar violations of procedure, thinking, "If he can get away with it, why can't I?" So what starts out as a small thing, a violation that may seem not to warrant disciplinary action, may actually ruin the efficiency of the entire department, putting the people the department serves at risk.

1. Detail question:_____
_____

   a.

   b.

   c.

   d.

2. Main idea question: _____
_____

   a.

   b.

   c.

   d.

3. Inference question:_____
_____

   a.

   b.

   c.

   d.

4. Vocabulary question: _____

_____

a.

b.

c.

d.

Possible Questions

Here is one question of each type based on the passage. Your questions may be very different, but these will give you an idea of the kinds of questions that could be asked.

1. Detail question: According to the passage, which of the following could happen "overnight"?
   a. The building will be burned down.
   b. The department may become unmanageable.
   c. A management crisis might erupt.
   d. The windows will all be broken.

2. Main idea question: Which of the following best expresses the main idea of the passage?
   a. Even minor infractions warrant disciplinary action.
   b. Broken windows must be repaired immediately.
   c. People shouldn't be disrespectful to their superiors.
   d. Reports must be taken seriously.

3. Inference question: The passage suggests that
   a. the broken window theory is inadequate.
   b. managers need to know how to handle a crisis.
   c. reports are unnecessary.
   d. people will get away with as much as they can.

4. Vocabulary question: In this passage, *condoned* most nearly means
   a. punished.
   b. overlooked.
   c. condemned.
   d. applauded.

Answers

1. c.
2. a.
3. d.
4. b.

Additional Resources

Here are some other ways you can build the vocabulary and knowledge that will help you do well on reading comprehension questions.

- Practice asking the four sample question types about passages you read for information or pleasure.
- Use a Web search engine to find articles related to the career you'd like to pursue. Exchange views with others on the Internet. All of these exchanges will help expand your knowledge of job-related material that may appear in a passage on the test.
- Use your library. Many public libraries have sections, sometimes called "Lifelong Learning Centers," that contain materials for adult learners. In these sections, you can find books with exercises in reading and study skills. It's also a good idea to enlarge your base of information by reading related books and articles. Many libraries have computer systems that allow you to access information quickly and easily. Library personnel will show you how to use the computers and microfilm and microfiche machines.
- Begin now to build a broad knowledge of your potential profession. Get in the habit of reading articles in newspapers and magazines on job-related issues. Keep a clipping file of those articles. This will help keep you informed of trends in the profession and familiarize you with pertinent vocabulary.
- If you need more help building your reading skills and taking reading comprehension tests, consider *Reading Comprehension Success in 20 Minutes a Day, 4th Edition,* published by LearningExpress.

ARITHMETIC REASONING

CHAPTER SUMMARY

This chapter gives you some important tips for dealing with the Arithmetic Reasoning questions on the TEA exam and reviews some of the most commonly tested concepts. If you've forgotten most of your high school math or have math anxiety, this chapter is for you.

Knowledge of basic arithmetic, as well as the more complex kinds of reasoning necessary for algebra and geometry problems, is an important qualification for almost any profession. Certainly math skills will be necessary at some point in your career as a Treasury Enforcement Agent. You will have to be able to add up dollar figures, evaluate budgets, compute percentages, and perform other such tasks in your job just as you do in your personal life.

The Arithmetic Reasoning portion of the TEA exam covers the subjects you probably studied in grade school and high school—that is, it emphasizes arithmetic skills and word problems.

Math Strategies

- **Don't work in your head! Use your test book or scratch paper to take notes, draw pictures, and calculate.** Although you might think that you can solve math questions more quickly in your head, that's a good way to make mistakes. Write out each step.

- **Read a math question in *chunks* rather than straight through from beginning to end.** As you read each chunk, stop to think about what it means and make notes or draw a picture to represent that chunk.
- **When you get to the actual question, circle it.** This will keep you more focused as you solve the problem.
- **Glance at the answer choices for clues.** If they're fractions, you probably should do your work in fractions; if they're decimals, you should probably work in decimals, etc.
- **Make a plan of attack** to help you solve the problem.
- **If a question stumps you, try one of the *backdoor* approaches** explained in the next section. These are particularly useful for solving word problems.
- **When you get your answer, reread the circled question to make sure you've answered it.** This helps avoid the careless mistake of answering the wrong question.
- **Check your work after you get an answer.** Test takers get a false sense of security when they get an answer that matches one of the multiple-choice answers. Here are some good ways to check your work *if you have time:*
  - Ask yourself if your answer is reasonable, if it makes sense.
  - Plug your answer back into the problem to make sure the problem holds together.
  - Do the question a second time, but use a different method.
- **Approximate when appropriate.** For example:
  - $5.98 + $8.97 is a little less than $15. (Add: $6 + $9)
  - .9876 × 5.0342 is close to 5. (Multiply: 1 × 5)
- **Skip hard questions and come back to them later.** Mark them in your test book so you can find them quickly.

Backdoor Approaches for Answering Questions That Puzzle You

Remember those word problems you dreaded in high school? Many of them are actually easier to solve by backdoor approaches. The two techniques that follow are terrific ways to solve multiple-choice word problems that you don't know how to solve with a straightforward approach. The first technique, *nice numbers*, is useful when there are unknowns (like x) in the text of the word problem, making the problem too abstract for you. The second technique, *working backward*, presents a quick way to substitute numeric answer choices back into the problem to see which one works.

Nice Numbers

1. When a question contains unknowns, like x, plug nice numbers in for the unknowns. A nice number is one that is easy to calculate with and makes sense in the problem.
2. Read the question with the nice numbers in place. Then solve it.
3. If the answer choices are all numbers, the choice that matches your answer is the right one.
4. If the answer choices contain unknowns, substitute the same nice numbers into all the answer choices. The choice that matches your answer is the right one. If more than one answer matches, do the problem again with different nice numbers. You will have to check only the answer choices that have already matched.

Example:

Judi went shopping with *p* dollars in her pocket. If the price of shirts was *s* shirts for *d* dollars, what is the maximum number of shirts Judi could buy with the money in her pocket?

a. *psd*

b. $\frac{ps}{d}$

c. $\frac{pd}{s}$

d. $\frac{ds}{p}$

e. none of these

To solve this problem, let's try these nice numbers: *p* = $100, *s* = 2; *d* = $25. Now reread it with the numbers in place:

Judi went shopping with **$100** in her pocket. If the price of shirts was **2** shirts for **$25**, what is the maximum number of shirts Judi could buy with the money in her pocket?

Since two shirts cost $25, that means that four shirts cost $50, and eight shirts cost $100. So our answer is **8**. Let's substitute the nice numbers into all four answers:

a. $100 \times 2 \times 25 = 5{,}000$

b. $\frac{100 \times 2}{25} = 8$

c. $\frac{100 \times 25}{2} = 1{,}250$

d. $\frac{25 \times 2}{100} = \frac{1}{2}$

e. none of these

The answer is choice **b,** because it is the only one that matches our answer of **8**.

Working Backward

You can frequently solve a word problem by plugging the answer choices back into the text of the problem to see which one fits all the facts stated in the problem. The process is faster than you think, because you will probably have to substitute only one or two answers to find the right one.

This approach works only when:

- All of the answer choices are numbers.
- You are asked to find a simple number, not a sum, product, difference, or ratio.

Here's what to do:

1. Look at all the answer choices and begin with the one in the middle of the range. For example, if the answers are 14, 8, 2, 20, and 25, begin by plugging 14 into the problem.
2. If your choice doesn't work, eliminate it. Determine if you need a bigger or smaller answer.

3. Plug in one of the remaining choices.

4. If none of the answers works, you may have made a careless error. Begin again or look for your mistake.

Example:

Juan ate $\frac{1}{3}$ of the jelly beans. Maria then ate $\frac{3}{4}$ of the remaining jelly beans, which left 10 jelly beans. How many jelly beans were there to begin with?

a. 60

b. 80

c. 90

d. 120

e. none of these

Starting with one of the middle answers, let's assume there were **90** jelly beans to begin with:

Since Juan ate $\frac{1}{3}$ of them, that means he ate 30 ($\frac{1}{3} \times 90 = 30$), leaving 60 of them (90 − 30 = 60). Maria then ate $\frac{3}{4}$ of the 60 jelly beans, or 45 of them ($\frac{3}{4} \times 60 = 45$). That leaves 15 jelly beans (60 − 45 = 15).

The problem states that there were **10** jelly beans left, and we wound up with 15 of them. That indicates that we started with too big a number. Thus, 90 and 120 are both wrong! With only two choices left, let's use common sense to decide which one to try. The next lower answer is only a little smaller than 90 and may not be small enough. So, let's try **60**:

Since Juan ate $\frac{1}{3}$ of them, that means he ate 20 ($\frac{1}{3} \times 60 = 20$), leaving 40 of them (60 − 20 = 40). Maria then ate $\frac{3}{4}$ of the 40 jelly beans, or 30 of them ($\frac{3}{4} \times 40 = 30$). That leaves 10 jelly beans (40 − 30 = 10).

Because this result of **10** jelly beans left agrees with the problem, the correct answer is choice **a**.

Word Problems

Many of the math problems on tests are word problems. A word problem can include any kind of math, including simple arithmetic, fractions, decimals, percentages, even algebra and geometry.

The hardest part of any word problem is translating English into math. When you read a problem, you can frequently translate it *word for word* from English statements into mathematical statements. At other times, however, a key word in the word problem hints at the mathematical operation to be performed. Here are the translation rules:

EQUALS key words: *is, are, has*	
ENGLISH	**MATH**
Bob **is** 18 years old.	$b = 18$
There **are** seven hats.	$h = 7$
Judi **has** five books.	$j = 5$

ADDITION   key words: *sum; more, greater, or older than; total; altogether*

ENGLISH	MATH
The **sum** of two numbers is 10.	$x + y = 10$
Karen has $5 **more than** Sam.	$k = 5 + s$
The base is 3" **greater than** the height.	$b = 3 + h$
Judi is two years **older than** Tony.	$j = 2 + t$
The **total** of three numbers is 25.	$a + b + c = 25$
How much do Joan and Tom have **altogether**?	$j + t = ?$

SUBTRACTION   key words: *difference; fewer, less, or younger than; remain; left over*

ENGLISH	MATH
The **difference** between two numbers is 17.	$x - y = 17$
Mike has 5 **fewer** cats than twice the number Jan has.	$m = 2j - 5$
Jay is two years **younger than** Brett.	$j = b - 2$
After Carol ate three apples, r apples **remained**.	$r = a - 3$

MULTIPLICATION   key words: *of, product, times*

ENGLISH	MATH
20% **of** Matthew's baseball caps	$0.20 \times m$
Half **of** the boys	$\frac{1}{2} \times b$
The **product** of two numbers is 12.	$a \times b = 12$

DIVISION   key word: *per*

ENGLISH	MATH
15 drops **per** teaspoon	$\frac{15 \text{ drops}}{\text{teaspoon}}$
22 miles **per** gallon	$\frac{22 \text{ miles}}{\text{gallon}}$

Distance Formula: Distance = Rate × Time

The key words are movement words like: plane, train, boat, car, walk, run, climb, swim, travel.

- How far did the **plane** travel in 4 hours if it averaged 300 miles per hour?

  $d = 300 \times 4$

  $d = 1,200$ miles
- Ben **walked** 20 miles in 4 hours. What was his average speed?

  $20 = r \times 4$

  5 miles per hour $= r$

Solving a Word Problem Using the Translation Table

Remember the earlier problem about the jelly beans?

> Juan ate $\frac{1}{3}$ of the jelly beans. Maria then ate $\frac{3}{4}$ of the remaining jelly beans, which left 10 jelly beans. How many jelly beans were there to begin with?
>
> **a.** 60
>
> **b.** 80
>
> **c.** 90
>
> **d.** 120
>
> **e.** none of these

We solved it by *working backward.* Now let's solve it using our translation rules.

Assume Juan started with J jelly beans. Eating $\frac{1}{3}$ **of** them means eating $\frac{1}{3} \times J$ jelly beans. Maria ate a fraction of the **remaining** jelly beans, which means we must **subtract** to find out how many are left: $J - \frac{1}{3} \times J = \frac{2}{3} \times J$. Maria then ate $\frac{3}{4}$, leaving $\frac{1}{4}$ **of** the $\frac{2}{3} \times J$ jelly beans, or $\frac{1}{4} \times \frac{2}{3} \times J$ jelly beans. Multiplying out $\frac{1}{4} \times \frac{2}{3} \times J$ gives $\frac{1}{6}J$ as the number of jelly beans left. The problem states that there were **10 jelly beans left**, meaning that we set $\frac{1}{6} \times J$ **equal to** 10:

$$\frac{1}{6} \times J = 10$$

Solving this equation for J gives $J = 60$. Thus, the right answer is choice **a** (the same answer we got when we *worked backward).* As you can see, both methods—working backward and translating from English to math—work. You should use whichever method is more comfortable for you.

Practice Word Problems

You will find word problems using fractions, decimals, and percentages in those sections of this lesson. For now, practice using the translation table on problems that just require you to work with basic arithmetic. Answers are found at the end of the lesson.

1. A police officer checked out 250 rounds of practice ammunition at the firing range. After practice, he returned 64 rounds. How many rounds did he shoot for practice?
   a. 186
   b. 166
   c. 196
   d. 176
   e. none of these

2. A sheriff's department Search and Rescue (SAR) unit has eight teams with nine personnel in each team. How many total personnel are assigned to the SAR unit?
   a. 89
   b. 68
   c. 90
   d. 72
   e. none of these

_____ **3.** A clerk can process 38 records into a ledger in one hour. How many hours will it take to process 228 records?

   a. 5
   b. 6
   c. 7
   d. 8
   e. none of these

_____ **4.** A federal officer completed a trip for official business and is submitting her voucher for payment. Airfare cost $310.22 and her rental car cost $135.16. The hotel she stayed at incurred a cost of $142.50 per night for three nights, plus three days per diem at $72.50 per day. What is the total amount she is to be reimbursed for the trip?

   a. $660.38
   b. $1,190.38
   c. $1,091.00
   d. $645.00
   e. none of these

Fraction Review

Problems involving fractions may be straightforward calculation questions, or they may be word problems. Typically, they ask you to add, subtract, multiply, divide, or compare fractions.

Working with Fractions

A fraction is a part of something.

Example:

Let's say that a pizza was cut into eight equal slices and you ate three of them. The fraction $\frac{3}{8}$ tells you what part of the pizza you ate. The following pizza shows this: Three of the eight pieces (the ones you ate) are shaded.

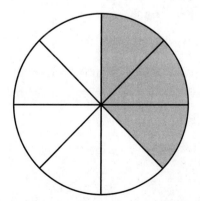

THREE KINDS OF FRACTIONS	
Proper fraction	The top number is less than the bottom number: $\frac{1}{2}$; $\frac{2}{3}$; $\frac{4}{9}$; $\frac{8}{13}$ The value of a proper fraction is less than 1.
Improper fraction	The top number is greater than or equal to the bottom number: $\frac{3}{2}$; $\frac{5}{3}$; $\frac{14}{9}$; $\frac{12}{12}$ The value of an improper fraction is 1 or more.
Mixed number	A fraction written to the right of a whole number: $3\frac{1}{2}$; $4\frac{2}{3}$; $12\frac{3}{4}$; $24\frac{3}{4}$ The value of a mixed number is more than 1: It is the sum of the whole number plus the fraction.

Changing Improper Fractions into Mixed or Whole Numbers

It's easier to add and subtract fractions that are mixed numbers rather than improper fractions. To change an improper fraction, say $\frac{13}{2}$, into a mixed number, follow these steps:

1. Divide the bottom number (2) into the top number (13) to get the whole number portion (6) of the mixed number:

$$\begin{array}{r} 6 \\ 2\overline{)13} \\ \underline{12} \\ 1 \end{array}$$

2. Write the remainder of the division (1) over the old bottom number (2): $6\frac{1}{2}$
3. Check: Change the mixed number back into an improper fraction (see following steps).

Changing Mixed Numbers into Improper Fractions

It's easier to multiply and divide fractions when you're working with improper fractions rather than mixed numbers. To change a mixed number, say $2\frac{3}{4}$, into an improper fraction, follow these steps:

1. Multiply the whole number (2) by the bottom number (4): $2 \times 4 = 8$
2. Add the result (8) to the top number (3): $8 + 3 = 11$
3. Put the total (11) over the bottom number (4): $\frac{11}{4}$
4. Check: Reverse the process by changing the improper fraction into a mixed number. If you get back the number you started with, your answer is right.

Reducing Fractions

Reducing a fraction means writing it in *lowest terms*, that is, with smaller numbers. For instance, 50¢ is $\frac{50}{100}$ of a dollar, or $\frac{1}{2}$ of a dollar. In fact, if you have 50¢ in your pocket, you say that you have half a dollar. Reducing a fraction does not change its value.

Follow these steps to reduce a fraction:

1. Find a whole number that divides *evenly* into both numbers that make up the fraction.
2. Divide that number into the top of the fraction, and replace the top of the fraction with the quotient (the answer you got when you divided).
3. Do the same thing to the bottom number.
4. Repeat the first three steps until you can't find a number that divides evenly into both numbers of the fraction.

For example, let's reduce $\frac{8}{24}$. We could do it in two steps: $\frac{8 \div 4}{24 \div 4} = \frac{2}{6}$; then $\frac{2 \div 2}{6 \div 2} = \frac{1}{3}$. Or we could do it in a single step: $\frac{8 \div 8}{24 \div 8} = \frac{1}{3}$.

Shortcut: When the top and bottom numbers both end in zeros, cross out the same number of zeros in both numbers to begin the reducing process. For example $\frac{300}{4,000}$ reduces to $\frac{3}{40}$ when you cross out two zeros in both numbers.

Whenever you do arithmetic with fractions, reduce your answer. On a multiple-choice test, don't panic if your answer isn't listed. Try to reduce it and then compare it to the choices.

Reduce these fractions to lowest terms.

_____ **5.** $\frac{3}{12} =$

_____ **6.** $\frac{14}{35} =$

_____ **7.** $\frac{27}{72} =$

Raising Fractions to Higher Terms

Before you can add and subtract fractions, you have to know how to raise a fraction to higher terms. This is actually the opposite of reducing a fraction.

Follow these steps to raise $\frac{2}{3}$ to 24ths:

1. Divide the old bottom number (3) into the new one (24): $\quad 3\overline{)24} = 8$

2. Multiply the answer (8) by the old top number (2): $\quad 2 \times 8 = 16$

3. Put the answer (16) over the new bottom number (24): $\quad \frac{16}{24}$

4. Check: Reduce the new fraction to see if you get back the original one: $\quad \frac{16 \div 8}{24 \div 8} = \frac{2}{3}$

Raise these fractions to higher terms.

_____ **8.** $\frac{13}{16} = \frac{}{64}$

_____ **9.** $\frac{8}{27} = \frac{}{81}$

_____ **10.** $\frac{11}{30} = \frac{}{240}$

Adding Fractions

If the fractions have the same bottom numbers, just add the top numbers together and write the total over the bottom number.

Examples: $\frac{2}{9} + \frac{4}{9} = \frac{2+4}{9} = \frac{6}{9}$ Reduce the sum: $\frac{2}{3}$.

$\frac{5}{8} + \frac{7}{8} = \frac{12}{8}$ Change the sum to a mixed number: $1\frac{4}{8}$; then reduce: $1\frac{1}{2}$.

There are a few extra steps to add mixed numbers with the same bottom numbers, say $2\frac{3}{5} + 1\frac{4}{5}$:

1. Add the fractions: $\frac{3}{5} + \frac{4}{5} = \frac{7}{5}$

2. Change the improper fraction into a mixed number: $\frac{7}{5} = 1\frac{2}{5}$

3. Add the whole numbers: $2 + 1 = 3$

4. Add the results of steps 2 and 3: $1\frac{2}{5} + 3 = 4\frac{2}{5}$

Finding the Least Common Denominator

If the fractions you want to add don't have the same bottom number, you will have to raise some or all of the fractions to higher terms so that they all have the same bottom number, called the **common denominator**. All of the original bottom numbers divide evenly into the common denominator. If it is the smallest number that they all divide evenly into, it is called the **least common denominator (LCD)**.

   Here are a few tips for finding the LCD, the smallest number that all the bottom numbers evenly divide into:

- See if all the bottom numbers divide evenly into the biggest bottom number.
- Look at a multiplication table of the largest bottom number until you find a number that all the other bottom numbers evenly divide into.
- When all else fails, multiply all the bottom numbers together.

   Example: $\frac{2}{3} + \frac{4}{5}$

1. Find the LCD. Multiply the bottom numbers: $3 \times 5 = 15$

2. Raise each fraction to 15ths: $\frac{2}{3} = \frac{10}{15}$

$+\frac{4}{5} = \frac{12}{15}$

3. Add as usual: $\frac{22}{15}$

Try these addition problems.

_____ **11.** $\frac{3}{4} + \frac{1}{6} =$

_____ **12.** $\frac{7}{8} + \frac{2}{3} + \frac{3}{4} =$

_____ **13.** $4\frac{1}{3} + 2\frac{3}{4} + \frac{1}{6} =$

Subtracting Fractions

If the fractions have the same bottom numbers, just subtract the top numbers and write the difference over the bottom number.

> *Example:* $\frac{4}{9} - \frac{3}{9} = \frac{4-3}{9} = \frac{1}{9}$

If the fractions you want to subtract don't have the same bottom number, you will have to raise some or all of the fractions to higher terms so that they all have the same bottom number, or LCD. If you forgot how to find the LCD, just read the section on adding fractions with different bottom numbers.

> *Example:* $\frac{5}{6} - \frac{3}{4}$

1. Raise each fraction to 12ths because 12 is the LCD, the smallest number that both 6 and 4 divide into evenly:

2. Subtract as usual:

$$\frac{5}{6} = \frac{10}{12}$$
$$-\frac{3}{4} = \frac{9}{12}$$
$$\overline{\frac{1}{12}}$$

Subtracting mixed numbers with the same bottom number is similar to adding mixed numbers.

> *Example:* $4\frac{3}{5} - 1\frac{2}{5}$

1. Subtract the fractions: $\qquad \frac{3}{5} - \frac{2}{5} = \frac{1}{5}$

2. Subtract the whole numbers: $\qquad 4 - 1 = 3$

3. Add the results of steps 1 and 2: $\qquad \frac{1}{5} + 3 = 3\frac{1}{5}$

Sometimes, there is an extra "borrowing" step when you subtract mixed numbers with the same bottom numbers, say $7\frac{3}{5} - 2\frac{4}{5}$:

1. You can't subtract the fractions the way they are because $\frac{4}{5}$ is bigger than $\frac{3}{5}$. So, you borrow 1 from the 7, making it 6, and change that 1 to $\frac{5}{5}$ because 5 is the bottom number: $\qquad 7\frac{3}{5} = 6\frac{5}{5} + \frac{3}{5}$

2. Add the numbers from step 1: $\qquad 6\frac{5}{5} + \frac{3}{5} = 6\frac{8}{5}$

3. Now you have a different version of the original problem: $\qquad 6\frac{8}{5} - 2\frac{4}{5}$

4. Subtract the fractional parts of the two mixed numbers: $\qquad \frac{8}{5} - \frac{4}{5} = \frac{4}{5}$

5. Subtract the whole number parts of the two mixed numbers: $\qquad 6 - 2 = 4$

6. Add the results of the last two steps together: $\qquad 4 + \frac{4}{5} = 4\frac{4}{5}$

Try these subtraction problems.

_____ **14.** $\frac{5}{6} - \frac{1}{4} =$

_____ **15.** $\frac{15}{16} - \frac{3}{32} - \frac{1}{64} =$

_____ **16.** $66\frac{2}{3} - 7\frac{1}{4} =$

Now let's put what you have learned about adding and subtracting fractions to work in some real-life problems.

_____ **17.** A package courier travels from a warehouse to the start of his route, a distance of $7\frac{3}{4}$ miles. His first stop is $5\frac{1}{2}$ miles after that, a second stop is $2\frac{7}{8}$ miles farther, and a third stop is $2\frac{1}{4}$ miles farther than the second. The route back to the warehouse is $8\frac{1}{2}$ miles. What is the total mileage the courier drove?

    a. $19\frac{1}{8}$

    b. $24\frac{1}{4}$

    c. $34\frac{5}{8}$

    d. $26\frac{7}{8}$

    e. none of these

_____ **18.** A federal agent recorded the beginning mileage on a government-issued vehicle as 1,714.2 and turned it in several months later with an ending mileage of 6,740.2. He received another vehicle with a beginning mileage of 2,739.9 and noted his ending mileage upon turning it in as 3,242.5. What is the combined mileage he added to both of these vehicles?

    a. 9,982.7

    b. 5,026

    c. 5,528.6

    d. 4,454.1

    e. none of these

Multiplying Fractions

Multiplying fractions is actually easier than adding them. All you do is multiply the top numbers and then multiply the bottom numbers.

Examples: $\frac{2}{3} \times \frac{5}{7} = \frac{2 \times 5}{3 \times 7} = \frac{10}{21}$ $\frac{1}{2} \times \frac{3}{5} \times \frac{7}{4} = \frac{1 \times 3 \times 7}{2 \times 5 \times 4} = \frac{21}{40}$

Sometimes, you can *cancel* before multiplying. Canceling is a shortcut that makes the multiplication go faster because you're multiplying with smaller numbers. It's very similar to reducing: If there is a number that divides evenly into a top number and bottom number, do that division before multiplying. If you forget to cancel, you'll still get the right answer, but you'll have to reduce it.

Example: $\frac{5}{6} \times \frac{9}{20}$

1. Cancel the 6 and the 9 by dividing 3 into both of them: $6 \div 3 = 2$ and $9 \div 3 = 3$. Cross out the 6 and the 9:

$$\frac{5}{\cancel{6}} \times \frac{\cancel{9}^{3}}{20}$$
$$_{2}$$

2. Cancel the 5 and the 20 by dividing 5 into both of them: $5 \div 5 = 1$ and $20 \div 5 = 4$. Cross out the 5 and the 20:

$$\frac{\cancel{5}^{1}}{\cancel{6}} \times \frac{\cancel{9}^{3}}{\cancel{20}}$$
$$_{2} \quad _{4}$$

3. Multiply across the new top numbers and the new bottom numbers:

$$\frac{1 \times 3}{2 \times 4} = \frac{3}{8}$$

Try these multiplication problems.

———— **19.** $\frac{1}{5} \times \frac{2}{3}$

———— **20.** $\frac{2}{3} \times \frac{4}{7} \times \frac{3}{5}$

———— **21.** $\frac{3}{4} \times \frac{8}{9}$

To multiply a fraction by a whole number, first rewrite the whole number as a fraction with a bottom number of 1.

Example: $5 \times \frac{2}{3} = \frac{5}{1} \times \frac{2}{3} = \frac{10}{3}$

To multiply with mixed numbers, it's easier to change them to improper fractions before multiplying.

Example: $4\frac{2}{3} \times 5\frac{1}{2}$

1. Convert $4\frac{2}{3}$ to an improper fraction:

$$4\frac{2}{3} = \frac{(4 \times 3 + 2)}{3} = \frac{14}{3}$$

2. Convert $5\frac{1}{2}$ to an improper fraction:

$$5\frac{1}{2} = \frac{(5 \times 2 + 1)}{2} = \frac{11}{2}$$

3. Cancel and multiply the fractions:

$$\frac{\cancel{14}^{7}}{3} \frac{11}{\cancel{2}_{1}} = \frac{77}{3}$$

4. Optional: Convert the improper fraction to a mixed number:

$$\frac{77}{3} = 25\frac{2}{3}$$

Now try these multiplication problems with mixed numbers and whole numbers.

———— **22.** $4\frac{1}{3} \times \frac{2}{5}$

———— **23.** $2\frac{1}{2} \times 6$

———— **24.** $3\frac{3}{4} \times 4\frac{2}{5}$

Here are a few more real-life problems to test your skills.

_____ **25.** After driving $\frac{2}{3}$ of the 15 miles to work, Mr. Stone stopped to make a phone call. How many miles had he driven when he made his call?
  a. 5
  b. $7\frac{1}{2}$
  c. 10
  d. 12
  e. none of these

_____ **26.** If Henry worked $\frac{3}{4}$ of a 40-hour week, how many hours did he work?
  a. $7\frac{1}{2}$
  b. 10
  c. 25
  d. 30
  e. none of these

_____ **27.** Technician Chin makes $14.00 an hour. When she works more than eight hours a day, she gets overtime pay of $1\frac{1}{2}$ times her regular hourly wage for the extra hours. How much did she earn for working 11 hours in one day?
  a. $77
  b. $154
  c. $175
  d. $210
  e. none of these

Dividing Fractions

To divide one fraction by a second fraction, invert the second fraction (that is, flip the top and bottom numbers) and then multiply. That's all there is to it!

Example: $\frac{1}{2} \div \frac{3}{5}$

1. Invert the second fraction ($\frac{3}{5}$):
2. Change the division sign ($\div$) to a multiplication sign ($\times$).
3. Multiply the first fraction by the new second fraction:

$$\frac{5}{3}$$
$$\frac{1}{2} \times \frac{3}{5}$$
$$\frac{1}{2} \times \frac{5}{3} = \frac{1 \times 5}{2 \times 3} = \frac{5}{6}$$

To divide a fraction by a whole number, first change the whole number to a fraction by putting it over 1. Then follow the preceding division steps.

Example: $\frac{3}{5} \div 2 = \frac{3}{5} \div \frac{2}{1} = \frac{3}{5} \times \frac{1}{2} = \frac{3 \times 1}{5 \times 2} = \frac{3}{10}$

When the division problem has a mixed number, convert it to an improper fraction and then divide as usual.

Example: $2\frac{3}{4} \div \frac{1}{6}$

1. Convert $2\frac{3}{4}$ to an improper fraction: $\qquad\qquad 2\frac{3}{4} = \frac{2 \times 4 + 3}{4} = \frac{11}{4}$

2. Divide $\frac{11}{4}$ by $\frac{1}{6}$: $\qquad\qquad\qquad\qquad \frac{11}{4} \div \frac{1}{6} = \frac{11}{4} \times \frac{6}{1}$

3. Flip $\frac{1}{6}$ to $\frac{6}{1}$, change $\div$ to $\times$, cancel and multiply: $\qquad \frac{11}{\underset{2}{4}} \times \frac{\overset{3}{6}}{1} = \frac{11 \times 3}{2 \times 1} = \frac{33}{2}$

Here are a few division problems to try.

_____ **28.** $\frac{1}{3} \div \frac{2}{3}$

_____ **29.** $2\frac{3}{4} \div \frac{1}{2}$

_____ **30.** $\frac{3}{5} \div 3$

_____ **31.** $3\frac{3}{4} \div 2\frac{1}{3}$

Let's wrap this up with some real-life problems.

_____ **32.** A gallon of ice cream will yield 42 scoops. Giving each guest at a party two scoops, how many gallons are required for 189 guests?

    a. $4\frac{1}{2}$

    b. 9

    c. 12

    d. 16

    e. none of these

_____ **33.** The rental rate of a tiller for a garden is $5.30 per hour. The rental bill was $39.75. How many hours was the tiller rented?

    a. $9\frac{1}{4}$

    b. $8\frac{3}{4}$

    c. $7\frac{1}{2}$

    d. $6\frac{3}{4}$

    e. none of these

_____ **34.** Three campers have a total of 25 pounds of food they must carry to their campsite in backpacks. If the weight is split evenly, how many pounds must each camper carry?

    a. $8\frac{1}{3}$

    b. $7\frac{7}{8}$

    c. $9\frac{1}{8}$

    d. $6\frac{3}{4}$

    e. none of these

Decimals

What Is a Decimal?

A decimal is a special kind of fraction. You use decimals every day when you deal with money—$10.35 is a decimal that represents 10 dollars and 35 cents. The decimal point separates the dollars from the cents. Because there are 100 cents in one dollar, 1¢ is $\frac{1}{100}$ of a dollar, or $.01.

Each decimal digit to the right of the decimal point has a name:

Examples: $.1 = 1$ tenth $= \frac{1}{10}$

$.02 = 2$ hundredths $= \frac{2}{100}$

$.003 = 3$ thousandths $= \frac{3}{1,000}$

$.0004 = 4$ ten-thousandths $= \frac{4}{10,000}$

When you add zeros after the rightmost decimal place, you don't change the value of the decimal. For example, 6.17 is the same as all of these:

6.170

6.1700

6.17000000000000000

If there are digits on both sides of the decimal point (like 10.35), the number is called a mixed decimal. If there are digits only to the right of the decimal point (like .53), the number is called a decimal. A whole number (like 15) is understood to have a decimal point at its right (15.). Thus, 15 is the same as 15.0, 15.00, 15.000, and so on.

Changing Fractions to Decimals

To change a fraction to a decimal, divide the bottom number into the top number after you put a decimal point and a few zeros on the right of the top number. When you divide, bring the decimal point up into your answer.

Example: Change $\frac{3}{4}$ to a decimal.

1. Add a decimal point and two zeros to the top number (3):   3.00
2. Divide the bottom number (4) into 3.00:
   Bring the decimal point up into the answer:

$$\begin{array}{r} .75 \\ 4\overline{)3.00} \\ \underline{2\,8} \\ 20 \\ \underline{20} \\ 0 \end{array}$$

3. The quotient (result of the division) is the answer: .75

Some fractions may require you to add many decimal zeros in order for the division to come out evenly. In fact, when you convert a fraction like $\frac{2}{3}$ to a decimal, you can keep adding decimal zeros to the top number forever because the division will never come out evenly! As you divide 3 into 2, you will keep getting 6's:

$$2 \div 3 = .6666666666 \text{ etc.}$$

This is called a **repeating decimal**, and it can be written as $.\overline{666}$ or as $.66\frac{2}{3}$. You can approximate it as .67, .667, .6667, and so on.

Changing Decimals to Fractions

To change a decimal to a fraction, write the digits of the decimal as the top number of a fraction and write the decimal's name as the bottom number of the fraction. Then reduce the fraction, if possible.

>   *Example:* .018

1. Write 18 as the top of the fraction: $\underline{18}$
2. Three places to the right of the decimal means *thousandths*, so write 1,000 as the bottom number: $\frac{18}{1,000}$
3. Reduce by dividing the top and bottom numbers by 2: $\frac{18 \div 2}{1,000 \div 2} = \frac{9}{500}$

>   Change these decimals or mixed decimals to fractions.

_____ **35.** .005

_____ **36.** 17.76

_____ **37.** 27.399

Comparing Decimals

Because decimals are easier to compare when they have the same number of digits after the decimal point, tack zeros onto the end of the shorter decimals. Then all you have to do is compare the numbers as if the decimal points weren't there:

>   *Example:*   Compare .08 and .1

1. Tack one zero at the end of .1:   .10
2. To compare .10 to .08, just compare 10 to 8.
3. Since 10 is larger than 8, .1 is larger than .08.

Adding and Subtracting Decimals

To add or subtract decimals, line them up so their decimal points are even. You may want to tack on zeros at the end of shorter decimals so you can keep all your digits lined up evenly. Remember, if a number doesn't have a decimal point, then put one at the right end of the number.

>   *Example:*   1.23 + 57 + .038

1. Line up the numbers like this:

$$\begin{array}{r} 1.230 \\ 57.000 \\ \underline{+\ .038} \\ 58.268 \end{array}$$

2. Add.

>   *Example:*   1.23 − .038 =

1. Line up the numbers like this:
2. Subtract.

$$\begin{array}{r} 1.230 \\ \underline{-\ .038} \\ 1.192 \end{array}$$

Try these addition and subtraction problems.

_____ **38.** 925.5026 + 27.399 + 836.0984 =

_____ **39.** 0.625 + 4.05 + 2 =

_____ **40.** 3.378 - 3.155 =

_____ **41.** 123.456 – 122

_____ **42.** Officer Peterson drove 3.7 miles to the state park. He then walked 1.6 miles around the park to make sure everything was all right. He got back into the car, drove 2.75 miles to check on a broken traffic light, and then drove 2 miles back to the police station. How many miles did he drive in total?
a. 8.05
b. 8.45
c. 8.8
d. 10
e. none of these

_____ **43.** The average number of emergency room visits at City Hospital fell from 486.4 per week to 402.5 per week. By how many emergency room visits per week did the average fall?
a. 73.9
b. 83
c. 83.1
d. 83.9
e. none of these

Multiplying Decimals

To multiply decimals, ignore the decimal points and just multiply the numbers. Then count the total number of decimal digits (the digits to the *right* of the decimal point) in the numbers you are multiplying. Count off that number of digits in your answer beginning at the right side and put the decimal point to the *left* of those digits.

Example: 215.7×2.4

1. Multiply 2157 times 24:

$$
\begin{array}{r}
2157 \\
\times\,24 \\
\hline
8628 \\
4314 \\
\hline
51768
\end{array}
$$

2. Because there is a total of two decimal digits in 215.7 and 2.4, count off two places from the right in 51768, placing the decimal point to the *left* of the last two digits:

517.68

If your answer doesn't have enough digits, tack zeros on to the left of the answer.

Example: .03 × .006

1. Multiply 3 times 6: $3 \times 6 = 18$

2. You need five decimal digits in your answer, so tack on three zeros: 00018

3. Put the decimal point at the front of the number (which is five digits in from the right): .00018

You can practice multiplying decimals with these problems.

_____ **44.** .05 × .6

_____ **45.** .053 × 6.4

_____ **46.** 38.1 × .0184

_____ **47.** Joe earns $14.50 per hour. Last week, he worked 37.5 hours. How much money did he earn that week?
   a. $518.00
   b. $525.00
   c. $536.50
   d. $543.75
   e. none of these

_____ **48.** Nuts cost $3.50 per pound. Approximately how much will 4.25 pounds of nuts cost?
   a. $12.50
   b. $12.88
   c. $14.50
   d. $14.88
   e. none of these

Dividing Decimals

To divide a decimal by a whole number, set up the division $(8\overline{).256})$ and immediately bring the decimal point straight up into the answer $(8\overline{).256})$. Then divide as you would normally divide whole numbers.

Example:

$$
\begin{array}{r}
.032 \\
8\overline{).256} \\
\underline{0} \\
25 \\
\underline{24} \\
16 \\
\underline{16} \\
0
\end{array}
$$

To divide any number by a decimal, there is an extra step to perform before you can divide. Move the decimal point to the very right of the number you are dividing by, counting the number of places you are moving it. Then move the decimal point the same number of places to the right in the number you are dividing into. In other words, first change the problem to one in which you are dividing by a whole number.

Example: $.06\overline{)1.218}$

1. Because there are two decimal digits in .06, move the decimal point two places to the right in both numbers and move the decimal point straight up into the answer:

$$.06.\overline{)1.21.8}$$

2. Divide using the new numbers:

$$
\begin{array}{r}
20.3 \\
6\overline{)121.8} \\
\underline{12} \\
01 \\
\underline{00} \\
18 \\
\underline{18} \\
0
\end{array}
$$

Under certain conditions, you have to tack on zeros to the right of the last decimal digit in the number you are dividing into:

- If there aren't enough digits for you to move the decimal point to the right, or
- If the answer doesn't come out evenly when you do the division, or
- If you're dividing a whole number by a decimal, then you will have to tack on the decimal point as well as some zeros.

Try your skills on these division problems.

_____ **49.** 7)9.8

_____ **50.** .0004).0512

_____ **51.** .5)28.6

_____ **52.** .14)196

_____ **53.** If James Worthington drove his truck 92.4 miles in 2.1 hours, what was his average speed in miles per hour?
  a. 41
  b. 44
  c. 90.3
  d. 94.5
  e. none of these

_____ **54.** Mary Sanders walked a total of 18.6 miles in four days. On average, how many miles did she walk each day?
  a. 4.15
  b. 4.60
  c. 4.65
  d. 22.60
  e. none of these

Percents

What Is a Percent?

A percent is a special kind of fraction or part of something. The bottom number (the *denominator*) is always 100. For example, 17% is the same as $\frac{17}{100}$. Literally, the word *percent* means *per 100 parts*. The root *cent* means 100: A *century* is 100 years, there are 100 *cents* in a dollar, etc. Thus, 17% means 17 parts out of 100. Because fractions can also be expressed as decimals, 17% is also equivalent to .17, which is 17 hundredths.

You come into contact with percents every day. Sales tax, interest, and discounts are just a few common examples.

If you're shaky on fractions, you may want to review the fraction section again before reading further.

Changing a Decimal to a Percent and Vice Versa

To change a decimal to a percent, move the decimal point two places to the **right** and tack on a percent sign (%) at the end. If the decimal point moves to the very right of the number, you don't have to write the decimal point. If there aren't enough places to move the decimal point, add zeros on the **right** before moving the decimal point.

To change a percent to a decimal, drop off the percent sign and move the decimal point two places to the **left**. If there aren't enough places to move the decimal point, add zeros on the **left** before moving the decimal point.

Try changing these decimals to percents.

_____ **55.** .45

_____ **56.** .008

_____ **57.** $.16\frac{2}{3}$

Now, change these percents to decimals.

_____ **58.** 12%

_____ **59.** $87\frac{1}{2}$%

_____ **60.** 250%

Changing a Fraction to a Percent and Vice Versa

To change a fraction to a percent, there are two techniques. Each is illustrated by changing the fraction $\frac{1}{4}$ to a percent:

Technique 1:   Multiply the fraction by 100%.

Multiply $\frac{1}{4}$ by 100%:
$$\frac{1}{\underset{1}{4}} \times \frac{\overset{25}{\cancel{100}}\%}{1} = 25\%.$$

Technique 2:   Divide the fraction's bottom number into the top number; then move the decimal point two places to the **right** and tack on a percent sign (%).
Divide 4 into 1 and move the decimal point two places to the right:

$$4\overline{)1.00}^{\,.25} \qquad .25 = 25\%$$

To change a percent to a fraction, remove the percent sign and write the number over 100. Then, reduce if possible.

Example: Change 4% to a fraction.

1. Remove the % and write the fraction 4 over 100:

$$\frac{4}{100}$$

2. Reduce:

$$\frac{4 \div 4}{100 \div 4} = \frac{1}{25}$$

Here's a more complicated example: Change $16\frac{2}{3}$% to a fraction.

1. Remove the % and write the fraction $16\frac{2}{3}$ over 100:

$$\frac{16\frac{2}{3}}{100}$$

2. Since a fraction means "top number divided by bottom number," rewrite the fraction as a division problem:

$$16\frac{2}{3} \div 100$$

3. Change the mixed number ($16\frac{2}{3}$) to an improper fraction ($\frac{50}{3}$):

$$\frac{50}{3} \div \frac{100}{1}$$

4. Flip the second fraction ($\frac{100}{1}$) and multiply:

$$\frac{\overset{1}{\cancel{50}}}{3} \times \frac{1}{\underset{2}{\cancel{100}}} = \frac{1}{6}$$

Try changing these fractions to percents.

_____ **61.** $\frac{1}{8}$

_____ **62.** $\frac{13}{25}$

_____ **63.** $\frac{7}{12}$

Now change these percents to fractions.

_____ **64.** 95%

_____ **65.** $37\frac{1}{2}$%

_____ **66.** 125%

Sometimes, it is more convenient to work with a percentage as a fraction or a decimal. Rather than have to *calculate* the equivalent fraction or decimal, consider memorizing the following equivalence table. Not only will this increase your efficiency on the math test, but it will also be practical for real-life situations.

CONVERSION TABLE		
Decimal	**%**	**Fraction**
.25	25%	$\frac{1}{4}$
.50	50%	$\frac{1}{2}$
.75	75%	$\frac{3}{4}$
.10	10%	$\frac{1}{10}$
.20	20%	$\frac{1}{5}$
.40	40%	$\frac{2}{5}$
.60	60%	$\frac{3}{5}$
.80	80%	$\frac{4}{5}$
.33$\overline{3}$	33$\frac{1}{3}$%	$\frac{1}{3}$
.66$\overline{6}$	66$\frac{2}{3}$%	$\frac{2}{3}$

Percent Word Problems

Word problems involving percents come in three main varieties:

- Find a percent of a whole.
  Example: What is 30% of 40?
- Find what percent one number is of another number.
  Example: 12 is what percent of 40?
- Find the whole when the percent of it is given.
  Example: 12 is 30% of what number?

While each variety has its own approach, there is a single shortcut formula you can use to solve each of these:

$$\frac{is}{of} = \frac{\%}{100}$$

The **is** is the number that usually follows or is just before the word **is** in the question.
The **of** is the number that usually follows the word **of** in the question.
The % is the number that is in front of the % or **percent** in the question.
Or you may think of the shortcut formula as:

$$\frac{part}{whole} = \frac{\%}{100}$$

To solve each of the three varieties, let's use the fact that the **cross products** are equal. The cross products are the products of the numbers diagonally across from each other. Remembering that *product* means *multiply,* here's how to create the cross products for the percent shortcut:

$$\frac{part}{whole} = \frac{\%}{100}$$
$$part \times 100 = whole \times \%$$

Here's how to use the shortcut with cross products:

- Find a percent of a whole.
  What is 30% of 40?
  30 is the % and 40 is the *of* number:
  Cross multiply and solve for *is*:

$$\frac{is}{40} = \frac{30}{100}$$
$$is \times 100 = 40 \times 30$$
$$is \times 100 = 1,200$$
$$\mathbf{12} \times 100 = 1,200$$

  Thus, **12 *is*** 30% of 40.

- Find what percent one number is of another number.
  12 is what percent of 40?
  12 is the *is* number and 40 is the *of* number:
  Cross multiply and solve for %:

$$\frac{12}{40} = \frac{\%}{100}$$
$$12 \times 100 = 40 \times \%$$
$$1,200 = 40 \times \%$$
$$1,200 = 40 \times \mathbf{30}$$

  Thus, 12 is **30%** of 40.

- Find the whole when the percent of it is given.
  12 is 30% of what number?
  12 is the *is* number and 30 is the %:
  Cross multiply and solve for the *of* number:

$$\frac{12}{of} = \frac{30}{100}$$
$$12 \times 100 = of \times 30$$
$$1,200 = of \times 30$$
$$1,200 = \mathbf{40} \times 30$$

  Thus 12, is 30% ***of* 40.**

You can use the same technique to find the percent increase or decrease. The *is* number is the actual increase or decrease, and the *of* number is the original amount.

Example: If a merchant puts his $20 hats on sale for $15, by what percent does he decrease the selling price?

1. Calculate the decrease, the *is* number: $20 - $15 = $5
2. The *of* number is the original amount, $20.
3. Set up the equation and solve for *of* by cross multiplying:

$$\frac{5}{20} = \frac{\%}{100}$$
$$5 \times 100 = 20 \times \%$$
$$500 = 20 \times \%$$
$$500 = 20 \times 25$$

4. Thus, the selling price is decreased by **25%**.

If the merchant later raises the price of the hats from $15 back to $20, don't be fooled into thinking that the percent increase is also 25%! It's actually more, because the increase amount of $5 is now based on a lower original price of only $15:

Thus, the selling price is increased by **33%**.

$$\frac{5}{15} = \frac{\%}{100}$$
$$5 \times 100 = 15 \times \%$$
$$500 = 15 \times \%$$
$$500 = 15 \times 33\frac{1}{3}$$

Find a percent of a whole.

_____ **67.** 1% of 25

_____ **68.** 18.2% of 50

_____ **69.** $37\frac{1}{2}$% of 100

_____ **70.** 125% of 60

Find what percent one number is of another number.

_____ **71.** 10 is what % of 20?

_____ **72.** 4 is what % of 12?

_____ **73.** 12 is what % of 4?

Find the whole when the percent of it is given.

_____ **74.** 15% of what number is 15?

_____ **75.** $37\frac{1}{2}$% of what number is 3?

_____ **76.** 200% of what number is 20?

Now try your percent skills on some real-life problems.

_____ **77.** Last Monday, 20% of 140-member nursing staff was absent. How many nurses were absent that day?
a. 14
b. 20
c. 28
d. 112
e. none of these

_____ **78.** 40% of Vero's postal service employees are women. If there are 80 women in Vero's postal service, how many men are employed there?
   a. 32
   b. 112
   c. 120
   d. 160
   e. none of these

_____ **79.** Of the 840 crimes committed last month, 42 involved petty theft. What percent of the crimes involved petty theft?
   a. .5%
   b. 2%
   c. 5%
   d. 20%
   e. none of these

_____ **80.** Sam's Shoe Store put all of its merchandise on sale for 20% off. If Jason saved $10 by purchasing one pair of shoes during the sale, what was the original price of the shoes before the sale?
   a. $12
   b. $20
   c. $40
   d. $50
   e. none of these

Averages

An **average**, also called an **arithmetic mean**, is a number that _typifies_ a group of numbers, a measure of central tendency. You come into contact with averages on a regular basis: your bowling average, the average grade on a test, the average number of hours you work per week.

To calculate an average, add up the numbers being averaged and divide by the number of items.

Example: What is the average of 6, 10, and 20?
Solution: Add the three numbers together and divide by 3: $\frac{6 + 10 + 20}{3} = 12$

Shortcut
Here's a neat shortcut for some average problems.

- Look at the numbers being averaged. If they are equally spaced, like 5, 10, 15, 20, and 25, then the average is the number in the middle, or 15 in this case.
- If there is an even number of such numbers, say 10, 20, 30, and 40, then there is no middle number. In this case, the average is halfway between the two middle numbers. In this case, the average is halfway between 20 and 30, or 25.

■ If the numbers are almost evenly spaced, you can probably estimate the average without going to the trouble of actually computing it. For example, the average of 10, 20, and 32 is just a little more than 20, the middle number.

Try these average questions.

_____ **81.** Bob's bowling scores for the last five games were 180, 182, 184, 186, and 188. What was his average bowling score?
 a. 182
 b. 183
 c. 184
 d. 185
 e. none of these

_____ **82.** Conroy averaged 30 miles per hour for the two hours he drove in town and 60 miles per hour for the two hours he drove on the highway. What was his average speed in miles per hour?
 a. 18
 b. $22\frac{1}{2}$
 c. 45
 d. 60
 e. none of these

_____ **83.** There are 10 females and 20 males in a history class. If the females achieved an average score of 85 and the males achieved an average score of 95, what was the class average? (Hint: Don't fall for the trap of taking the average of 85 and 95; there are more 95s being averaged than 85s, so the average is closer to 95.)
 a. $90\frac{2}{3}$
 b. $91\frac{2}{3}$
 c. 92
 d. $92\frac{2}{3}$
 e. none of these

Algebra

Algebra questions do not appear on every test. However, when they do, they typically cover the material you learned in prealgebra or in the first few months of your high school algebra course. Popular topics for algebra questions include:

- solving equations
- positive and negative numbers
- algebraic expressions

What Is Algebra?

Algebra is a way to express and solve problems using numbers and symbols. These symbols, called *unknowns* or *variables,* are letters of the alphabet that are used to represent numbers.

For example, let's say you are asked to find out what number, when added to 3, gives you a total of 5. Using algebra, you could express the problem as $x + 3 = 5$. The variable x represents the number you are trying to find.

Here's another example, this time using only variables. To find the distance traveled, multiply the rate of travel (speed) by the amount of time traveled: $d = r \times t$. The variable d stands for *distance, r* stands for *rate,* and t stands for *time.*

In algebra, the variables may take on different values. In other words, they *vary,* and that's why they're called *variables.*

Operations

Algebra uses the same operations as arithmetic: addition, subtraction, multiplication, and division. In arithmetic, we might say $3 + 4 = 7$, while in algebra, we would talk about two numbers whose values we don't know that add up to 7, or $x + y = 7$. Here's how each operation translates to algebra:

ALGEBRAIC OPERATIONS	
The sum of two numbers	$x + y$
The difference of two numbers	$x - y$
The product of two numbers	$x \times y$ or $x \bullet y$ or xy
The quotient of two numbers	$\frac{x}{y}$ or $x \div y$

Equations

An equation is a mathematical sentence stating that two quantities are equal. For example:

$$2x = 10$$
$$x + 5 = 8$$

The idea is to find a replacement for the unknown that will make the sentence true. That's called *solving* the equation. Thus, in the first example, $x = 5$ because $2 \times 5 = 10$. In the second example, $x = 3$ because $3 + 5 = 8$.

Sometimes you can solve an equation by inspection, as with the previous examples. Other equations may be more complicated and require a step-by-step solution, for example:

$$\frac{n+2}{4} + 1 = 3$$

The general approach is to consider an equation like a balance scale, with both sides equally balanced. Essentially, whatever you do to one side, you must also do to the other side to maintain the balance. Thus, if you were to add 2 to the left side, you would also have to add 2 to the right side.

Let's apply this *balance* concept to our earlier complicated equation. Remembering that we want to solve it for *n*, we must somehow rearrange it so the *n* is isolated on one side of the equation. Its value will then be on the other side. Looking at the equation, you can see that *n* has been increased by 2 and then divided by 4 and ultimately added to 1. Therefore, we will undo these operations to isolate *n*.

Begin by subtracting 1 from both sides of the equation:

$$\frac{n+2}{4} + 1 = 3$$
$$\underline{ -1 \quad -1}$$
$$\frac{n+2}{4} = 2$$

Next, multiply both sides by 4:

$$4 \times \frac{n+2}{4} = 2 \times 4$$
$$n + 2 = 8$$

Finally, subtract 2 from both sides:

$$\underline{ -2 \quad -2}$$

This isolates *n* and solves the equation:

$$n = 6$$

Notice that each operation in the original equation was undone by using the inverse operation. That is, addition was undone by subtraction, and division was undone by multiplication. In general, each operation can be undone by its *inverse:*

ALGEBRAIC INVERSES	
OPERATION	**INVERSE**
Addition	Subtraction
Subtraction	Addition
Multiplication	Division
Division	Multiplication

After you solve an equation, check your work by plugging the answer back into the original equation to make sure it balances. Let's see what happens when we plug 6 in for *n:*

$$\frac{6+2}{4} + 1 = 3$$
$$\frac{8}{4} + 1 = 3$$
$$2 + 1 = 3$$
$$3 = 3 ✔$$

Solve each equation for *x:*

_____ **84.** $x + 5 = 12$

_____ **85.** $3x + 6 = 18$

_____ **86.** $\frac{1}{4}x = 7$

Positive and Negative Numbers

Positive and negative numbers, also known as *signed* numbers, are best shown as points along the number line:

Numbers to the left of 0 are *negative* and those to the right are *positive.* Zero is neither negative nor positive. If a number is written without a sign, it is assumed to be *positive.* Notice that when you are on the negative side of the number line, numbers with bigger values are actually smaller. For example, –5 is *less than* –2. You come into contact with negative numbers more often than you might think; for example, very cold temperatures are recorded as negative numbers.

As you move to the right along the number line, the numbers get larger. Mathematically, to indicate that one number, say 4, is *greater than* another number, say –2, the *greater than* sign (>) is used:

$$4 > -2$$

On the other hand, to say that –2 is *less than* 4, we use the *less than* sign, (<):

$$-2 < 4$$

Arithmetic with Positive and Negative Numbers

The following table illustrates the rules for doing arithmetic with signed numbers. Notice that when a negative number follows an operation (as it does in the second example), it is enclosed in parentheses to avoid confusion.

RULE	EXAMPLE
ADDITION	
If both numbers have the same sign, just add them. The answer has the same sign as the numbers being added. If both numbers have different signs, subtract the smaller number from the larger. The answer has the same sign as the larger number. If both numbers are the same but have opposite signs, the sum is zero.	$3 + 5 = 8$ $-3 + (-5) = -8$ $-3 + 5 = 2$ $3 + (-5) = -2$ $3 + (-3) = 0$
SUBTRACTION	
Change the sign of the number to be subtracted and then add as above.	$3 - 5 = 3 + (-5) = -2$ $-3 - 5 = -3 + (-5) = -8$ $-3 - (-5) = -3 + 5 = 2$
MULTIPLICATION	
Multiply the numbers together. If both numbers have the same sign, the answer is positive; otherwise, it is negative.	$3 \times 5 = 15$ $-3 \times (-5) = 15$ $-3 \times 5 = -15$ $3 \times (-5) = -15$
If one number is zero, the answer is zero.	$3 \times 0 = 0$
DIVISION	
Divide the numbers. If both numbers have the same sign, the answer is positive; otherwise, it is negative.	$15 \div 3 = 5$ $-15 \div (-3) = 5$ $15 \div (-3) = -5$ $-15 \div 3 = -5$
If the top number is zero, the answer is zero.	$0 \div 3 = 0$

When more than one arithmetic operation appears, you must know the correct sequence in which to perform the operations. For example, do you know what to do first to calculate $2 + 3 \times 4$? You're right if you said, "multiply first." The correct answer is 14. If you add first, you will get the wrong answer of 20. The correct sequence of operations is:

1. parentheses
2. exponents
3. multiplication
4. division
5. addition
6. subtraction

} If you remember this saying, you will know the order of operations: **Please Excuse My Dear Aunt Sally.**

Even when signed numbers appear in an equation, the step-by-step solution works exactly as it does for positive numbers. You just have to remember the arithmetic rules for negative numbers. For example, let's solve $14x + 2 = 5$.

1. Subtract 2 from both sides:

$$-14x + 2 = -5$$
$$\underline{\quad -2 \quad -2 \quad}$$
$$-14x = -7$$

2. Divide both sides by -14:

$$-14x \div -14 = -7 \div -14$$
$$x = \frac{1}{2}$$

Now try these problems with signed numbers.

———— **87.** $1 - 3 \times (-4) = x$

———— **88.** $-3x + 6 = -18$

———— **89.** $\frac{x}{-4} + 3 = -7$

Algebraic Expressions

An algebraic expression is a group of numbers, unknowns, and arithmetic operations, like: $3x - 2y$. This one may be translated as "3 times some number minus 2 times another number." To *evaluate* an algebraic expression, replace each variable with its value. For example, if $x = 5$ and $y = 4$, we would evaluate $3x - 2y$ as follows:

$$3(5) - 2(4) = 15 - 8 = 7$$

Evaluate these expressions.

———— **90.** $4a + 3b$; $a = 2$ and $b = -1$

———— **91.** $3mn - 4m + 2n$; $m = 3$ and $n = -3$

———— **92.** $-2x - \frac{1}{2}y + 4z$; $x = 5$, $y = -4$, and $z = 6$

———— **93.** The volume of a cylinder is given by the formula $V = \pi r^2 h$, where r is the radius of the base and h is the height of the cylinder. What is the volume of a cylinder with a base radius of 3 and height of 4? (Leave π in your answer.)

———— **94.** If $x = 3$, what is the value of $3x - x$?

Length, Weight, and Time Units

The questions involving length, weight, and time on the math test will ask you either to convert between different measurement units or to add or subtract measurement values.

Common Terms

You may encounter questions that expect you to understand basic geometric concepts, such as the following:

- **perimeter**: the distance around a two-dimensional figure. To determine the perimeter of a shape, add the lengths of each side.
- **square footage**: unit of measurement used to define the size of a rectangular area. To determine square footage, multiply length by width.

Converting

You may encounter questions that ask you to convert between units of measurement in length, weight, or time. To convert from a smaller unit (such as inches) to a larger unit (such as feet), divide the smaller unit by the number of those units necessary to equal the larger unit. To convert from a larger unit to a smaller unit, multiply the larger unit by the conversion number.

> *Example:* Convert 36 inches to feet.

- Since 1 foot = 12 inches, divide 36 by 12: $36 \div 12 = 3$ feet

> *Example:* Convert 4 feet to inches.

- Since 1 foot = 12 inches, multiply 4 by 12: $4 \times 12 = 48$ inches

> *Example:* Convert 32 ounces to pounds.

- Since 1 pound = 16 ounces, divide 32 by 16: $32 \div 16 = 2$ pounds

> *Example:* Convert 2 pounds to ounces.

- Since 1 pound = 16 ounces, multiply 2 by 16: $2 \times 16 = 32$ ounces

> *Example:* Convert 180 minutes to hours.

- Since 1 hour = 60 minutes, divide 180 by 60: $180 \div 60 = 3$ hours

> *Example:* Convert 4 hours to minutes.

- Since 1 hour = 60 minutes, multiply 4 by 60: $4 \times 60 = 240$ minutes

Now try some on your own. Convert as indicated. The answers are at the end of this section on page 125.

95. 2 feet = _____ inches

96. 3 pounds = _____ ounces

Calculating with Length, Weight, and Time Units

On the test, you may be asked to add or subtract length, weight, and time units. The only trick to doing this correctly is to remember to convert the smaller units to larger units and vice versa, if need be.

Example: Find the perimeter of the figure:

To add the lengths, add each column of length units separately:

$$
\begin{array}{ll}
5 \text{ ft.} & 7 \text{ in.} \\
2 \text{ ft.} & 6 \text{ in.} \\
6 \text{ ft.} & 9 \text{ in.} \\
+\ 3 \text{ ft.} & 5 \text{ in.} \\
\hline
\mathbf{16 \text{ ft.}} & \mathbf{27 \text{ in.}}
\end{array}
$$

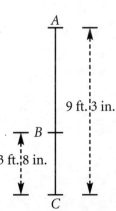

3 ft. 5 in.

6 ft. 9 in.

5 ft. 7 in.

2 ft. 6 in.

Since 27 inches is more than 1 foot, the total of 16 ft. 27 in. must be simplified:

- Convert 27 inches to feet and inches:
$27 \text{ in.} \times \frac{1 \text{ ft.}}{12 \text{ in.}} = \frac{27}{12} \text{ ft.} = 2\frac{3}{12} \text{ ft.} = 2 \text{ ft. } 3 \text{ in.}$

- Add:
$$
\begin{array}{l}
16 \text{ ft.} \\
+\ 2 \text{ ft. } 3 \text{ in.} \\
\hline
\mathbf{18 \text{ ft.} \quad 3 \text{ in.}}
\end{array}
$$
Thus, the perimeter is **18 feet 3 inches.**

Finding the length of a line segment may require subtracting lengths of different units. For example, find the length of line segment *AB*:

To subtract the lengths, subtract each column of length units separately, starting with the rightmost column.

$$
\begin{array}{l}
9 \text{ ft. } 3 \text{ in.} \\
-3 \text{ ft. } 8 \text{ in.} \\
\hline
\end{array}
$$

Warning: You can't subtract 8 inches from 3 inches because 8 is larger than 3! As in regular subtraction, you have to *borrow* 1 from the column on the left. However, borrowing *1 ft.* is the same as borrowing *12 inches*; adding the borrowed 12 inches to the 3 inches gives 15 inches. Thus:

A

B

C

9 ft. 3 in.

3 ft. 8 in.

$$\overset{8}{\cancel{9}} \text{ ft. } \overset{\overset{15}{12}}{\cancel{3}} \text{ in.}$$
$$- 3 \text{ ft. } 8 \text{ in.}$$
$$\overline{5 \text{ ft. } 7 \text{ in.}}$$

Thus, the length of $\overline{AB}$ is **5 feet 7 inches.**

Add or subtract, and simplify. Answers are at the end of this lesson.

97.   5 ft. 3 in.
     + 2 ft. 9 in.

98.   5 hr. 38 min.
   − 3 hr. 45 min.

Now, try these time word problems.

99. During finals week, Jan took three tests and each required 45 minutes. If she then took one last test, and all four tests required a total of $3\frac{1}{4}$ hours, how long did the last test take?

a. $\frac{1}{2}$ hour

b. $\frac{2}{3}$ hour

c. $\frac{3}{4}$ hour

d. 1 hour

e. none of these

100. If each of eight biology classrooms is in use for 5 hours 15 minutes per day, and a total of 84 student experiments are done, how long does each experiment take on average?

a. 20 minutes

b. 30 minutes

c. 40 minutes

d. 50 minutes

e. none of these

Answers

Word Problems
1. a.
2. d.
3. b.
4. e.

Fractions
5. $\frac{1}{4}$
6. $\frac{2}{5}$
7. $\frac{3}{8}$
8. 52
9. 24
10. 88
11. $\frac{11}{12}$
12. $\frac{55}{24}$ or $2\frac{7}{24}$
13. $7\frac{1}{4}$
14. $\frac{7}{12}$
15. $\frac{53}{64}$
16. $59\frac{5}{12}$
17. d.
18. c.
19. $\frac{2}{15}$
20. $\frac{8}{35}$
21. $\frac{2}{3}$
22. $\frac{26}{15}$ or $1\frac{11}{15}$
23. 15
24. $\frac{33}{2}$ or $16\frac{1}{2}$
25. c.
26. d.
27. c.
28. $\frac{1}{2}$
29. $5\frac{1}{2}$
30. $\frac{1}{5}$
31. $\frac{45}{28}$ or $1\frac{17}{28}$

32. b.
33. c.
34. a.

Decimals
35. $\frac{5}{1,000}$ or $\frac{1}{200}$
36. $17\frac{19}{25}$
37. $27\frac{399}{1000}$
38. 1789
39. 6.675
40. .223
41. 1.456
42. b.
43. d.
44. 0.03
45. 0.3392
46. 0.70104
47. d.
48. d.
49. 1.4
50. 128
51. 572
52. 1,400
53. b.
54. c.

Percents
55. 45%
56. 0.8%
57. 16.67% or $16\frac{2}{3}$%
58. 0.12
59. 0.875
60. 2.5
61. 12.5% or $12\frac{1}{2}$%
62. 52%
63. 58.33% or $58\frac{1}{3}$%
64. $\frac{19}{20}$
65. $\frac{3}{8}$
66. $\frac{5}{4}$ or $1\frac{1}{4}$

67. $\frac{1}{4}$ or .25
68. 9.1
69. $37\frac{1}{2}$ or 37.5
70. 75
71. 50%
72. $33\frac{1}{3}$%
73. 300%
74. 100
75. 8
76. 10
77. c.
78. c.
79. c.
80. d.

Averages
81. c.
82. c.
83. b.

Basic Algebra
84. 7
85. 4
86. 28
87. 13
88. 8
89. 40
90. 5
91. −45
92. 16
93. 36π
94. 6

Length, Weight, and Time Units
95. 24
96. 48
97. 8 ft.
98. 1 hr. 53 min.
99. d.
100. b.

8 ▶ PROBLEMS FOR INVESTIGATION

CHAPTER SUMMARY
In this chapter, you will learn how to approach the Problems for Investigation portion of your Treasury Enforcement Agent exam. The chapter also contains definitions of terms you need to know in order to ace this part of the test.

In a sense, the Problems for Investigation portion of the Treasury Enforcement Agent exam is really an extension of the Verbal Reasoning portion—that is, the first qualification for doing well is the ability to read well. However, it is not necessary for you to be a fast reader; you have one hour to answer the 30 questions in this section, so time isn't usually a problem. What you absolutely must be able to do is to *read closely* and comprehend every detail of what you read. Complete concentration on what you're reading and attention to detail are the essential abilities for doing well on these questions.

What the Questions Are Like

For each problem in the Problems for Investigation portion of the TEA exam, you will be presented with a short narrative, about a paragraph long, that describes a criminal event or possibly criminal event. This narrative is followed by a list of ten or 11 statements that were made while the event was being investigated, followed by several questions about the statements. You will be asked to select one of the five answer choices that follow the question.

The Narrative Fact Pattern

An example of a narrative fact pattern might be:

Local police have become suspicious of the activities in which Lobster Lines, Inc., a transport service for fresh seafood, is engaged. Located in Portland, Maine, Lobster Lines receives seafood from the boats that fish out of Casco Bay and transports the seafood to several different distributors, most of whom supply restaurants. Lobster Lines owns four trucks and two cargo airplanes. After observing Lobster Lines over a period of five years, police suspect the company is engaged in the trafficking of narcotics. They contact the Organized Crime Drug Enforcement Task Force.

The first steps to take in approaching this problem are to pay very close attention to the narrative fact pattern and to think of it in conjunction with the list of statements that follow it (discussed next), because the fact pattern and statements are interrelated. You will notice that the narrative provides only a minimum of background information. You should proceed on the basis that all of the information in the narrative is true. This necessarily means that any statement in the list that contradicts the narrative fact pattern is probably false. Let's look at what this means in terms of the statements.

The Statements

On the basis of the narrative fact pattern you just read, it is easy to see that if one of the statements made during the course of the investigation is "Ralph Manson said Lobster Lines is located in San Francisco," this statement is probably not true because it contradicts the narrative. In the real TEA exam, you will no doubt be presented with a question that asks whether a certain statement is a lie, and you will have to analyze what that means for the investigation. Of course, not all statements are such obvious lies. Another possible statement might be "Lobster Lines owns a Lear Jet that no one knows about." In this case, you shouldn't

immediately assume, without question, that the person who made this statement is lying, although it is certainly reasonable to suspect the statement is a lie. There is a fine line between truth and lie, and this is important knowledge to have when you are engaged in most law enforcement work. Its importance should become more clear as you read on.

Examples of statements that follow the Lobster Lines narrative might be:

1. Janet Mills, former bookkeeper for Lobster Lines, said that over the last five years, the business grew only slightly.

2. Merlin Webster, owner of Lobster Lines, said that his income has not changed over the last five years.

3. Donald Carp, Webster's neighbor, said that over the last five years, Webster has remodeled his house twice (once adding an apartment for his sister), put in a swimming pool, and purchased two new Mercedes.

4. Local police records show that Webster has a prior conviction for fraud.

5. Jan Garfield, one of Lobster Lines' two pilots, said she met Webster ten years ago when both of them were in the military and stationed at Ft. Leonard Wood.

6. The Maine Secretary of State office said that the two Mercedes that Merlin is known to drive are registered to Bob and Shirley Webster, his parents.

7. Zach Miller, Lobster Lines' other pilot, said that Garfield handles all flights to Chicago, while his (Zach's) destinations vary, depending on the orders. The four trucks handle the New England area.

8. Patti Webster, Merlin's sister, said she operates a small landscape business and has little contact with her brother.

9. Fisherman Whit Gromley said that Lobster Lines can always be counted on to buy his catch, no matter what its quality or size may be.

10. Company records show that Lobster Lines regularly supplies distributors in Illinois, Vermont, Rhode Island, New Hampshire, Massachusetts, and Connecticut. Records indicate no clients in other locations.

11. The Portland Assessor's office said the house where Merlin Webster lives is owned by Jan Herman, his wife, and there is no mortgage outstanding.

You can see that these statements provide a great deal of diverse information of varying usefulness, just as is the case in the real world. While you should read over these statements at the same time as the narrative, you don't need to make any effort to memorize them or try to figure out what they mean. You'll have plenty of time to do that when you start answering the questions.

The Questions
After the list of statements, you will find seven to ten questions that ask you to draw conclusions about the information you have just read. The five answer choices—**a**, **b**, **c**, **d**, and **e**—are always taken from the statement list, so a question might look like this:

1. Which statement along with Statement 7 casts suspicion on Zach Miller?
   a. Statement 8
   b. Statement 9
   c. Statement 10
   d. Statement 11
   e. Statement 6

It is also possible for each choice to list more than one statement, that is, some of the questions might ask you "Which two statements" provide certain information. Then, the choices would be, for example, "Statements 3 and 6," and so on.

A Systematic Approach to Problems for Investigation

The Problems for Investigation portion of the TEA exam is designed to test how well you think analytically. In answering the questions, you will use both common sense and intuition as you analyze the problem; however, you should be sure to maintain your objectivity about the narrative (more about that soon).

Following are the steps you should take in approaching the problems.

Read the Narrative Carefully
Your approach to this section of the test begins with reading the narrative. As previously noted, you need to read carefully and with attention to detail; however, you should not spend time trying to fill in any of the gaps in the narrative. In other words, it does not matter if you don't know that the Organized Crime Drug Enforcement Task Force consists of agents from the IRS, FBI, DEA, ATF, Bureau of Immigration and Customs Enforcement, Department of Homeland Security, and others. Nor do you need to be concerned about whether the narrative is accurate as to things like jurisdiction. Everything you need to know to answer the questions is contained in the fact pattern and the statements. The only trick is to think about them in the right way.

Read the Statements Carefully
After you have read the narrative, read through the statements made during the course of the investigation. You shouldn't try to analyze them at this point, but they do provide you with some information, such as in which direction the investigation is going and how

many suspects there are. For example, the statements in the sample indicate that agents are following the money in an effort to find out about any involvement by Lobster Lines or its employees in narcotics trafficking.

Read Each Question Carefully

For each question, the first step, and a very important one, is to read thoroughly and accurately. Be careful not to read so fast that you see "implicate" and think "intimidate." It makes a huge difference in answering the question, as do things like "most helpful" versus "least helpful" and "remove suspicion" versus "cast suspicion." In our sample question, it is important to note that you are to choose an answer that relates to Statement 7; so you should reread Statement 7 before you try to answer the question.

Be Objective

You may think that an officer acted inappropriately or come to a conclusion about who you believe committed the crime. These kinds of impressions will only get in your way as you answer the questions. Most of the narratives are constructed so that the criminal could be one or more of several people. So, in our sample narrative, it is not a good use of your time to ask yourself if the local police should have acted sooner or whether you think Zach Miller or Merlin Webster (or both, or someone else) is the guilty party. After all, as a special agent, you will want to remain open to all possibilities in the course of an investigation.

Let the Questions Focus Your Thinking

When you first approach the problems, the narrative and statements may seem like just a lot of random information. The questions are designed to focus your thinking in particular areas and test your ability to analyze that information. For instance, you may be asked which statement or statements indicate that someone is lying. Or you may be asked whether certain statements contradict each other, support each other,

cast suspicion in a certain direction, or are not helpful at all to the investigation.

After you have read the question carefully, analyze the problem by asking yourself the following:

- Which details of the random information in the narrative are actually pertinent to the question?
- How does the sequence of events in the narrative relate to the question, and how are the events interrelated?
- Which of the statements are verifiable fact and which are based on conjecture or hearsay?
- Which of the sources are reliable?
- What are the possible motives of the people making the statements?

Eliminate the Irrelevant

Once you've read everything carefully and know what the question is asking, you can eliminate those elements that are irrelevant. Look at the answer choices in the example. It would be a colossal waste of your time if, in question 1, you were to look at each of the statements to see which ones cast suspicion on Zach Miller. You need to look only at statements 6, 8, 9, 10, and 11. Even if you think that statement 5 casts suspicion on Miller, you can't give it as an answer because it is not one of the choices. So, you want to look at only statements offered as possibilities in the answer choices. At the same time, you may be able to eliminate some options completely, making your final decision even easier. The statements that are applicable to the sample question are:

6. The Maine Secretary of State office said that the two Mercedes that Merlin is known to drive are registered to Bob and Shirley Webster, his parents.

8. Patti Webster, Merlin's sister, said she operates a small landscape business and has little contact with her brother.

9. Fisherman Whit Gromley said that Lobster Lines can always be counted on to buy his catch, no matter what its quality or size may be.

10. Company records show that Lobster Lines regularly supplies distributors in Illinois, Vermont, Rhode Island, New Hampshire, Massachusetts, and Connecticut. Records indicate no clients in other locations.

11. The Portland Assessor's office said the house where Merlin Webster lives is owned by Jan Herman, his wife, and there is no mortgage outstanding.

The question is asking you, when you know that Miller does not fly to Chicago and the trucks handle deliveries in New England (statement 7), which of these four statements casts suspicion on Miller? The answer is choice c, statement 10. Since Chicago is in Illinois and all the other states are in New England, and these are the only places Lobster Lines has customers, Miller must be making undocumented flights. That casts suspicion on him because that could mean he is trafficking narcotics. It could also mean that he is transporting illegal seafood or that he doesn't think Rhode Island and Connecticut are in New England. The information does not solve the crime, but it does, as the question asks, cast suspicion on Miller. Note, too, that in this example, you could have arrived at the correct answer by eliminating the obviously wrong choices.

To sum up, the steps you learned in this lesson will take you a long way toward successful completion of the Problems for Investigation portion of your TEA exam:

- Read closely with attention to detail
- Remain objective
- Allow the questions to focus your thinking
- Eliminate the irrelevant

Though all the information you need to answer these questions is on the test, you can go a step further by studying the information in the next section.

Some Helpful Definitions

On a very basic level, you can answer Problems for Investigation questions using common sense. Common sense consists of two parts—commonality and sense (or knowledge). In other words, common sense starts with the premise that some knowledge is common to all of us. In the Problems for Investigation, there is an assumption that you will have a general understanding of certain legal terms. They're common terms, and if you've ever watched courtroom drama in movies or on television or read one of the proliferation of novels by lawyers around today, you probably have enough understanding of these terms to make it through the TEA exam. However, there is some additional information that will give you an extra edge.

Legal terms have essentially the same definitions whether they are used in a courtroom or during an investigation, but the way the evidence itself is used may be quite different, and it is important to keep that in mind. For example, most of us have a general notion that hearsay is information of which the speaker has no real knowledge. An example would be if a witness said, "I heard that Patricia Sanchez closed her bank account last week." It is pretty obvious that the speaker has no real knowledge of this transaction. Even if this was said by a bank employee, clearly it was not the same employee who waited on Patricia Sanchez. Rather, this person heard someone say that the bank account was closed. If this witness were testifying in a trial or other court proceeding, this evidence probably would not be allowed. Although there are some exceptions that you may have seen in court, generally a witness can testify only to facts about which he or she has direct knowledge. So if there was no other evidence that Sanchez had closed her bank account, the jury would never hear the information and would not, obviously, be able to use it in reaching their decision.

During the course of an investigation, evidence is used in quite a different manner. If the statement about Patricia's bank account was made in an investigation, officers would no doubt follow up on the information. Hearsay is not as reliable as other kinds of information, but that does not mean it is always false. An officer in this case would obtain bank records (which could, by the way, be used in a trial) and check the truth of the statement. This distinction should be pretty clear if you think about it this way: Imagine a lawyer following each agent around during the course of an investigation. If an agent talked to a witness who said "I heard Patricia Sanchez closed her bank account last week," the lawyer would shout, "Objection, hearsay!" and the officer would not be able to use the information. That scenario is, to say the least, ludicrous. Of course agents use hearsay. The fact that it is hearsay makes it less reliable and may determine how much time is spent following up the information, but it certainly would not be ignored. The box on the next page gives you a rundown of some common legal terms whose definitions may help you answer some Problems for Investigation questions.

Sample Problem for Investigation Questions

If you are prepared to read closely, remain objective, and think analytically, you should be ready to try the sample Problems for Investigation that follow. Don't worry about your time right now, just try to answer the questions and then check the explanations that follow the questions. Go back and look again at any questions you got wrong to see where the problem is. Good luck!

Answer questions 1–9 on the basis of the following narrative and the statements that come after it.

You are an ICE agent assigned to investigate narcotics trafficking at the southern border. You receive a call from the Port of Entry Supervisory inspector. He states that some border inspectors were monitoring incoming traffic and noticed a driver that seemed to be confused. Several inspectors observed the driver for about ten to 15 minutes as he was waiting in traffic to cross the border. When he approached the primary inspection position, he could not answer some of the questions. He was sent to secondary inspection and some narcotics were discovered in the vehicle. The driver was detained while you begin an investigation.

During the course of the investigation, the following statements were made.

1. Inspector Juan Torres stated he was the primary inspector. When the driver, Julian Delgado, presented himself for entry, he could not say who owned the vehicle he was driving. When he was asked if there were any registration or insurance papers for the vehicle, he stated he borrowed it from his uncle, Ignacio, to get some parts to repair his car, and that he was just going to get the parts and return to Mexico. Inspector Torres referred him for further in-depth inspection.

2. The secondary inspector, Sally Kelly, stated that Julian Delgado arrived at her secondary inspection station sweating profusely and seemed in distress. When she asked him in Spanish his name and address, he could not reply. After a few moments, he got out of the vehicle and asked for some water, which he was given. He was then put in a secure waiting area.

continued on page 134

Legal Terms You Should Know

Here are some definitions that should be helpful for you as you are taking the TEA exam. Some of these are types of evidence; others are simply common terms used in law enforcement that it will be useful for you to know.

- **Alibi.** An alibi places the person at another place at the time the crime is committed. In an investigation, an agent would check the accuracy of the statement—that is, suspects have been known to lie about alibis.

- **Circumstantial evidence.** Circumstantial evidence is evidence not based on personal knowledge or observation of facts or events, but rather based on other facts that lead to certain conclusions. For example, you may deduce that a person has recently obtained some money if you know for a fact that person just bought a new car and took a vacation. Again, it would cause agents to follow up to find out if extra money was obtained and where it came from.

- **Coincidence.** A coincidence is when two or more occurrences happen at the same general time, or one right after the other, but they are not related. The fact that you take a Caribbean cruise right after money is discovered missing from your employer doesn't prove you took it. Maybe you coincidentally won the lottery.

- **Collusion.** Collusion is an agreement between two or more people to obtain something illegally or to defraud another person of what is legally his or hers. It implies the presence of fraud. For instance, collusion happens when a doctor and patient agree to lie about the patient's injuries in order to defraud an insurance company.

- **Conspiracy.** Conspiracy is similar to collusion, except it does not necessarily carry the implication of fraud. A conspiracy occurs when two or more people agree to engage in criminal activity. They may either work together or agree that one of them will commit the crime, with the other aiding in the planning or commission of the crime. A conspiracy also happens when a person solicits another person to commit a crime, as in hiring a "hit man." If Bob robs a bank, which he is able to do because Mary gave him the combination to the safe (and Mary knew why Bob wanted the combination), Bob and Mary are guilty of conspiracy to commit bank robbery.

- **Contradiction.** Two or more facts contradict each other when they say opposite things, or when it is impossible for both of them to be true. If I say the mugger was over six feet and you say the mugger was short—and we are talking about the same mugger—we are contradicting each other.

- **Corroboration.** Corroboration occurs when one fact supports another. If one suspect says, "I couldn't possibly have driven the getaway car because I don't drive," another person's saying, "That's right, the suspect is legally blind" corroborates the fact that the suspect doesn't drive.

- **Hearsay.** Hearsay happens when you hear something and then you say it. It is the difference between a witness saying, "I'm having an affair" and a witness saying, "I heard Mary was having an affair."

- **Implication.** An implication is something that is inferred or implied. A suspect who says, "I loaded the ATM on to the truck; Murray just drove" creates the implication that Murray probably did help load the machine or that a third person was involved, assuming ATMs are too heavy for one person to lift.

- **Motive.** A motive is what exists to cause a person to commit a crime. Owing money to a loan shark is a motive for robbing a store; being second in line to an inheritance is motive for murdering whoever is first.

- **Opportunity (or access).** Opportunity is one of the conditions, along with motive, for considering someone a serious suspect. A person who owes money to a loan shark but was in the hospital when the store was robbed has motive but does not have opportunity. Opportunity often means access, that is, the ability to be in or go to the right place for committing a crime.

- **Suspicion.** In the course of an investigation, several people may seem suspicious, that is, be considered suspects. A person need not be arrested, nor must an officer be convinced the person is guilty, in order for a person to be a suspect. Anyone who has motive and opportunity, or lies about an element of the case, can legitimately be considered a suspect. Colonel Mustard and Miss Scarlet may both be suspects, but only one of them is guilty.

3. Border K9 Officer Reed Connelly with his K9 "Rambo" inspected the outside of the vehicle, and Rambo alerted to the presence of narcotics in the vehicle. Rambo had been trained and had previously alerted 276 other times, and all were confirmed as valid for the presence of narcotics. Officer Connelly provided a written report of these facts.

4. After the K9 alert, Inspectors Mary Bartlett and Travis Craig searched the vehicle and discovered narcotics packages. The inspectors noted that some were labeled "Kings court," and others were labeled "for Tudor." The packages were in the trunk of the vehicle and under all of the seats.

5. Inspectors Bartlett and Craig both stated that they had observed Delgado in his vehicle waiting to cross into the United States. They both stated he seemed agitated and kept looking down at the floor of the vehicle and into the backseat area.

6. Border Inspector Tim Martin stated that he had heard from another inspector that a lot of the narcotics loads were destined to be driven to Los Angeles.

7. Border Inspector Campbell said that a check of the border crossing information disclosed that the vehicle had crossed 42 times in the last 90 days, driven by Veronica Chase. The driver, Julian Delgado, had no record of ever crossing the border in that vehicle.

8. Supervisory Inspector Michael Jarvis stated that he had seen the same pattern of smuggling attempted many times and that Julian Delgado knew that the narcotics were in the vehicle.

9. The vehicle registration information states that the vehicle is owned by a Veronica Chase, 1313 Tudor Lane, San Diego, California. The vehicle had been reported stolen two days earlier.

10. A preliminary interview of Julian Delgado indicated that he lived at 1333 King's Court, San Diego, California. Julian Delgado stated he would like to talk with someone about a misunderstanding. When asked what he was talking about, Delgado stated that his uncle William owned the vehicle and would explain the lack of insurance and registration papers.

1. Which statements indicate that Veronica Chase and Julian Delgado may be involved in the narcotics smuggling?
   a. Statements 1, 2, and 10
   b. Statements 4, 9, and 10
   c. Statements 6, 8, and 9
   d. Statements 5, 7, and 8
   e. none of these

2. What statement is hearsay and cannot be used?
   a. Statement 6
   b. Statement 7
   c. Statement 8
   d. Statement 9
   e. none of these

3. Which statement indicates there is legal reason to search the vehicle for narcotics?
   a. Statement 1
   b. Statement 2
   c. Statement 3
   d. Statement 7
   e. none of these

4. Which statement has little value to the investigation?
  a. Statement 2
  b. Statement 4
  c. Statement 5
  d. Statement 6
  e. none of these

5. Which statements indicate that Julian Delgado lied about his reasons for driving the vehicle across the border?
  a. Statements 2 and 9
  b. Statements 2 and 8
  c. Statements 7 and 10
  d. Statements 1 and 10
  e. none of these

6. Which statement indicates that the vehicle may have been used before to smuggle narcotics?
  a. Statement 5
  b. Statement 6
  c. Statement 7
  d. Statement 9
  e. none of these

7. What statements would cast suspicion that Veronica Chase may have been involved in narcotics smuggling prior to the incident with Julian Delgado?
  a. Statements 1, 2, and 6
  b. Statements 4, 7, and 9
  c. Statements 3, 6, and 8
  d. Statements 6, 7, and 10
  e. none of these

8. What statements contradict each other?
  a. Statements 2 and 9
  b. Statements 3 and 6
  c. Statements 4 and 7
  d. Statements 1 and 10
  e. none of these

9. What two statements corroborate each other?
  a. Statements 1 and 4
  b. Statements 4 and 5
  c. Statements 5 and 10
  d. Statements 1 and 10
  e. none of these

Answer questions 10–19 on the basis of the following narrative and the statements that come after it.

On March 10, firefighters received a call to respond to a fire at Jane Godowsky's shoe manufacturing business, Walk On Air, Inc. The blaze was extensive when firefighters arrived; by the time the fire was extinguished, the plant was a total loss. The next morning, Jane Godowsky announced she would not rebuild the plant and filed an insurance claim. Local authorities contacted the Bureau of Alcohol, Tobacco, Firearms and Explosives. Agents began an investigation.

During the course of the investigation, the following statements were made.

1. Firefighter Jason Columbus said that the fire appeared to have started in the northeast corner of the building.

2. Mason Fletcher, line supervisor at Walk On Air, said he called 911 when he saw smoke coming from the storeroom in the southwest corner of the building.

3. Fire Marshall Monica Stern said the dogs used in the investigation located pieces of metal that appeared to belong to a gas can.

4. Don Larson, line worker at Walk On Air, said that his sewing machine had been throwing sparks.

5. Ralph Michaels, owner of Blue Suede Shoes, Inc., said Godowsky had been losing business for the last five years.

6. Sarah Rand, buyer for The Shoe Boutique, said that she had recently stopped ordering from Blue Suede Shoes and started ordering from Walk On Air, because the shoes were of better quality.

7. The city building inspector said that Walk On Air had received five safety citations last month, including storing flammable materials improperly and poor ventilation in the storeroom.

8. Bill Walters, Jane Godowsky's administrative assistant, said Godowsky told him she was sick of the shoe business and wanted to find a buyer to take over the plant.

9. Gary Sterling, owner of United Marble Company, which is next door to Walk On Air, said that Walk On Air's employees were always parking in his lot, even though he had repeatedly asked them not to.

10. John Witt, Jane Godowsky's ex-husband, said Godowsky never had good business sense and he knew her business would fail.

11. Linda Falstaff, Walk On Air's banker, said Godowsky had recently been talking about a loan to expand the business.

10. Which two statements indicate the fire might NOT have been arson?
a. Statements 5 and 6
b. Statements 9 and 11
c. Statements 8 and 9
d. Statements 10 and 11
e. Statements 4 and 7

11. Which two statements indicate a motive for Jane Godowsky to commit arson?
a. Statements 4 and 7
b. Statements 3 and 10
c. Statements 5 and 8
d. Statements 9 and 11
e. Statements 8 and 10

12. Which statement is hearsay?
a. Statement 5
b. Statement 6
c. Statement 7
d. Statement 8
e. Statement 9

13. Which statement provides the best evidence that arson was the cause of the fire?
a. Statement 8
b. Statement 2
c. Statement 4
d. Statement 1
e. Statement 3

14. Which statement leads one to question the reliability of the speaker?
a. Statement 2
b. Statement 10
c. Statement 6
d. Statement 9
e. Statement 1

15. Which two statements seem to corroborate each other?
a. Statements 1 and 8
b. Statements 7 and 9
c. Statements 6 and 11
d. Statements 5 and 10
e. Statements 3 and 4

16. Which two statements indicate that more than one person was involved in setting the fire?
   a. Statements 7 and 8
   b. Statements 3 and 4
   c. Statements 9 and 10
   d. Statements 1 and 2
   e. Statements 5 and 6

17. Which statement is least helpful to officers investigating the fire?
   a. Statement 9
   b. Statement 10
   c. Statement 4
   d. Statement 5
   e. Statement 1

18. Which statement does NOT implicate Jane Godowsky?
   a. Statement 8
   b. Statement 5
   c. Statement 6
   d. Statement 9
   e. Statement 10

19. Which statement is most likely to be mere coincidence?
   a. Statement 3
   b. Statement 4
   c. Statement 7
   d. Statement 10
   e. Statement 1

Answers

1. b. These three statements contain information that Veronica Chase's and Julian Delgado's addresses may be indicated on the narcotics packaging

2. a. The statement has nebulous information that is not of investigative value in this case, as there is no indication that the vehicle was going to the Los Angeles area. Choice **c** seems to be hearsay, but it is from direct knowledge of Supervisory Inspector Jarvis.

3. b. This statement shows a proven record of indications by the K9 "Rambo" and show that narcotics may be present in the vehicle.

4. d. This statement is not proven, has no informational value, and does not pertain to this investigation.

5. d. These statements indicate that Julian Delgado said he was driving a borrowed car to get parts to fix his own car, but he admits to living in the United States.

6. c. The statement shows that the vehicle has crossed a number of times with the owner of the vehicle driving it. This information should be used to further investigate Veronica Chase.

7. b. These statements would indicate that she had been crossing the border many times prior to the incident, and she is implicated in the current investigation. The fact that her address may be noted on some of the narcotics packages warrants further investigation.

8. d. These statements have Delgado naming two different people as the owner of the vehicle. They could be used to document an attempt at lying in a subsequent interview with Delgado.

9. b. These statements both indicated where the narcotics were hidden, and has Julian Delgado seemingly looking at the hidden locations.

10. e. Statements 4 and 7 indicate there may have been fire hazards in the factory.

11. c. Statements 5 and 8 indicate that Godowsky's business is not doing well and that she wants to get out of the business, both motives for arson.

12. d. Statement 8 is a statement made without personal knowledge, simply repeating what others said.

13. e. Statement 3 indicates that physical evidence was found at the scene. This is always more reliable than information gathered from witnesses.

14. b. Statement 10 is made by Godowsky's ex-husband, who may harbor ill will toward her.

15. c. Statements 6 and 11 both indicate that Walk On Air's business was doing well.

16. d. Statements 1 and 2 place the fire's starting point in two different locations, which could indicate a person in each location setting a fire.

17. a. Statement 9 may indicate some animosity between Gary Sterling and Jane Godowsky, but probably not serious enough to lead one to arson.

18. c. Statement 6 is made by a satisfied customer and does not indicate any reason for Godowsky to commit arson.

19. b. Many factory machines throw sparks; however, investigators should follow up on this information.

9 ▶ TREASURY ENFORCEMENT AGENT PRACTICE EXAM 1

CHAPTER SUMMARY

Here is another sample test based on the TEA exam. After reviewing the sample questions in Chapter 3 and working through instructional Chapters 6, 7, and 8, take this test to see how much your score has improved.

Like the real TEA exam, the test that follows is made up of three sections. Part A, the Verbal Reasoning portion, consists of 25 short reading passages, each accompanied by a multiple-choice question. Part B, the Arithmetic Reasoning portion, consists of 20 word or numeric problems, each accompanied by a multiple-choice question. Part C, the Problems for Investigation portion, consists of several short narratives that describe a criminal or possibly criminal event, each accompanied by a list of ten or eleven statements that were made while the event was being investigated, followed by several questions about the statements.

For this exam, you should simulate the actual test-taking experience as closely as you can. Find a quiet place to work where you won't be disturbed. Tear out the answer sheet on the next page and find some number 2 pencils to fill in the circles. You will have 50 minutes to complete Part A, 50 minutes to complete Part B, and one hour to complete Part C. Set a timer or stopwatch for each part, but do not worry too much if you go over the allotted time on this practice exam. You can work more on timing when you take the second practice exam in Lesson 10.

Part A: Verbal Reasoning

1.	ⓐ ⓑ ⓒ ⓓ ⓔ	10.	ⓐ ⓑ ⓒ ⓓ ⓔ	19.	ⓐ ⓑ ⓒ ⓓ ⓔ
2.	ⓐ ⓑ ⓒ ⓓ ⓔ	11.	ⓐ ⓑ ⓒ ⓓ ⓔ	20.	ⓐ ⓑ ⓒ ⓓ ⓔ
3.	ⓐ ⓑ ⓒ ⓓ ⓔ	12.	ⓐ ⓑ ⓒ ⓓ ⓔ	21.	ⓐ ⓑ ⓒ ⓓ ⓔ
4.	ⓐ ⓑ ⓒ ⓓ ⓔ	13.	ⓐ ⓑ ⓒ ⓓ ⓔ	22.	ⓐ ⓑ ⓒ ⓓ ⓔ
5.	ⓐ ⓑ ⓒ ⓓ ⓔ	14.	ⓐ ⓑ ⓒ ⓓ ⓔ	23.	ⓐ ⓑ ⓒ ⓓ ⓔ
6.	ⓐ ⓑ ⓒ ⓓ ⓔ	15.	ⓐ ⓑ ⓒ ⓓ ⓔ	24.	ⓐ ⓑ ⓒ ⓓ ⓔ
7.	ⓐ ⓑ ⓒ ⓓ ⓔ	16.	ⓐ ⓑ ⓒ ⓓ ⓔ	25.	ⓐ ⓑ ⓒ ⓓ ⓔ
8.	ⓐ ⓑ ⓒ ⓓ ⓔ	17.	ⓐ ⓑ ⓒ ⓓ ⓔ		
9.	ⓐ ⓑ ⓒ ⓓ ⓔ	18.	ⓐ ⓑ ⓒ ⓓ ⓔ		

Part B: Arithmetic Reasoning

1.	ⓐ ⓑ ⓒ ⓓ ⓔ	8.	ⓐ ⓑ ⓒ ⓓ ⓔ	15.	ⓐ ⓑ ⓒ ⓓ ⓔ
2.	ⓐ ⓑ ⓒ ⓓ ⓔ	9.	ⓐ ⓑ ⓒ ⓓ ⓔ	16.	ⓐ ⓑ ⓒ ⓓ ⓔ
3.	ⓐ ⓑ ⓒ ⓓ ⓔ	10.	ⓐ ⓑ ⓒ ⓓ ⓔ	17.	ⓐ ⓑ ⓒ ⓓ ⓔ
4.	ⓐ ⓑ ⓒ ⓓ ⓔ	11.	ⓐ ⓑ ⓒ ⓓ ⓔ	18.	ⓐ ⓑ ⓒ ⓓ ⓔ
5.	ⓐ ⓑ ⓒ ⓓ ⓔ	12.	ⓐ ⓑ ⓒ ⓓ ⓔ	19.	ⓐ ⓑ ⓒ ⓓ ⓔ
6.	ⓐ ⓑ ⓒ ⓓ ⓔ	13.	ⓐ ⓑ ⓒ ⓓ ⓔ	20.	ⓐ ⓑ ⓒ ⓓ ⓔ
7.	ⓐ ⓑ ⓒ ⓓ ⓔ	14.	ⓐ ⓑ ⓒ ⓓ ⓔ		

Part C: Problems for Investigation

1.	ⓐ ⓑ ⓒ ⓓ ⓔ	11.	ⓐ ⓑ ⓒ ⓓ ⓔ	21.	ⓐ ⓑ ⓒ ⓓ ⓔ
2.	ⓐ ⓑ ⓒ ⓓ ⓔ	12.	ⓐ ⓑ ⓒ ⓓ ⓔ	22.	ⓐ ⓑ ⓒ ⓓ ⓔ
3.	ⓐ ⓑ ⓒ ⓓ ⓔ	13.	ⓐ ⓑ ⓒ ⓓ ⓔ	23.	ⓐ ⓑ ⓒ ⓓ ⓔ
4.	ⓐ ⓑ ⓒ ⓓ ⓔ	14.	ⓐ ⓑ ⓒ ⓓ ⓔ	24.	ⓐ ⓑ ⓒ ⓓ ⓔ
5.	ⓐ ⓑ ⓒ ⓓ ⓔ	15.	ⓐ ⓑ ⓒ ⓓ ⓔ	25.	ⓐ ⓑ ⓒ ⓓ ⓔ
6.	ⓐ ⓑ ⓒ ⓓ ⓔ	16.	ⓐ ⓑ ⓒ ⓓ ⓔ	26.	ⓐ ⓑ ⓒ ⓓ ⓔ
7.	ⓐ ⓑ ⓒ ⓓ ⓔ	17.	ⓐ ⓑ ⓒ ⓓ ⓔ	27.	ⓐ ⓑ ⓒ ⓓ ⓔ
8.	ⓐ ⓑ ⓒ ⓓ ⓔ	18.	ⓐ ⓑ ⓒ ⓓ ⓔ	28.	ⓐ ⓑ ⓒ ⓓ ⓔ
9.	ⓐ ⓑ ⓒ ⓓ ⓔ	19.	ⓐ ⓑ ⓒ ⓓ ⓔ	29.	ⓐ ⓑ ⓒ ⓓ ⓔ
10.	ⓐ ⓑ ⓒ ⓓ ⓔ	20.	ⓐ ⓑ ⓒ ⓓ ⓔ	30.	ⓐ ⓑ ⓒ ⓓ ⓔ

Part A: Verbal Reasoning

Read each of the following paragraphs carefully, and answer the question that follows it by choosing the best of the five possible answer choices. You have 50 minutes for this section.

For most judges, sentencing a person who has been convicted of a crime is a difficult decision. In the majority of jurisdictions throughout the country, judges have few sentencing options from which to choose. Generally, their options are confined to a fine, probation, or incarceration. Crimes, however, cover a wide spectrum of criminal behavior, and a wide variety of sanctions must be available.

1. The author of this paragraph would probably approve most of
   a. giving judges more sentencing options from which to choose.
   b. having laws that dictate which sentence a judge should hand down.
   c. allowing someone other than a judge to sentence a criminal.
   d. making incarceration for all serious crimes mandatory.
   e. spending more money on the criminal justice system.

In the 1966 Supreme Court decision *Miranda v. Arizona*, the court held that before the police can obtain statements from a person subjected to an interrogation, the person must be given a *Miranda* warning. This warning means that a person must be told that he or she has the right to remain silent during the police interrogation. Violation of this right means that any statement that the person makes is not admissible in a court hearing.

2. The paragraph best supports the statement that
   a. police who do not warn persons of their *Miranda* rights are guilty of a crime.
   b. a *Miranda* warning must be given before a police interrogation can begin.
   c. the police may no longer interrogate persons suspected of a crime unless a lawyer is present.
   d. the 1966 Supreme Court decision in *Miranda* should be reversed.
   e. persons who are interrogated by police should always remain silent until their lawyer comes.

Every few decades for more than 150 years, the public library has endured another cycle of change. We're in the middle of one of these cycles today as librarians try to be responsive to the trends of the times. The Internet and CD-ROM technology have had their effect on the public library. This trend is changing libraries in a significant way.

3. The paragraph best supports the statement that
   a. public libraries today are not as responsive to the needs of readers as in past decades.
   b. the Internet and CD-ROM should be part of any public library system.
   c. technologies like the Internet and CD-ROM are changing public libraries.
   d. librarians are responsible for making the Internet and CD-ROM more popular.
   e. widespread use of computers is threatening our public libraries.

Desktop videoconferencing may be a relatively new meeting technology, but it may not be for everyone. Before you recommend that your company buy a desktop videoconferencing system, you need to examine your goals and needs. Technologies need to complement how people operate within a company.

4. The paragraph best supports the statement that
  a. desktop videoconferencing is the wave of the future for most businesses.
  b. before buying a new technology, a company should identify why and how it will be used.
  c. technologies such as desktop videoconferencing are changing the role of the business meeting.
  d. how people interrelate within a company is one way of judging whether a company can afford technology.
  e. many companies cannot afford to buy a desktop videoconferencing system.

Detectives would be able to solve more crimes if they could compare information about cases with files of past crimes. An artificial intelligence (AI) system, designed by computer scientists, may allow them to do just that. The system, which could run around the clock, would look for patterns and similarities between crimes that may be separated by time and geographical location. Because the amount of available data about crimes is always increasing, having a system that could "data mine"—sift through the data—would save time and human effort. A test run of the system showed that it could detect ten times as many patterns as detectives.

5. The paragraph best supports the statement that
  a. AI systems should replace human detectives.
  b. an AI system is always the most reliable option for "data mining."
  c. detectives have intuitions about crimes that a computer system could never have.
  d. an AI system that detects crime patterns could greatly help detectives solve crimes.
  e. because the AI system would run 24 hours a day, it would never miss a pattern between crimes.

In criminal cases, the availability of readable fingerprints is often critical in establishing evidence of a major crime. It is therefore necessary to follow proper procedures when taking fingerprints. For elimination purposes, major case prints should be obtained from all persons who may have touched areas associated with a crime scene.

6. With which of the following statements is the author most likely to agree?
  a. No crimes can be solved without readable fingerprints.
  b. Most fingerprint experts do not follow proper procedures.
  c. All persons who have touched an area in a crime scene are suspects.
  d. All fingerprints found at a crime scene are used in court as evidence.
  e. All persons who have touched a crime-scene area should be fingerprinted.

Video surveillance is a valuable tool for the investigator. If a crime is committed in view of the video cameras, details about the crime can be viewed over and over again to assist the investigator in the details. Eyewitnesses making statements may not have the ability to recall minor details that may be very important in solving the crime. Over time, eyewitness accounts may change as they hear or read about the crime, and witnesses may try to fill in their memory by guessing about events and actions they did not actually see.

7. The paragraph best supports the statement that
   a. video cameras should be placed in all known crime locations.
   b. an eyewitness to a crime should carry a video camera.
   c. a video recording of a crime is better evidence than an eyewitness in providing details of a crime.
   d. an investigator should discount a witness statement if he or she has a video recording.
   e. not all eyewitnesses have the ability to correctly recall what they see.

People who want to persuade others about a particular issue often use argumentation tactics. Most of these can advance the argument in an honest way, but some tactics are meant to distract the listener from the real issues.

8. The paragraph best supports the statement that
   a. most arguments do not settle the issue at hand.
   b. argumentation is an art requires a great deal of study.
   c. although most people argue in a fair way, often they do not succeed.
   d. the most effective way to persuade people is to distract them.
   e. some people use argumentation tactics that are dishonest.

According to research scientists, sleep loss may lead to gaining weight. Studies show that that sleep deprivation affects the part of the brain that regulates hunger, increasing hormone levels that make you feel hungry and decreasing hormone levels that make you feel full. The result could mean overeating and gaining weight. It may explain why sleep-deprived college students, new parents, and shift workers tend to gain weight.

9. The paragraph best supports the statement that
   a. sleep deprivation may be an important part of the puzzle of why some people gain weight.
   b. sleep loss is the top reason so many people are overweight.
   c. if people made sure they got eight hours of sleep each night, they would not gain weight.
   d. only a small portion of people are sleep deprived, so the link between sleep loss and weight gain is not significant.
   e. this study is only relevant to college students, new parents, and shift workers.

Frequently, law enforcement officers use powerful DNA analysis techniques to investigate "cold cases"—unsolved crimes from the past. Some agencies are forming "cold-case squads" that review old cases for DNA evidence and other new leads. Just as investigators collect biological evidence from crime scenes today, they can create a DNA profile from old evidence—clothing or bedding—that was collected years, even decades, before. Unlike other kinds of evidence, like eyewitness accounts, that may become less reliable over time, DNA evidence can be reliable 10, 15, even 20 years after a crime was committed.

10. The writer believes that DNA evidence
   a. is the most reliable type of evidence from a crime scene.
   b. has the power to reveal the truth about a crime long after it has occurred.
   c. can be used to solve cold cases only when legal issues are appropriately addressed.
   d. has led to crime-solving advancements so great that the laws cannot keep up.
   e. collected from old crime scenes is very different from new biological evidence.

Electronic mail (e-mail) technology has made it possible for people around the world to communicate with each other about many topics—from sharing research to developing personal friendships. In the realm of business, e-mail simplifies the flow of ideas, connects people from distant offices, eliminates the need for meetings, and often boosts productivity. But e-mail for business purposes should be carefully managed to avoid unclear and inappropriate communication. E-mail messages should be concise, with the most important topics in the first paragraph. When confidential or highly complex issues need to be addressed, phone calls or face-to-face conversations are best.

11. The paragraph best supports the statement that e-mail

   a. is not always the easiest way to connect people from distant offices.

   b. has changed considerably since it first emerged as a technology.

   c. causes people to be unproductive when it is used incorrectly.

   d. is most effective when it is used to address uncomplicated matters.

   e. is most effective when it is used to address minor matters.

Between 1983 and 2000, the number of practicing physicians increased by about 39%. During the same time period, the number of healthcare managers increased by more than 700%. These percentages mean that many doctors have lost the authority to make their own schedules, determine the fees that they charge, and decide on prescribed treatments.

12. The paragraph best supports the statement that doctors

   a. resent the interference of heathcare managers.

   b. no longer have adequate training.

   c. care a great deal about their patients.

   d. are less independent than they use to be.

   e. are making a lot less money than they used to make.

By the time they reach adulthood, most people can perform many different activities involving motor skills. Motor skills involve such diverse tasks as riding a bicycle, threading a needle, and cooking dinner. What all these activities have in common is their dependence on precision and timing of muscular movement.

13. The paragraph best supports the statement that

   a. most adults have refined their motor skills through practice.

   b. most adults know how to ride a bicycle, thread a needle, and cook dinner.

   c. threading a needle is a precise motor skill.

   d. children perform fewer fine motor activities in a day than adults do.

   e. refined motor skills are limited to adults.

Close-up images of Mars by the *Mariner 9* probe indicated networks of valleys that looked like the stream beds on Earth. These images also implied that Mars once had an atmosphere that was thick enough to trap the sun's heat. If this were true, something happened to Mars billions of years ago that stripped away the planet's atmosphere.

14. The paragraph best supports the statement that
   a. Mars now has little or no atmosphere.
   b. Mars once had a thicker atmosphere than Earth does.
   c. the *Mariner 9* probe took the first pictures of Mars.
   d. Mars is closer to the sun than Earth is.
   e. Mars is more mountainous than Earth is.

Forest fires feed on decades-long accumulations of debris and leap from the tops of young trees into the branches of mature trees. Fires that jump from tree-top to treetop can be devastating. In old-growth forests, however, the shade of mature trees keeps thickets of small trees from sprouting, and the lower branches of mature trees are too high to catch the flames.

15. The paragraph best supports the statement that
   a. forest fire damage is reduced in old-growth forests.
   b. small trees should be cut down to prevent forest fires.
   c. mature trees should be thinned out to prevent forest fires.
   d. forest fires do the most damage in old-growth forests.
   e. old-growth forests have a larger accumulation of forest debris.

Originating in the 1920s, the pyramid scheme is one of the oldest con games going. Honest people are often pulled in, thinking the scheme is a legitimate investment enterprise. The first customer to "fall for" the pyramid scheme will actually make big money and will therefore persuade friends and relatives to join also. The chain then continues with the con artist who originated the scheme pocketing, rather than investing, the money. Finally, the pyramid collapses, but by that time the scam artist will usually have moved out of town, leaving no forwarding address.

16. The paragraph best supports the statement that
   a. it is fairly easy to spot a pyramid scheme in the making.
   b. the first customer of a pyramid scheme is the most gullible.
   c. the con artist who sets up a pyramid scheme must have a modicum of patience.
   d. the pyramid scheme had its heyday in the 1920s.
   e. the pyramid scheme got its name from its structure.

Although romanticized in fiction, the job of a private investigator is often very boring. The real PI can spend hours or days looking into a not-particularly-lucrative insurance fraud scheme or sitting outside a sleazy motel waiting to catch some not-particularly-attractive philandering husband or wife of a client in the act. In fact, there would be very few private investigators in detective fiction if their jobs had to be portrayed realistically.

17. The paragraph best supports the statement that private investigators
   a. routinely do work related to industrial or family disputes.
   b. usually have disreputable clients.
   c. embellish their experience so they can write more exciting detective fiction.
   d. sometimes choose their line of work because they think it will be romantic.
   e. are not usually well paid.

Chicago police are using new technologies to see and hear what's going on in the city's streets. Video surveillance cameras that also record sound have been installed in the city's high-crime neighborhoods. These devices can recognize the sound of a gunshot, narrow in on its source, and place a 911 call. Opponents of the technology say that the city's camera system infringes on citizens' privacy rights. But as long as cameras are set up in public spaces, they do not violate the law. And the reduction in Chicago's crime rate—which is at its lowest in 40 years—far outweighs any privacy issues.

18. The author of the paragraph believes that
    a. a citizen's right to privacy is a bogus issue.
    b. surveillance cameras should not be restricted to public spaces.
    c. the cameras used in Chicago should be used in cities around the country.
    d. Chicago's reduction in crimes is a result of its surveillance camera system.
    e. maintaining the right to privacy is more important than cutting crime.

Although Darwin's theory of evolution revolutionized the natural sciences, Herbert Spencer's theory of social evolution was a blight on American history. Robber barons used Spencer's theory as an excuse for grabbing power, perverting Darwin's idea of "survival of the fittest." According to the robber barons' theory—which still survives in subtler forms today—the poor were simply not "fit," or they'd be rich!

19. The paragraph best supports the statement that
    a. Darwin's idea of fitness was not necessarily synonymous with "having the most power."
    b. Darwin objected to Spencer's perverting his theory of evolution in order to take advantage of the poor.
    c. Spencer's theory flourished in the days of the robber barons but has since mostly fallen into disfavor.
    d. Spencer's theory of social evolution is unscientific.
    e. to be economically successful, one must be fit.

Because of her gender, Maria Mitchell was offered virtually no opportunity for a career in science; however, she created an opportunity for herself. In 1847, using a telescope her father had set up on the roof of the building where he worked, she discovered a new comet. As a result, in 1848, she became the first female member of the prestigious American Academy of Arts and Sciences and, in 1865, became a professor of astronomy at the newly founded Vassar College.

20. The paragraph best supports the statement that
    a. people who are not handed opportunities can generally create them.
    b. Maria Mitchell was encouraged by her father to become an astronomer.
    c. Maria Mitchell fought for a woman's right to work in science.
    d. the discovery of new heavenly bodies is a status symbol in the science of astronomy.
    e. Vassar College has a strong Department of Astronomy.

One reason people have difficulty solving problems on the job is that they look for complex solutions. Often, it is much easier and more productive to look for a simpler answer to a problem. Looking for a simpler answer first will frequently lead you toward a more comprehensive and lasting solution.

21. The paragraph best supports the statement that
    a. it is difficult to solve complex problems on the job.
    b. if a problem is complex, the answer will be complex.
    c. it is easier to solve a complex problem than a simple one.
    d. one good way to solve problems is to look for simple answers.
    e. being able to solve complex problems quickly makes one more productive.

Even though some companies offer "family-friendly" policies like parental leaves and flexible work arrangements, employees do not always use them. A company's culture—its attitudes about work and family—often influence whether employees take advantage of such policies. In particular, managers can have a key effect. Employees may not use family-friendly benefits because they feel that their manager will not approve and that that their status in the workplace and their career advancement will be compromised.

22. The paragraph best supports the statement that
  a. using family-friendly policies hinders workers' career advancement.
  b. if family-friendly benefits are available, employees will use them.
  c. even when work-family policies are available, employees do not always use them.
  d. flexible work arrangements often result in high employee productivity.
  e. supportive managers increase employee satisfaction and loyalty.

Handling computer repairs does not have to frustrate a well-organized office staff. Many office professionals have an in-house checklist for initially handling computer problems. The checklist consists of the common causes of computer down time: disconnected cables, competing electrical devices, dirty equipment, the wrong type of paper. By going through the checklist before phoning a computer technician, office assistants will often correct the problem quickly.

23. The paragraph best supports the statement that
  a. computer downtime is usually the result of a mistake by an office worker.
  b. a technician should be called in for computer repairs only after an office worker has completed an in-house checklist.
  c. to avoid costly repairs, office workers should clean computer equipment several times each month.
  d. computer breakdowns cause more frustration to office workers than most other problems do.
  e. a technician should be called in for computer repairs if the problem is too complex for an office worker.

Identity theft is when someone uses your personal information—your name, Social Security number, or any account number—without your permission to commit fraud or other crimes. In some cases, criminals have used someone else's personal data to take funds from bank accounts. In the worst cases, criminals assume another's identity entirely, running up huge debts and committing crimes under the stolen identity. Victims of identity theft may incur substantial costs in order to correct the situation and reestablish their reputation.

24. The paragraph best supports the statement that
  a. computer technology has led to the rise in identity theft.
  b. your personal information is unique to you, like your fingerprints.
  c. identity theft is a federal crime.
  d. identity theft is not committed for financial gain.
  e. criminals can cause substantial damage to a victim's assets, credit, and reputation.

More and more office workers telecommute from offices in their own homes. The upside of telecommuting is both greater productivity and greater flexibility. Telecommuters produce, on average, 20% more than if they were to work in an office, and their flexible schedule allows them to balance both their family and work responsibilities.

25. The paragraph best supports the statement that telecommuters
   a. tend to have more family responsibilities than workers who travel to the office.
   b. get more work done in a given time period than workers who travel to the office.
   c. produce a better quality work product than workers who travel to the office.
   d. are more flexible in their personal lives than workers who travel to the office.
   e. are more productive if they have families to help them balance responsibilities.

Part B: Arithmetic Reasoning

Analyze the following paragraphs, set up the problem for each one, and choose the correct solution from choices **a**, **b**, **c**, and **d**. If none of these four choices is correct, choose option **e**, "none of these." You have 50 minutes for this section.

1. After making purchases, you look at the three receipts from the purchases. They are for $7.62, $22.38, and $20.26. You started with $58.25. How much change should you have left?
   a. $13.61
   b. $6.99
   c. $7.99
   d. $15.61
   e. none of these

2. If a vehicle is driven 22 miles on Monday, 25 miles on Tuesday, and 19 miles on Wednesday, what is the average number of miles driven each day?
   a. 19
   b. 21
   c. 22
   d. 23.5
   e. none of these

3. The directions on an exam allow $2\frac{1}{2}$ hours to answer 50 questions. If you want to spend an equal amount of time on each of the 50 questions, about how much time should you allow for each one?
   a. 45 seconds
   b. $1\frac{1}{2}$ minutes
   c. 2 minutes
   d. 3 minutes
   e. none of these

4. If a worker is given a salary increase of $1.25 per hour, what it the total amount of the salary increase for one 40-hour week?
   a. $49.20
   b. $50.00
   c. $50.25
   d. $51.75
   e. none of these

5. Five cans of tomatoes cost $6.50. At this rate, how much will nine cans of tomatoes cost?
   a. $10.55
   b. $11.70
   c. $11.90
   d. $12.40
   e. none of these

6. The basal metabolic rate (BMR) is the rate at which our body uses calories. The BMR for a man in his twenties is about 1,700 calories per day. If 204 of these calories should come from protein, about what percent of this man's diet should be protein?
 a. 1.2%
 b. 8.3%
 c. 12%
 d. 16%
 e. none of these

7. A piece of ribbon 3 feet 4 inches long was divided in 5 equal parts. How long was each part?
 a. 1 foot 2 inches
 b. 10 inches
 c. 8 inches
 d. 6 inches
 e. none of these

8. In half of migraine sufferers, a certain drug reduces the number of migraines by 50%. What percentage of all migraines can be eliminated by this drug?
 a. 25%
 b. 50%
 c. 75%
 d. 80%
 e. none of these

9. You are downloading a file for work and it will take 22 minutes to complete. It is now 15:35 and you have to shut down the computer at 16:00. What time will the file download be complete?
 a. 15:44
 b. 15:47
 c. 15:57
 d. 16:07
 e. none of these

10. Out of 100 citizens polled, 80 said they believed street crime was on the rise. How many citizens out of 30,000 could be expected to say they believe street crime is on the rise?
 a. 2,400
 b. 6,000
 c. 22,000
 d. 26,000
 e. none of these

11. Lefty keeps track of the length of each fish that he catches. Following are the lengths in inches of the fish that he caught one day:

12, 13, 8, 10, 8, 9, 17

What is the median fish length that Lefty caught that day?
 a. 8 inches
 b. 10 inches
 c. 11 inches
 d. 12 inches
 e. none of these

12. Dimitri has 40 math problems to do for homework. If he does 40% of the assignment in one hour, how long will it take for Dimitri to complete the whole assignment?
 a. 1.5 hours
 b. 2.0 hours
 c. 2.5 hours
 d. 4.0 hours
 e. none of these

13. A fencing project for an uneven lot is being completed. The premade fence sections are available in six-foot lengths and four-foot lengths and cannot be cut. The measurements of the lot are two sides of 22 feet, one side of 30 feet and one side of 24 feet, for a total fence length of 98 feet. How many of each section of fence must be purchased?
  a. 14 six-foot sections and 3 four-foot sections
  b. 15 six-foot sections and 2 four-foot sections
  c. 16 six-foot sections and 1 four-foot section
  d. 15 six-foot sections and 3 four-foot sections
  e. none of these

14. The population of Smithtown increases at a rate of 3% annually. If the population is currently 2,500, what will the population be at the same time next year?
  a. 2,530
  b. 2,560
  c. 2,570
  d. 2,800
  e. none of these

15. The radius of a circle is 13. What is the approximate area of the circle?
  a. 81.64
  b. 530.66
  c. 1,666.27
  d. 169
  e. none of these

16. Rashaard went fishing six days in the month of June. He caught 11, four, zero, five, four, and six fish, respectively. On the days that Rashaard fished, what was his average catch?
  a. 4
  b. 5
  c. 6
  d. 7
  e. none of these

17. An office uses two dozen pencils and $3\frac{1}{2}$ reams of paper each week. If pencils cost five cents each and a ream of paper costs $7.50, how much does it cost to supply the office for a week?
  a. $7.55
  b. $12.20
  c. $26.25
  d. $28.45
  e. none of these

18. Mr. James Rossen is just beginning a computer consulting firm and has purchased the following equipment:

Three telephone sets, each costing $125
Two computers, each costing $1,300
Two computer monitors, each costing $950
One printer costing $600
One answering machine costing $50

Mr. Rossen is reviewing his finances. What should he write as the total value of the equipment he has purchased so far?
  a. $3,025
  b. $3,275
  c. $5,400
  d. $5,525
  e. none of these

19. Roger earned $24,355 this year and $23,000 the year before. To the nearest $100, what did Roger earn in the past two years?
  a. $47,300
  b. $47,400
  c. $47,455
  d. $47,500
  e. none of these

20. Which of the following numeric values contains a six in the hundredths decimal place?
a. 0.0923
b. 626.0357
c. 16.0076
d. 4611.03556
e. none of these

Part C: Problems for Investigation

Carefully read each of the following paragraphs and the statements that come after it, and then answer the questions by choosing the best of the five possible answer choices. You have 60 minutes for this section.

Bert Hines was imprisoned in a federal facility for forgery. Hines, along with three other prisoners and two guards, was taken from lockup to a local optometrist's office on January 17. The four prisoners were secured by handcuffs to an 8-foot length of chain during transport and while sitting in the optometrist's waiting room. Hines was released from the chain and taken to the examination room where a preliminary eye exam was conducted. He was then escorted back to the waiting room. As another prisoner was being released, Hines, who had not been reshackled, seized a gun from one of the guards and managed to escape. He took the optometrist's receptionist, Michelle Rogers, hostage and fled with her. He released her within 30 minutes, when he stole a car.

During the course of the investigation, the following statements were made.

1. Jeff Reynolds, one of the four prisoners, said that Hines's cellmate told him Hines had a girlfriend in town.

2. The optometrist said that Hines acted "weird" during the exam.

3. Jessie Seymour, one of the guards, said that Hines was not reshackled because his exam was not complete.

4. Mary Hobbes, the guard whose gun was stolen, said that the gun was not regulation.

5. Maurice Chang, one of the four prisoners, said that Hines made eye contact with a female passerby as the prisoners were led into the office.

6. Martin Steffins, Michelle Rogers's fiancé, said that Michelle was always afraid on the days prisoners came to the office.

7. Michelle Rogers said that Hines retrieved a package from the planter in front of the office and later showed her a passport and an envelope containing several thousand dollars.

8. Rachel Firth, the owner of the car Hines stole, said that one of her husband's suits, which she had picked up at the dry cleaner, was hanging in the car.

9. Michael Jones, Rachel's husband, said that the car tended to "cut out" at speeds over 60 miles per hour.

10. Raymond Diaz, Hines's cellmate, said that Hines spoke French fluently.

1. Which statement is hearsay?
a. Statement 1
b. Statement 2
c. Statement 4
d. Statement 7
e. Statement 10

2. Which two statements indicate that Hines may have been planning to leave the country?
   a. Statements 7 and 8
   b. Statements 2 and 10
   c. Statements 8 and 10
   d. Statements 2 and 8
   e. Statements 7 and 10

3. Which two statements along with statement 2 are least likely to be of use in this investigation?
   a. Statements 3 and 5
   b. Statements 4 and 6
   c. Statements 1 and 7
   d. Statements 8 and 10
   e. Statements 1 and 9

4. Which two statements indicate the escape was planned, rather than spontaneous?
   a. Statements 2 and 5
   b. Statements 3 and 7
   c. Statements 2 and 3
   d. Statements 5 and 7
   e. Statements 8 and 10

5. Which statement indicates an avoidable mistake on the part of prison guards?
   a. Statement 2
   b. Statement 3
   c. Statement 1
   d. Statement 5
   e. Statement 6

6. Assuming law enforcement officers spot Hines driving Firth's car, which statement would lead officers to consider commencing a high-speed chase?
   a. Statement 7
   b. Statement 8
   c. Statement 6
   d. Statement 4
   e. Statement 9

7. Which statement indicates officers should contact security at the local airport?
   a. Statement 7
   b. Statement 8
   c. Statement 9
   d. Statement 10
   e. Statement 6

The president was scheduled to speak at the Civic Arena. There was no charge to attend the event, but audience members had to obtain a ticket beforehand in order to be admitted to the arena the day of the speech. One week before the event, the Secret Service arrived to finalize security plans. The next day, the box office at the arena received a letter containing a threat on the president's life.

During the course of the investigation, the following statements were made.

1. Edna Thurber, box office manager, said that mail was always delivered into a locked box and only she and Bob White, the arena manager, had a key.

2. Randy Shoemaker, a box office employee, said that the tickets were all distributed two weeks before the speech.

3. After examining the envelope in which the threat arrived, Police Officer Connie Hall noted that the stamp was not canceled.

4. Rita Lawe, a box office employee, said that several people had tried to obtain tickets in the last week; a short, thin, scruffy man had come to the box office several times.

5. Bob White said he knew for a fact that Edna Thurber had volunteered for a "get out the vote drive" in the last election.

6. Randy Shoemaker said that Rita Lawe was mad at the president because she was being harassed to repay her student loans.

7. Special agent Maury Thurston said that several members of the public had spoken to him while he was examining the exterior of the arena. He remembered a thin man in a shabby raincoat who asked if there would be bomb-sniffing dogs.

8. Edna Thurber said that Alan Pip, Bob White's assistant, was always talking about how members of the government were also members of a satanic cult.

9. Bob White said that prior to getting the job managing the arena, he was in the military.

10. Alan Pip said that, last week when he went out on the loading dock to have a cigarette, he saw a man looking around the area. He said the man was thin and wearing a dirty sweatshirt.

8. Which statements along with statement 4 indicate the threat was made by someone who does not work at the arena?
   a. Statements 3 and 6
   b. Statements 7 and 10
   c. Statements 1 and 5
   d. Statements 6 and 8
   e. Statements 3 and 7

9. Which statement leads one to question the reliability of Alan Pip?
   a. Statement 1
   b. Statement 10
   c. Statement 3
   d. Statement 8
   e. Statement 7

10. Which two statements are most damaging to Bob White?
    a. Statements 1 and 3
    b. Statements 5 and 9
    c. Statements 4 and 8
    d. Statements 2 and 10
    e. Statements 5 and 10

11. Which statement is least damaging to Edna Thurber?
    a. Statement 8
    b. Statement 1
    c. Statement 5
    d. Statement 3
    e. Statement 7

12. Which statement represents an idle threat?
    a. Statement 4
    b. Statement 6
    c. Statement 7
    d. Statement 9
    e. Statement 10

13. Which two statements indicate cooperation between the Secret Service and local police?
    a. Statements 5 and 9
    b. Statements 1 and 3
    c. Statements 5 and 7
    d. Statements 1 and 7
    e. Statements 3 and 7

14. Which statement is the least helpful in solving the case?
    a. Statement 8
    b. Statement 6
    c. Statement 5
    d. Statement 2
    e. Statement 4

Immigration and Customs Enforcement Agent Ellen Mitchell noticed several boxes marked "Assorted hand-carved wooden figures from Cameroon," which were being unloaded from a United Express cargo plane. The boxes were from Mandara Exports, Ltd., and to Freddy Jones Imports. Inspector Mitchell was suspicious of the shipment for several reasons. It was a large shipment, and she had never heard of Freddy Jones Imports before; the boxes were triple-sealed; and Jones himself was there waiting to claim the boxes. Mitchell opened one of the crates and found figures carved of ivory.

During the course of the investigation, the following statements were made.

1. Freddy Jones stated that he had ordered wooden figures and he had the invoice to prove it.

2. Margaret Woo, United Express employee, said she picked up this shipment from another plane in Madrid and looked only at the bill of lading, which indicated the crates contained hand-carved wooden figures from Cameroon. Her supervisor happened to be present at the pickup.

3. In Cameroon, Michelle Eseka, president of Mandara Exports, Ltd., stated she obtains the carved figurines from several suppliers and cooperatives.

4. William Calabar, head of purchasing for Mandara Exports, said that he has recently been dealing mostly with Francis Onitsha, a supplier from eastern Cameroon, for the wooden carvings.

5. Rosemary Ndele, Michelle Eseka's administrative assistant, said that William Calabar was a compulsive gambler.

6. Michelle Eseka said she had told Calabar not to deal with Onitsha, because Onitsha once asked her to send some contraband along with one of her regular shipments.

7. Kenneth Yokadouma, Michelle Eseka's banker, said that Mandara Exports had been losing money lately and that Eseka was in danger of losing the business.

8. A member of Women's Hands, a cooperative that carves figures and makes jewelry, said that Francis Onitsha asked them to do some ivory carvings.

9. Francis Onitsha said that Rosemary Ndele put Freddy Jones in touch with Mandara Exports.

10. Customs officials in Douala, Cameroon, said that they had no record of this shipment.

15. Which statement is most damaging to Francis Onitsha?
   a. Statement 6
   b. Statement 8
   c. Statement 2
   d. Statement 4
   e. Statement 9

16. Which statement appears to be an attempt by the speaker to establish innocence?
   a. Statement 7
   b. Statement 9
   c. Statement 10
   d. Statement 6
   e. Statement 5

17. Which statement indicates that United Express employees knew nothing about the illegal shipment?
  a. Statement 4
  b. Statement 6
  c. Statement 2
  d. Statement 10
  e. Statement 8

18. Which statement causes one to be suspicious of the information provided by Rosemary Ndele?
  a. Statement 9
  b. Statement 8
  c. Statement 4
  d. Statement 5
  e. Statement 7

19. Which statement provides a motive for Michelle Eseka to make the illegal shipment?
  a. Statement 6
  b. Statement 8
  c. Statement 9
  d. Statement 10
  e. Statement 7

20. Which two statements cast the greatest suspicion on William Calabar?
  a. Statements 3 and 4
  b. Statements 7 and 10
  c. Statements 1 and 2
  d. Statements 5 and 6
  e. Statements 8 and 9

21. Which statement illustrates cooperation between U.S. and Cameroon law enforcement agencies?
  a. Statement 8
  b. Statement 3
  c. Statement 10
  d. Statement 7
  e. Statement 6

22. Which statement implies Freddy Jones had knowledge of the illegal shipment?
  a. Statement 1
  b. Statement 9
  c. Statement 2
  d. Statement 10
  e. Statement 6

23. Which two statements indicate the bill of lading may have been tampered with?
  a. Statements 2 and 10
  b. Statements 1 and 6
  c. Statements 3 and 9
  d. Statements 2 and 6
  e. Statements 6 and 9

Henry Allen, fiscally conservative candidate for city council, contacted the Internal Security Division of the Internal Revenue Service and alleged that an IRS employee was giving Allen's tax information to an opponent, Susan Vickers. Vickers was threatening to release information that Allen's business had been operating at a loss the last five years. Molly Hepplewhite, an Internal Security Inspector for the IRS, commences an investigation.

During the course of the investigation, the following statements were made.

1. Milton Banks, Susan Vickers's neighbor, said that he once caught Vickers going through his trash.

2. Bill Pushman, Henry Allen's campaign manager, said that he dated Alice West in college. Alice now works at the IRS.

3. Shelby Gray, Susan Vickers's sister, said that Susan would always do whatever she needed to do to get what she wanted.

4. Calvin Morris, Susan Vickers's campaign manager, said that his sister-in-law, Mary Yate, works at the IRS, but they haven't spoken in months.

5. IRS employee Doug Edwards said that Mary Yate and Alice West have lunch together almost every day.

6. Frank Luther, Henry Allen's neighbor, said that Allen has no business running for city council when he can't even keep his dog in his own yard.

7. Felicia Dial said that she plans to vote for Henry Allen because he promises to run the city as efficiently as he runs his business.

8. IRS employee Mary Yate said that Frank Luther and Doug Edwards have been friends since grade school.

9. IRS employee Avery Page said that Alice West makes a lot of personal phone calls and once he heard her say, "He can't treat you like that!"

10. Henry Allen said that current council member Mavis Wright said that Susan Vickers said she'd do anything to win this election.

24. Which statement is most damaging to the Susan Vickers campaign?
- **a.** Statement 1
- **b.** Statement 3
- **c.** Statement 4
- **d.** Statement 10
- **e.** Statement 5

25. Which statement is least helpful to the investigation?
- **a.** Statement 1
- **b.** Statement 8
- **c.** Statement 2
- **d.** Statement 6
- **e.** Statement 4

26. Which two statements are hearsay?
- **a.** Statements 1 and 2
- **b.** Statements 9 and 10
- **c.** Statements 5 and 6
- **d.** Statements 3 and 4
- **e.** Statements 1 and 6

27. Which statement represents circumstantial evidence?
- **a.** Statement 5
- **b.** Statement 2
- **c.** Statement 4
- **d.** Statement 7
- **e.** Statement 3

28. Which statement indicates that an IRS employee is providing information to the Vickers campaign?
- **a.** Statement 1
- **b.** Statement 3
- **c.** Statement 10
- **d.** Statement 4
- **e.** Statement 8

29. Which two statements imply the possibility that the Allen campaign is attempting to make the Vickers campaign appear guilty?
- **a.** Statements 4 and 8
- **b.** Statements 1 and 3
- **c.** Statements 2 and 5
- **d.** Statements 8 and 10
- **e.** Statements 3 and 10

30. Which two statements tend to implicate Frank Luther?
- **a.** Statements 6 and 8
- **b.** Statements 1 and 5
- **c.** Statements 2 and 9
- **d.** Statements 4 and 5
- **e.** Statements 4 and 6

Answers

Part A: Verbal Reasoning

1. a. The paragraph stresses that more options in sentencing should be made available to judges. Choice **b** contradicts the author's opinion. There is no support for choice **c**. Choice **d** is also contradictory because it would limit a judge's options. There is no support for choice **e** in the paragraph.

2. b. This answer is clearly supported in the second sentence. Nothing in the paragraph suggests that it is a crime not to give a Miranda warning, so choice **a** is incorrect. Choice **c** is also wrong because police may interrogate as long as a warning is given. There is no support given for either choice **d** or choice **e**.

3. c. The last two sentences give direct support for this response. Choice **a** is somewhat of a contradiction because the author believes that librarians are trying to respond to the needs of readers. Choice **b** is attractive but is not in the passage. There is no indication that librarians have increased the popularity of CD-ROM and the Internet (choice **d**). Choice **e** is not in the passage.

4. b. The second sentence points out that goals and needs should be established before a company purchases a new technology such as videoconferencing. Choice **a** is incorrect because the paragraph indicates that videoconferencing is happening now; it is not necessarily the wave of the future. Choices **c**, **d**, and **e** are incorrect because none of these is mentioned in the paragraph.

5. d. The first and last sentences of the paragraph provide support for choice **d**. Choices **a** and **c** are incorrect—the paragraph does not go so far as to suggest that humans should be replaced by an AI system, nor does it make an argument for why the human component of crimefighting is irreplaceable. Choices **b** and **e** use the absolute terms "always" and "never"—red flags that these answer choices are overstating their claims.

6. e. The last sentence offers direct support for this response. Choice **a** is wrong because even though readable fingerprints are critical, the author does not say that crimes cannot be solved without them. There is no support for choice **b** or **c**. Choice **d** can be ruled out because the author indicates that there are fingerprints taken at a crime scene that are eliminated as evidence.

7. c. The passage makes note that a video has the ability to be reviewed as many times as necessary to get the facts and minutiae of the crime to assist the investigator. Choices **a** and **b** are incorrect, as those solutions are not feasible. Choice **d** is incorrect, as witnesses may have viewed the occurrence from a different perspective. Choice **e** is incorrect, as the ability of individuals to recall information varies from person to person.

8. e. The last sentence implies that some argumentation tactics are not honest. There is no support for choice **a** or **b**. Choice **c** is not related to the paragraph. Choice **d** is incorrect because even though people may be persuaded by distraction, this is not something that the writer has indicated is effective.

9. a. The paragraph establishes a possible link—"an important part of the puzzle"—between sleep loss and weight gain. Choice **b** is incorrect because it overstates the paragraph's claim by saying that sleep loss is not just one factor, but the "top reason" for weight gain. Again, choice **c** overstates the claims of the paragraph. Although the paragraph connects sleep loss with weight gain, it does not say that getting enough sleep could prevent weight gain. Choices **d** and **e** are incorrect because they focus on specific details from the passage but use them to draw incorrect conclusions. Although the passage names college students, new parents, and shift workers as examples of people affected by sleep loss and weight gain, it does not say that these are the only people who are affected.

10. b. This statement can be inferred from the last sentence of the passage: "DNA evidence can be reliable 10, 15, even 20 years after a crime is committed." Choice **a** is incorrect because the writer does not make a claim that DNA evidence is the "most reliable" evidence, only that it is "reliable" and "powerful." The writer does not discuss the legal issues surrounding DNA evidence anywhere in the passage; thus, choices **c** and **d** are incorrect. Choice **e** is contradicted by the third sentence in the paragraph.

11. d. The final sentence of the paragraph supports choice **d**. The other choices are not in the passage. Choice **e** may seem attractive at first, but the paragraph says that e-mail should be *concise with the most important topics in the first paragraph*; it does not say that topic must be *minor*.

12. d. The author of this statement suggests that doctors are less independent. The author stresses that many doctors have lost authority. There is no support for the opinion that doctors resent the healthcare managers, however—which rules out choice **a**. The doctors' training is never mentioned (choice **b**). Doctors may care about their patients (choice **c**), but this information is not part of the paragraph. Choice **e** is not mentioned.

13. c. The second sentence states that threading a needle involves motor skill. The other choices are not in the paragraph.

14. a. The paragraph states that Mars once had a thick atmosphere but that it was stripped away. The other choices, true or not, cannot be found in the passage.

15. a. The last sentence provides direct support for choice **a**. The author never suggests that any trees should be cut down or thinned out, which eliminates choices **b** and **c**. Choice **d** contradicts the author's opinion. The author suggests that old growth forests have less debris, which rules out choice **e**.

16. c. The fact that the pyramid-scheme con artist must actually allow the first customer to make money suggests that patience is necessary. Choices **a** and **b** are contradicted in the passage. The paragraph says that the pyramid scheme originated in the 1920s, but does not say it had its heyday then; thus, choice **d** is incorrect. Choice **e** is a fact but is not mentioned in the passage.

17. a. This is expressed in the second sentence. The other choices are not in the passage. Choice **c** may be attractive, but the paragraph does not say that private investigators actually write detective fiction.

18. d. Although the author does not state this explicitly, the last sentence of the passage infers it. The author links the Chicago's crime reduction with its camera system—although he or she does not provide any specific proof for his or her claim. Choice **a** is incorrect. Although the author compares the importance of privacy issues to crime reduction, there is no indication that he or she finds privacy issues "bogus." Choice **b** is contradicted by the fifth sentence in the passage: "As long as cameras are set up in public spaces, they do not violate the law." Choice **c** is incorrect because it raises the question of whether Chicago's camera system should be adopted by other cities—a matter not discussed in the passage. Choice **e** is contradicted by the author's assertion in the last sentence.

19. a. The paragraph states that the power-grabbing robber barons perverted Darwin's theory, so it can be inferred that Darwin's idea of fitness was not necessarily related to having power over others. Choice **b** is wrong because the paragraph does not say that Darwin knew about Spencer's theory. Choice **c** is contradicted in the passage. Choices **d** and **e** are not mentioned.

20. d. The fact that Maria Mitchell was admitted to a *prestigious* astronomical society as a result of her discovery of a comet supports this answer. Choice **a** is wrong because the paragraph does not deal with anyone except Maria Mitchell. The other choices are not mentioned in the passage.

21. d. The second sentence of the passage supports this answer choice. The other choices are not in the passage.

22. c. The essential information is contained in the first sentence of the paragraph. Choice **a** is incorrect because it represents a belief that employees may have, not a fact supported by evidence. Choice **b** is contradicted by the first sentence of the passage. Choices **d** and **e** are incorrect because they both raise topics that are not covered by the paragraph.

23. b. The fourth sentence points to the idea of completing a checklist before phoning for a repair person. Choices **a**, **c**, and **e** are not in the paragraph. Choice **c** may be a good idea, but it is not in the paragraph. Choice **d** is refuted in the paragraph.

24. e. The last two sentences in the paragraph support this statement. Choices **a** and **c** are incorrect because they make assertions that are not covered by the material in the passage. Choice **b** is contradicted by the paragraph—if personal data were unique to each individual like fingerprints, then others would not be able to steal it. Choice **d** is contradicted by the second sentence in the paragraph, which cites using another's personal data to take funds from bank accounts as an example of identity theft.

25. b. The third sentence reflects this answer choice. The other choices are not reflected in the passage.

Part B: Arithmetic reasoning

1. c. The amount of $7.99 can be found by adding the three amounts together ($7.62 + $22.38 + $20.26 = $50.26), and then subtracting from the starting amount ($58.25 - $50.26 = $7.99).

2. c. This is a two-step problem. First, add the three numbers, then divide the sum by 3 to find the average. 22 plus 25 plus 19 is 66. 66 divided by 3 is 22.

3. d. First, convert the $2\frac{1}{2}$ hours to minutes. Then, divide the answer by 50. 2 hours 30 minutes is 150 minutes. 150 divided by 50 is 3.

4. b. This is a multiplication problem. $1.25 times 40 is $50.00.

5. b. Find the cost for one can (unit rate) by dividing the cost of five cans by 5. $6.50 ÷ 5 = $1.30 per can. Multiply the cost per can by 9 cans. $1.30 × 9 = $11.70. A proportion can also be used: $\frac{5}{\$6.50} = \frac{9}{x}$. To solve the proportion, cross multiply and divide. $5x = \$58.50$, $\frac{5x}{5} = \frac{\$58.50}{5}$, $x = \$11.70$.

6. c. The problem is solved by dividing 204 by 1,700. The answer, 0.12, is then converted to a percentage.

7. c. Three feet 4 inches equals 40 inches; 40 divided by 5 is 8.

8. a. The drug is 50% effective for 50% of migraine sufferers, so it eliminates $(0.50)(0.50) = 0.25$, or 25% of all migraines.

9. c. The question is a simple one of adding minutes to the current time 15:35 plus 22 minutes. (35 + 22 = 57) Do not let the 24-hour format of the time confuse you, and the 16:00 deadline to shut down the computer is not significant in calculating this problem.

10. e. Eighty out of 100 is 80%. Eighty percent of 30,000 is 24,000, which is not one of the answer choices.

11. b. The median value is the middle value when the numbers are sorted in descending order. This is 10 inches.

12. c. If Dimitri does 40% of the assignment in one hour, he can do 16 problems per hour. To arrive at the answer, divide 40 by 16: $\frac{40 \text{ problems}}{16 \text{ problems per hour}} = 2.5$ hours.

13. c. This may seem like a simple division of six-foot sections of fence from the total length needed (98 feet) but the problem also states that the sections cannot be cut. Therefore, two of the sides will require three six-foot lengths and one four-foot length, while the remaining sides will each require four and five six-foot lengths, respectively.

14. e. 3% is equal to 0.03, so multiply 2,500 times 0.03 and add the result to the original 2,500 for a total of 2,575, which is not one of the answer choices.

15. b. The formula for finding the area of a circle is Area $= \pi r^2$. First, square the radius: 13 times 13 equals 169. Then, multiply by the approximate value of π, 3.14, to get 530.66.

16. b. The average is the sum divided by the number of times Rashaard went fishing: $11 + 4 + 0 + 5 + 4 + 6$ divided by 6 is 5.

17. e. First, find the total price of the pencils: (24 pencils)($0.05) = $1.20. Then, find the total price of the paper: (3.5 reams)($7.50 per ream) = $26.25. Next, add the two totals together: $1.20 + 26.25 = $27.45, which is not one of the answer choices.

18. d. It is important to remember to include all three telephone sets ($375 total), both computers ($2,600 total), and both monitors ($1,900 total) in the total value for the correct answer of $5,525.

19. b. $24,355 + $23,000 = $47,355. When this is rounded to the nearest $100, the answer is $47,400.

20. e. The hundredths position is the second place to the *right* of the decimal. None of the numeric values shown has a number 6 in that position. Do not be confused by a number than contains a 6 to the left of the decimal.

Part C: Problems for Investigation

1. a. Statement 1 is a statement made without personal knowledge, simply repeating what others said.

2. e. Statement 7 demonstrates that Hines has the means—a passport and money—to leave the country, and statement 10 contains the information that Hines speaks a foreign language, facilitating Hines going to another country.

3. b. Statements 4 and 6. The fact that the guard was carrying a nonregulation firearm has no bearing on the investigation into Hines's disappearance; neither does the fact that Michelle Rogers was not comfortable with the prisoners.

4. d. Statements 5 and 7 indicate that someone left the package outside the office for Hines, requiring prior planning.

5. b. Statement 3 was an entirely avoidable mistake; Hines should have been reshackled when he returned to the waiting room.

6. e. Statement 9 indicates that the car may experience mechanical difficulties at speeds over 60 miles an hour; if the officers can force Hines to drive faster than that, the car might be disabled.

7. a. Statement 7 provides information that Hines is planning to go where he will need a passport. Chances are, this will require him to travel by air.

8. b. Statements 7 and 10 both provide information about a member of the public, who may be the person mentioned in Statement 4.

9. d. Statement 8 indicates Alan Pip may be somewhat unstable.

10. a. Statements 1 and 3 provide information about White's ability to access a locked postal box along with the information that the envelope may not have gone through the U.S. Postal Service, but instead may have been simply placed with the mail.

11. c. Merely doing work to get more people to vote does not cast suspicion on a volunteer. Statements 1 and 3 might cast a little suspicion on Edna, and statement 8 could be an attempt by Edna to divert attention from herself.

12. b. Even if Lawe had been making angry comments about the president and her student loans, it is doubtful that would be a serious threat.

13. e. Statements 3 and 7 taken together refer to the involvement of local police and Secret Service in preparations for the president's visit and the threat investigation.

14. d. Statement 2 provides no information that would further the investigation.

15. b. Statement 8 indicates a direct link between Francis Onitsha and the making of ivory figurines.

16. d. In statement 6, Michelle Eseka may be trying to focus the investigation away from her and toward Onitsha.

17. c. Margaret Woo referred only to the paperwork and did not actually check the contents of crates. Her story can easily be checked through her supervisor.

18. a. Statement 9 presents the possibility that Rosemary Ndele is working in concert with Freddy Jones. Since Jones is a primary suspect, her association with him makes her information of questionable value.

19. e. Statement 7 indicates that Eseka's business is in financial trouble; that could be a motive for engaging in a lucrative smuggling scheme.

20. d. Statements 5 and 6 provide a possible motive for William Calabar (a gambling debt) and indicate that he disregarded a direct order from his boss.

21. c. Statement 10 states that Cameroon officials provided U.S. investigators information from official records.

22. b. Statement 9 indicates the possibility that Jones sought out Mandara Exports and that he knows an employee there. This is a deviation from the normal course of business.

23. a. Statement 2 states that the bill of lading contains what is now known to be inaccurate information about the shipment. Statement 10 indicates that Cameroon customs was avoided, because officials there might check the shipment against the bill of lading.

24. c. Statement 4 provides information on the opportunity the Vickers campaign had to receive information from the IRS.

25. d. Statement 6 is not related to the investigation at all.

26. b. Statements 9 and 10 are statements made without personal knowledge, simply repeating what others said.

27. a. Circumstantial evidence is evidence from which the presence of a principal fact of the case can be inferred. The fact that Mary Yate and Alice West frequently have lunch together by itself proves nothing; however, one may infer it means they have a close relationship.

28. d. Statement 4 provides the opportunity for the campaign to receive information from the IRS.

29. c. Statements 2 and 5 indicate a connection from the Allen campaign to the IRS and then to the Vickers campaign.

30. a. Statements 6 and 8 show that Luther holds a grudge against Allen and has access to the IRS through Doug Edwards.

Scoring

Once again, in order to evaluate how you did on this practice exam, start by scoring the three sections—Verbal Reasoning, Arithmetic Reasoning, and Problems for Investigation—separately but using the same method. First, find the number of questions you got right in each part. Questions you skipped or got wrong don't count; just add up the number of correct answers. Divide the number of questions you got right by the number of questions in each section to arrive at a percentage score. (If necessary, use the tables at the end of Lesson 5 to check your math.) If you achieve a score of at least 70% on the three parts, you will most likely pass the TEA exam.

You have probably seen improvement between your first practice exam score and this one; but if you didn't improve as much as you'd like, here are some options:

- **If you scored below 60%,** you should seriously consider whether you're ready for the TEA exam at this time. A good idea would be to take some brushup courses, either at a university or community college nearby or through correspondence, in the areas you feel less sure of. If you don't have time for a course, you might try private tutoring.

- **If your score is in the 60–70% range,** you need to work as hard as you can to improve your skills. The LearningExpress books *Reading Comprehension Success in 20 Minutes a Day* and *Practical Math Success in 20 Minutes a Day* or other books from your public library will undoubtedly help. Also, reread and pay close attention to the sample questions in Lesson 3 and all the advice in instructional Lessons 6, 7, and 8 of this book in order to improve your score. It might also be helpful to ask friends and family to make up mock test questions and quiz you on them.

- **If your score is between 70–90%,** you could still benefit from additional work by going back to the instructional lessons and by brushing up your reading comprehension and general math skills before the exam.

- **If you scored above 90%,** that's great! This kind of score should make you a good candidate for a Treasury Enforcement Agent position. Don't lose your edge, though; keep studying right up to the day before the exam.

Keep in mind that what's much more important than your scores, for now, is how you did on each of the basic skills tested by the exam. Using this advice, diagnose your strengths and weaknesses so that you can concentrate your efforts as you prepare for the exam. Your percentage scores in conjunction with the LearningExpress Test Preparation System in Lesson 4 of this book will help you revise your study plan if need be. After your study plan is revised, turn again to the instructional lessons that cover each of the basic skills tested on the TEA exam.

If you didn't score as well as you would like, ask yourself the following: Did I run out of time before I could answer all the questions? Did I go back and change my answers from right to wrong? Did I get flustered and sit staring at a difficult question for what seemed like hours? If you had any of these problems, be sure to go over the LearningExpress Test Preparation System in Lesson 4 again to learn how to avoid them.

After working on your reading and math skills and on the instructional lesson for the Problems for Investigation portion of the test, take the second practice exam in Lesson 10 to see how much you've improved.

10 ▶ TREASURY ENFORCEMENT AGENT PRACTICE EXAM 2

CHAPTER SUMMARY

This is the final practice test in this book based on the Treasury Enforcement Agent exam. Use this test to see how much you've improved.

For this exam, once again, simulate the actual test-taking experience as closely as possible. Work in a quiet place, away from interruptions. Tear out the answer sheet on the next page, and use your number 2 pencil to fill in the circles. Use a timer or stopwatch and allow yourself 50 minutes to complete Part A, 50 minutes to complete Part B, and one hour to complete Part C.

After the exam, again use the answer key that follows it to see your progress on each section and to find out why the correct answers are correct and the incorrect ones incorrect. Then use the scoring section at the end of the exam to see how you did overall.

Part A: Verbal Reasoning

1. ⓐ ⓑ ⓒ ⓓ ⓔ
2. ⓐ ⓑ ⓒ ⓓ ⓔ
3. ⓐ ⓑ ⓒ ⓓ ⓔ
4. ⓐ ⓑ ⓒ ⓓ ⓔ
5. ⓐ ⓑ ⓒ ⓓ ⓔ
6. ⓐ ⓑ ⓒ ⓓ ⓔ
7. ⓐ ⓑ ⓒ ⓓ ⓔ
8. ⓐ ⓑ ⓒ ⓓ ⓔ
9. ⓐ ⓑ ⓒ ⓓ ⓔ

10. ⓐ ⓑ ⓒ ⓓ ⓔ
11. ⓐ ⓑ ⓒ ⓓ ⓔ
12. ⓐ ⓑ ⓒ ⓓ ⓔ
13. ⓐ ⓑ ⓒ ⓓ ⓔ
14. ⓐ ⓑ ⓒ ⓓ ⓔ
15. ⓐ ⓑ ⓒ ⓓ ⓔ
16. ⓐ ⓑ ⓒ ⓓ ⓔ
17. ⓐ ⓑ ⓒ ⓓ ⓔ
18. ⓐ ⓑ ⓒ ⓓ ⓔ

19. ⓐ ⓑ ⓒ ⓓ ⓔ
20. ⓐ ⓑ ⓒ ⓓ ⓔ
21. ⓐ ⓑ ⓒ ⓓ ⓔ
22. ⓐ ⓑ ⓒ ⓓ ⓔ
23. ⓐ ⓑ ⓒ ⓓ ⓔ
24. ⓐ ⓑ ⓒ ⓓ ⓔ
25. ⓐ ⓑ ⓒ ⓓ ⓔ

Part B: Arithmetic Reasoning

1. ⓐ ⓑ ⓒ ⓓ ⓔ
2. ⓐ ⓑ ⓒ ⓓ ⓔ
3. ⓐ ⓑ ⓒ ⓓ ⓔ
4. ⓐ ⓑ ⓒ ⓓ ⓔ
5. ⓐ ⓑ ⓒ ⓓ ⓔ
6. ⓐ ⓑ ⓒ ⓓ ⓔ
7. ⓐ ⓑ ⓒ ⓓ ⓔ

8. ⓐ ⓑ ⓒ ⓓ ⓔ
9. ⓐ ⓑ ⓒ ⓓ ⓔ
10. ⓐ ⓑ ⓒ ⓓ ⓔ
11. ⓐ ⓑ ⓒ ⓓ ⓔ
12. ⓐ ⓑ ⓒ ⓓ ⓔ
13. ⓐ ⓑ ⓒ ⓓ ⓔ
14. ⓐ ⓑ ⓒ ⓓ ⓔ

15. ⓐ ⓑ ⓒ ⓓ ⓔ
16. ⓐ ⓑ ⓒ ⓓ ⓔ
17. ⓐ ⓑ ⓒ ⓓ ⓔ
18. ⓐ ⓑ ⓒ ⓓ ⓔ
19. ⓐ ⓑ ⓒ ⓓ ⓔ
20. ⓐ ⓑ ⓒ ⓓ ⓔ

Part C: Problems for Investigation

1. ⓐ ⓑ ⓒ ⓓ ⓔ
2. ⓐ ⓑ ⓒ ⓓ ⓔ
3. ⓐ ⓑ ⓒ ⓓ ⓔ
4. ⓐ ⓑ ⓒ ⓓ ⓔ
5. ⓐ ⓑ ⓒ ⓓ ⓔ
6. ⓐ ⓑ ⓒ ⓓ ⓔ
7. ⓐ ⓑ ⓒ ⓓ ⓔ
8. ⓐ ⓑ ⓒ ⓓ ⓔ
9. ⓐ ⓑ ⓒ ⓓ ⓔ
10. ⓐ ⓑ ⓒ ⓓ ⓔ

11. ⓐ ⓑ ⓒ ⓓ ⓔ
12. ⓐ ⓑ ⓒ ⓓ ⓔ
13. ⓐ ⓑ ⓒ ⓓ ⓔ
14. ⓐ ⓑ ⓒ ⓓ ⓔ
15. ⓐ ⓑ ⓒ ⓓ ⓔ
16. ⓐ ⓑ ⓒ ⓓ ⓔ
17. ⓐ ⓑ ⓒ ⓓ ⓔ
18. ⓐ ⓑ ⓒ ⓓ ⓔ
19. ⓐ ⓑ ⓒ ⓓ ⓔ
20. ⓐ ⓑ ⓒ ⓓ ⓔ

21. ⓐ ⓑ ⓒ ⓓ ⓔ
22. ⓐ ⓑ ⓒ ⓓ ⓔ
23. ⓐ ⓑ ⓒ ⓓ ⓔ
24. ⓐ ⓑ ⓒ ⓓ ⓔ
25. ⓐ ⓑ ⓒ ⓓ ⓔ
26. ⓐ ⓑ ⓒ ⓓ ⓔ
27. ⓐ ⓑ ⓒ ⓓ ⓔ
28. ⓐ ⓑ ⓒ ⓓ ⓔ
29. ⓐ ⓑ ⓒ ⓓ ⓔ
30. ⓐ ⓑ ⓒ ⓓ ⓔ

Part A: Verbal Reasoning

Read each of the following paragraphs carefully, and answer the question that follows it by choosing the best of the five possible answer choices. You have 50 minutes for this section.

In many police departments, detectives who want to be promoted further must first spend an extended period of time working in the internal affairs division. Not only do these officers become thoroughly versed in detecting police misconduct; they also become familiar with the circumstances and attitudes out of which such conduct might arise. Placement in internal affairs reduces the possibility that a commanding officer might be too lenient in investigating or disciplining a colleague. The transfer to internal affairs also separates a detective from his or her precinct, reducing the prospect of cronyism, and it familiarizes the detective with serving in a supervisory capacity.

1. The paragraph best supports the statement that detectives are transferred to internal affairs mainly in order to
   a. familiarize them with the laws regarding police misconduct.
   b. enable them to identify situations that might lead to police misconduct.
   c. ensure that they are closely supervised.
   d. augment the staff of the internal affairs division.
   e. promote solidarity within the police department.

Creativity is not just the domain of artists and musicians. Businesses also need creative people to come up with better ways to produce things, increase efficiency and quality, and discover market needs that have not yet been filled. Companies that know how to foster talent, ability, and creativity are the ones that will succeed in today's corporate world.

2. The author of the paragraph would most likely support the statement that
   a. businesses that want to attract creative people should hire artists and musicians.
   b. companies that prioritize creativity will be inefficient.
   c. creative people are rarely loyal employees.
   d. companies that encourage creativity will perform better.
   e. companies can foster creativity by finding ways to challenge workers.

The rules for obtaining evidence, set down in state and federal law, usually come to our attention when they work to the advantage of defendants in court, but these laws were not created with the courtroom in mind. They were formulated with the pragmatic intent of shaping police procedure before the arrest, in order to ensure justice, thoroughness, and the preservation of civil liberties. A good police officer must be as well schooled in the rules for properly obtaining evidence as is a defense lawyer or risk losing a conviction. When a case is thrown out of court or a defendant is released because of these evidentiary "technicalities," we are often angered and mystified, but we are not always aware of how these rules of evidence shape police procedure in positive ways every day.

3. The paragraph best supports the statement that
   a. the rules of evidence too often protect the rights of guilty defendants.
   b. police officers often do not follow the rules of evidence.
   c. the rules of evidence have more negative than positive effects.
   d. the rules of evidence need to be reviewed and perhaps revised.
   e. rules of evidence help shape police procedure.

Whether or not you can accomplish a specific goal or meet a specific deadline depends first on how much time you need to get the job done. What should you do when the demands of the job exceed the time you have available? The best approach is to divide the project into smaller pieces. Different goals will have to be divided in different ways, but one seemingly unrealistic goal can often be accomplished by working on several smaller, more reasonable goals.

4. The paragraph best supports the statement that
   a. demanding jobs often must remain only partially completed.
   b. the best way to complete projects is not to have too many goals.
   c. the best way to tackle a large project is to separate it into smaller parts.
   d. the best approach to a demanding job is to delegate responsibility.
   e. demanding jobs often have unrealistic time constraints.

Adolescents are at high risk for violent crime. Although they make up only 14% of the population age 12 and over, 30% of all violent crimes—1.9 million—are committed against them. Because crimes against adolescents are likely to be committed by offenders of the same age (as well as same sex and race), preventing violence among and against adolescents is a twofold challenge. New violence-prevention programs in urban middle schools help reduce the crime rate by teaching both victims and perpetrators the skills of conflict resolution and how to apply reason to disputes.

5. The paragraph best supports the statement that
   a. middle school violence-prevention programs are designed to teach school officials how to deal with problem adolescents.
   b. middle school students appreciate the conflict resolution skills they acquire in violence-prevention programs.
   c. violence against adolescents is increasing.
   d. violence committed by adolescents is increasing.
   e. middle school violence-prevention programs are designed to teach adolescents how they can avoid escalation of conflict into violence.

Every year Americans use over one billion sharp objects to administer healthcare in their homes. These sharp objects include lancets, needles, and syringes. If not disposed of in puncture-resistant containers, they can injure sanitation workers. Sharp objects should be disposed of in hard plastic or metal containers with secure lids. The containers should be clearly marked and puncture resistant.

6. The paragraph best supports the idea that sanitation workers can be injured if they
   a. do not place sharp objects in puncture-resistant containers.
   b. come in contact with sharp objects that have not been placed in secure containers.
   c. are careless with sharp objects such as lancets, needles, and syringes in their homes.
   d. do not mark the containers they pick up with a warning that those containers contain sharp objects.
   e. work too hastily and are sometimes injured by sharp objects used to administer healthcare.

Colds and the flu are mainly spread through coughing and sneezing. Droplets from a cough or sneeze may move through the air or be deposited on surfaces such as desks, tables, or doorknobs. When another person touches a contaminated surface and then touches his own eyes, mouth, or nose before washing his hands, he may become infected. To stop the spread of germs, wash your hands often with soap and warm water for 15 to 20 seconds.

7. The paragraph best supports the statement that
   a. many people do not practice proper hand hygiene.
   b. you should never shake another person's hand during flu season.
   c. droplets from a cough or sneeze that land on a surface can infect others.
   d. bacteria and viruses can live two hours or longer on surfaces such as tables.
   e. a 100% effective way to prevent colds is to wash your hands regularly.

Hearsay evidence, which is the secondhand reporting of a statement, is allowed in court only when the truth of the statement is irrelevant. Hearsay that depends on the statement's truthfulness is inadmissible because the witness does not appear in court for cross-examination; therefore, to introduce it would be to deprive the accused of the constitutional right to confront the accuser.

8. The paragraph best supports the idea that the writer's main purpose is to
   a. explain why hearsay evidence abridges the rights of the accused.
   b. question the credibility of hearsay evidence.
   c. argue that rules about the admissibility of hearsay evidence should be changed.
   d. specify which use of hearsay evidence is inadmissible and why.
   e. show that the concept of hearsay evidence is often misunderstood.

Members of your work team may have skills and abilities that you are not aware of, and they may be able to contribute to your team's as well as to your own success. Whenever a new responsibility is given to your work team, it is usually a good idea to have all the members come up with ideas and suggestions about how to perform the new tasks. This way, you are likely to discover special work-related skills you never suspected they had. So take time to explore your work team's talents.

9. The paragraph best supports the statement that one member of a work team
   a. may have abilities that others on the team don't know about.
   b. usually stands out as having more ideas than other members do.
   c. should be assigned the task of discovering the whole team's talents.
   d. should act as a leader for the entire team.
   e. can have more skills and abilities than all the rest.

Managing job and family is not simple. Both commitments make strong demands on people and are sometimes in direct opposition to each other. Saying yes to one means saying no to the other, and stress can often result. Being realistic and creating a balance in life can help set priorities.

10. The paragraph best supports the statement that
   a. most family responsibilities cause stress at home and at work.
   b. it is important to avoid making commitments to other people.
   c. because it pays the bills, a job must take priority over other commitments.
   d. it is important to have a balance between job and family responsibilities.
   e. because they are so important, family responsibilities must take priority over the job.

Detectives who routinely investigate violent crimes can't help but become somewhat jaded. Paradoxically, the victims and witnesses with whom they work closely are often in a highly vulnerable and emotional state. The emotional fallout from a sexual assault, for example, can be complex and long lasting. Detectives must be trained to handle people in emotional distress and must be sensitive to the fact that for the victim the crime is not routine. At the same time, detectives must recognize the limits of their role and resist the temptation to act as therapists or social workers, instead referring victims to the proper agencies.

11. The paragraph best supports the idea that
   a. detectives who investigate violent crime must not become jaded by the experience.
   b. therapists and social workers can do less for victims of violent crime than can the police.
   c. detectives should not become overly involved with victims of sexual assault.
   d. some victims can handle the emotional distress caused by a violent crime more easily than others.
   e. detectives should be especially sensitive to the emotional states of victims of violent crime.

In a 20-year period, more Americans died from extreme heat than from hurricanes, lightning, tornadoes, floods, and earthquakes put together. Most heat-related fatalities happen in the summer. Even though the elderly, children, and people with certain medical conditions are at the greatest risk, young and healthy people can also be vulnerable to heat. To prevent heat-related illness, drink plenty of water, wear lightweight, light-colored clothes, spend time in air conditioning, and avoid strenuous physical activity, especially during the hot parts of the day.

12. The paragraph best supports the statement that
   a. natural disasters such as earthquakes are more dangerous than hot summers.
   b. even healthy people can be affected by extreme heat.
   c. only the elderly and children are susceptible to heat-related illnesses.
   d. the best way to avoid heat illness is to stay in an air-conditioned environment.
   e. air conditioners emit a refrigerant that has a negative effect on the environment.

Lie detector tests are part of our culture. We all recognize the image of a polygraph pen making a jagged path across a chart—from police dramas, ads, even reality TV shows. However, the accuracy of polygraph testing has long been controversial. One problem is that no evidence exists that lying creates a distinctive physiological response. For instance, an honest person may be nervous when answering truthfully and a dishonest person may not be nervous at all.

13. The paragraph best supports the statement that lie detector tests
   a. are an accurate law enforcement tool.
   b. are more widespread in TV shows than in law enforcement agencies.
   c. are completely useless in finding deceptions.
   d. have been and continue to be controversial.
   e. have a validity rate of about 60%, slightly better than chance.

When searching a crime scene for evidence, an agent must take the utmost care to avoid contamination. Advanced planning is required to provide the search team with the proper tools and supplies necessary to conduct a search for evidence. Members of the team should be wearing rubber or latex gloves for safety and to avoid evidence contamination. Spare gloves must be available for team members if their gloves tear or become unusable. Each part of the area to be searched should be labeled to avoid duplication of effort, and to avoid missing an area. A scene manager will note the time of entry and exit and name of everyone that enters and leaves the search area. The scene manager will also note the location and description of evidence recovered, along with the name of the team member that discovered the item.

14. The paragraph best supports the statement that
  a. evidence will not be contaminated if the search team forgets to wear gloves.
  b. good planning will help search team properly collect evidence.
  c. a scene manager will help in searching for evidence.
  d. a search team must work together or the job will not be completed correctly.
  e. the team manager relies on the team members to make decisions at the search site.

Moscow has a history of chaotic periods of war that ended with the destruction of a once largely wooden city and the building of a "new" city on top of the rubble of the old. The result is a layered city, with each tier holding information about a part of Russia's past. In some areas of the city, archaeologists have reached the layer from 1147, the year of Moscow's founding. Among the findings from the various periods of Moscow's history are carved bones, metal tools, pottery, glass, jewelry, and crosses.

15. The paragraph best supports the inference that
  a. the people of Moscow are more interested in modernization than in preservation.
  b. Moscow has a history of invasions, with each new conqueror razing past structures.
  c. the Soviet government destroyed many of the historic buildings in Russia.
  d. Moscow is the oldest large city in Russia, founded in 1147.
  e. Moscow has endured many periods of uprising and revolution.

A book proposal has three major functions. First, it should sell a publisher on the commercial potential of the as-yet-to-be-written book. Second, the writing in the proposal itself should convince the publisher that the author has the ability to write the book. Finally, the proposal should show that the author has the background necessary to write the book.

16. The paragraph best supports the definition of the word *background*, as it is used in the passage, as
  a. something behind the main event.
  b. something in a subordinated position.
  c. events leading up to something.
  d. facts to help explain something.
  e. one's ability to do something.

Over the past century, the temperature of the earth's surface has risen by about 1° Fahrenheit. Scientists have strong evidence that human activities are the main cause of the warming that has occurred in the last 50 years. Burning fossil fuels for cars, trucks, homes, and factories as well as increased agriculture, deforestation, and industrial production have all contributed to a buildup of "greenhouse" gases that trap the sun's heat and warm the earth's atmosphere.

17. The passage best supports the statement that
  a. the warming of the earth's surface is a positive event.
  b. evidence for global warming is insufficient and controversial.
  c. humans are primarily responsible for the earth's warming in the past 50 years.
  d. human activities are the sole reason for the earth's warming in the past 50 years.
  e. the government should do more to slow the rate of global warming.

The Competitive Civil Service system is designed to give applicants fair and equal treatment and to ensure that federal applicants are hired based on objective criteria. Hiring has to be based solely on candidates' knowledge, skills, and abilities (which you'll sometimes see abbreviated as KSA) and not on any external factors such as race, religion, sex, and so on. Whereas employers in the private sector can hire employees for subjective reasons, federal employers must be able to justify their decisions with objective "evidence" that the candidate is qualified.

18. The paragraph best supports the statement that
  a. hiring in the private sector is inherently unfair.
  b. KSAs are not as important as test scores to federal employers.
  c. federal hiring practices are simpler than those employed by the private sector.
  d. getting a job with the civil service is more difficult than getting one in the private sector.
  e. the civil service strives to hire on the basis of a candidate's abilities.

Is bullying a normal part of growing up? Schools are increasingly deciding that bullying—which includes a whole list of behaviors that involve one person or a group trying to harm someone who is weaker or more vulnerable—is not an acceptable childhood rite of passage. Schools can effectively reduce bullying by raising awareness about the issue, involving teachers and parents in supervision, and creating clear rules and social expectations about bullying.

19. The paragraph best supports the statement that
  a. interest in reducing bullying has gone up.
  b. most American schools are now implementing programs to reduce bullying.
  c. bullying has long been considered an unacceptable form of violence.
  d. schools really cannot do much about bullying.
  e. bullying always involves name-calling and taunting.

For the safety of parachutists and persons on the ground, the Federal Aviation Association has made an important rule regarding jumping over or into congested, open-air assemblies of persons. No one may make a parachute jump over or into a congested area of a city, town, or settlement, or an open-air assembly of persons (for example, at a fair or air show), unless a certificate of authorization for that jump, issued by the FAA, has been given to the parachutist. A parachutist may, however, drift over that area with a fully deployed and properly functioning parachute if he or she is at a sufficient altitude to avoid creating a hazard.

20. The paragraph best supports the idea that
   a. parachutists may not jump over or into congested open-air assemblies of persons.
   b. a parachutist must be careful not to drift over congested open-air assemblies of persons.
   c. parachutists can obtain a certificate from the FAA to drift over, but not jump into, congested open-air assemblies of persons.
   d. parachutists must have permission of the FAA in order to jump over or into congested open-air assemblies of persons.
   e. only fully qualified parachutists can jump into or drift over congested open-air assemblies of persons.

Dinosaurs and birds may seem like unlikely cousins, but recent evidence is strengthening the case that the animals are evolutionary kin. This theory, first proposed in the late nineteenth century, fell out of favor, but is now becoming a more accepted view. For example, one recent analysis showed that predatory dinosaurs had a very birdlike lung system that allowed them to maintain a stable, high metabolism. This brings dinosaurs closer to warm-blooded creatures and farther from today's cold-blooded living reptiles, once considered their closest evolutionary relatives.

21. The passage implies that
   a. the theory that dinosaurs and birds are linked through evolution is bogus.
   b. dinosaurs were once believed to be cold-blooded.
   c. a birdlike lung system is inferior to reptiles' lung systems.
   d. the link between dinosaurs and birds is a recent hypothesis.
   e. there is no evidence linking dinosaurs and birds.

Medical waste has been a growing concern because of recent incidents of injury to members of the public due to exposure to discarded blood vials, needles (sharps), empty prescription bottles, and syringes. Medical waste can typically include general refuse, human blood and blood products, cultures and stocks of infectious agents, laboratory animal carcasses, contaminated bedding material, and pathological wastes. Hospitals attempt to cope with the problem through a variety of disposal methods, among them compaction or hydropulping, steam sterilization, and incineration, but new methods are being sought all the time to counteract this growing problem.

22. The paragraph best supports the statement that
   a. most excessive medical waste is the result of carelessness.
   b. most excessive medical waste is the result of poor planning.
   c. new ways of disposing of medical waste are badly needed.
   d. the main danger of exposure to medical waste is infection.
   e. medical waste disposal presents new problems in this day of new diseases.

The specific techniques used by federal investigators depend on the mission of the agency for which they work. An undercover narcotics agent will use different techniques and knowledge than an agent examining tax records in search of evidence of fraud. However, all investigators share the task of finding facts through sound investigative techniques and of backing up those facts in reports.

23. The paragraph best supports the statement that
  a. investigators often collaborate between agencies.
  b. only investigators from certain federal agencies need to write reports.
  c. all federal investigators must be able to recognize and explore leads to information and evidence.
  d. undercover narcotics work is more dangerous than other kinds of investigations.
  e. investigators from different agencies do not share common functions.

Firefighters know that the dangers of motor-vehicle fires are too often overlooked. In the United States, one out of five fires involves motor vehicles, resulting each year in 600 deaths, 2,600 civilian injuries, and 1,200 injuries to firefighters. The main reason for so many injuries and fatalities is that a vehicle can generate heat of up to 1500° F. Because of the intense heat generated in a vehicle fire, parts of the car or truck may burst, causing debris to shoot great distances and turning bumpers, tire rims, drive shafts, axles, and even engine parts into lethal shrapnel. Gas tanks may rupture and spray highly flammable fuel. In addition, hazardous materials such as battery acid, even without burning, can cause serious injury. Carbon monoxide, a toxic, odorless, and colorless gas that is produced during a fire, is also a deadly byproduct of a motor vehicle fire.

24. The paragraph best supports the statement that the principal cause of injury in motor-vehicle fires is
  a. battery acid.
  b. odorless gases.
  c. extremely high temperatures.
  d. firefighters' mistakes.
  e. flying car parts.

Data storage capability for home computers is increasing at a dramatic rate. When affordable home computers were first introduced, the data limits were such that software had to be small enough to not utilize the entire amount of space available. As a comparison, an estimate of the storage capacity of a 100-gigabyte drive could contain the equivalent information of over 1,543,209 paperback books. Considering that 300-, 400-, and 500-gigabyte drives are common, the amount of storage space available on home computers is impressive.

25. The paragraph best supports the statement that
  a. storage capacity of home computers has increased impressively.
  b. a home computer can be used to store books.
  c. previous versions of hard drives were too expensive.
  d. there is a great use of paperback books as a measuring tool.
  e. larger hard drives require bigger software packages.

Part B: Arithmetic Reasoning

Analyze the following paragraphs, set up the problem for each one, and choose the correct solution from choices **a**, **b**, **c**, and **d**. If none of these four choices is correct, choose choice **e**, "none of these." You have 50 minutes for this section.

1. A special agent receives an annual base pay and an Unscheduled Overtime (UOT) pay at the rate of 25% of the base pay. What would be the amount of the monthly UOT pay for an annual salary of $66,000?
  a. $5,500
  b. $2,640
  c. $6,875
  d. $1,375
  e. none of these

2. When Eduardo and Jean work together, they can load nine trucks in three hours. If Jean and Eduardo work together for two hours, and then Jean leaves while Eduardo continues to work, how long will it take to load 12 trucks?
a. 7 hours
b. 6 hours
c. 5 hours
d. 4 hours
e. none of these

3. A motorcycle has a two-gallon gas tank and gets 56 miles per gallon. If the rider starts with a full tank of gas, needs to fill the tank twice, and has $1\frac{1}{2}$ gallons of gas remaining when he reaches his destination, how far did he travel?
a. 140 miles
b. 196 miles
c. 252 miles
d. 308 miles
e. none of these

4. Rose earned $3.50 in interest. If she started with $500 and left it in the bank for 50 days, what annual rate did the bank give?
a. 7.5%
b. 7.0%
c. 6.5%
d. 6.0%
e. none of these

5. Gary's total at the hardware store was $53.21. If the sales tax is 6%, what is the cost without the tax?
a. $56.40
b. $54.37
c. $52.25
d. $50.20
e. none of these

6. A map used in Canada shows the distances in kilometers. Approximately how many miles is a distance of 1,250 kilometers? (1 kilometer = .62 miles)
a. 775 miles
b. 1,262 miles
c. 850 miles
d. 2,016 miles
e. none of these

7. A salesclerk receives time-and-a-half for any hours worked over 40. If she works 48 hours one week, and her overtime pay is $9.00 per hour, how much does she make that week?
a. $468
b. $432
c. $312
d. $288
e. none of these

8. Tara's car gets 15 miles per gallon in the city and 20 miles per gallon on the highway. If she drives 120 miles in the city and 200 on the highway, how many miles per gallon does she get?
a. $200 \div (200 \div 20 + 120 \div 15)$
b. $120 \div (200 \div 20 + 120 \div 15)$
c. $(20 + 15) \div 2$
d. $(200 + 120) \div (200 \div 20 + 120 \div 15)$
e. none of these

9. Land in development is selling for $60,000 per acre. If Jack purchases $1\frac{3}{4}$ acres, how much will he pay?
a. $45,000
b. $135,000
c. $105,000
d. $120,000
e. none of these

10. A police investigator is ordered to report to the scene of a crime eight miles away. If his car travels at an average rate of 50 miles an hour, how long will it take him to reach the destination?
   a. 7.5 minutes
   b. 8.1 minutes
   c. 8.5 minutes
   d. 9.6 minutes
   e. none of these

11. Two cars leave Omaha traveling west at different times. If the first car travels at 60 miles per hour and the second car leaves 20 minutes later, how fast should the second car travel in order to catch the first car two hours after the first car leaves?
   a. 65 mph
   b. 67 mph
   c. 72 mph
   d. 75 mph
   e. none of these

12. How much does $500 grow to if it is compounded semiannually for one year at 8% interest?
   a. $540.80
   b. $583.70
   c. $586.93
   d. $680.24
   e. none of these

13. If a property valued at $50,000 is taxed $325 in property taxes, what is the tax rate?
   a. $7.00 per $1,000
   b. $6.00 per $1,000
   c. $0.70 per $1,000
   d. $0.60 per $1,000
   e. none of these

14. A school purchases four televisions. If they receive a discount of 15% of the list price of $300, how much money do they save?
   a. $45
   b. $60
   c. $90
   d. $180
   e. none of these

15. A coffee shop has pledged all of its profits in one day to a charity. The total sales for the day were $3,250 and the expenses were 10% of that amount. How much will be donated to the charity?
   a. $3,100
   b. $2,625
   c. $2,925
   d. $325
   e. none of these

16. In a group of 55 men, 12 have sideburns, 22 have mustaches, and 30 have no facial hair. How many have both sideburns and a mustache?
   a. $(12 + 22) - (55 - 30)$
   b. $(55 - 22) - (12 + 30)$
   c. $55 - (12 + 30)$
   d. $55 - 30 - 33 - 12$
   e. none of these

17. The ratio of apples to oranges in a fruit basket is 3:1, and there are nine apples in the basket. How many pieces of fruit are in the basket?
   a. 3
   b. 6
   c. 12
   d. 15
   e. none of these

18. Natasha bought a set of golf clubs for $340. If she sold them for $255, what was her percent loss?
a. 75%
b. 65%
c. 35%
d. 25%
e. none of these

19. Mary has invested in two separate stocks. One was worth $10,500 at the beginning of the year, and the other was worth $7,535. They earned 23% and 17% last year, respectively. What was the overall percentage earned?
a. ($10,500 × 1.23 + $7,535 × 1.17) ÷ ($10,500 + $7,535)
b. ($10,500 × 1.23 + $7,535 × 1.17) ÷ ($10,500 + $7,535) − 1
c. ($10,500 × 0.23 + $7,535 × 0.17) ÷ $7,535
d. ($10,500 + $7,535) × (0.17 + 0.23) ÷ ($10,500 + $7,535) − 1
e. none of these

20. A salesperson receives a 10% commission selling VCRs and radios. If VCRs cost $225, and radios cost $75, how many radios would the salesperson have to sell in order to receive the same commission earned from three VCRs?
a. 3
b. 6
c. 8
d. 12
e. none of these

Part C: Problems for investigation

Carefully read each of the following paragraphs and the statements that come after it, and then answer the questions by choosing the best of the five possible answer choices. You have 60 minutes for this section.

Local police stop a car, driven by Robert Hanson, for speeding. On the seat next to Hanson, the officer notes an open beer can. Upon searching the car, he finds a .38 caliber handgun and an architect's diagram of the FBI fingerprint facility in the glove box. Because Hanson has no permit for the gun, he is arrested and the federal authorities are called.

During the course of the investigation, the following statements were made.

1. Andrea Wesson, an ATF forensic technician, reported finding a large quantity of nails, receipts for fertilizer, and a book called "The Coming World Domination" in the car.

2. Robert Hanson says that the car belongs to his cousin, John Wylie, and Hanson only borrowed it for the day. He says he doesn't know anything about the gun, map, fertilizer, or book, but he admits to drinking beer while driving.

3. John Wylie says that he lent his car to his sister, Mabel, last week to drive her kids to school.

4. Police in Virginia report that, last month, Robert Hanson was ticketed for failure to yield 32 miles from the FBI fingerprint facility.

5. John Wylie's neighbor, Sally West, says that Wylie lost his job at the post office two years ago.

6. Roger Beam, owner of a military surplus store, says that Mabel Wylie is a regular customer.

7. Police records show that the .38 caliber handgun found in the car is registered to Farley Stewart, who reported it stolen two months ago.

8. Mabel Wylie's neighbor says that Mabel is not a good mother.

9. Mabel Wylie says that Farley Stewart is her ex-husband.

10. Robert Hanson says that he was audited by the IRS five years ago and hasn't paid taxes since then.

1. Which statement indicates that Robert Hanson has been planning an action against the FBI fingerprint facility for at least four weeks?
   a. Statement 1
   b. Statement 3
   c. Statement 4
   d. Statement 10
   e. Statement 7

2. Which statement is opinion rather than fact?
   a. Statement 3
   b. Statement 8
   c. Statement 6
   d. Statement 5
   e. Statement 9

3. Which statement along with statement 7 implicates Farley Stewart in a plan to blow up the FBI fingerprint facility?
   a. Statement 6
   b. Statement 3
   c. Statement 9
   d. Statement 1
   e. Statement 8

4. Which statement is least helpful in solving the case?
   a. Statement 5
   b. Statement 4
   c. Statement 3
   d. Statement 2
   e. Statement 9

5. Which statement presents circumstantial evidence?
   a. Statement 1
   b. Statement 4
   c. Statement 7
   d. Statement 2
   e. Statement 5

6. Which statement does NOT implicate Robert Hanson in a crime?
   a. Statement 2
   b. Statement 10
   c. Statement 4
   d. Statement 5
   e. Statement 6

7. Which two statements along with statement 3 cast the greatest suspicion on Mabel Wylie?
   a. Statements 7 and 9
   b. Statements 6 and 8
   c. Statements 7 and 8
   d. Statements 6 and 9
   e. Statements 8 and 9

8. Which statement presents a possible motive for Robert Hanson's involvement in planning to blow up the FBI fingerprint facility?
   a. Statement 8
   b. Statement 2
   c. Statement 9
   d. Statement 4
   e. Statement 10

9. Which two statements indicate cooperation between the ATF and local police departments?
   a. Statements 1 and 5
   b. Statements 6 and 9
   c. Statements 8 and 10
   d. Statements 4 and 7
   e. Statements 2 and 3

10. Which statement indicates an attempt by John Wylie to establish his innocence?
   a. Statement 9
   b. Statement 3
   c. Statement 6
   d. Statement 5
   e. Statement 8

Neal Atkins, a gun salesman at the Gun N Tackle store, sees a couple come into the shop with a young child. The woman, Minerva Lake, follows the boy around the store while the man, Felix Lake, asks to look at various guns and examines a .32 caliber revolver that he says he collects. At that point, Minerva Lake comes to the counter to purchase the revolver and supplies the address of her residence as verification. Atkins sells her the gun, but as the Lakes leave the store, Fred Katz, the owner of the store, sees Minerva hand the gun to Felix. Katz has overheard the sale and is concerned that Minerva has bought the gun for Felix and not for herself, which is illegal. He writes down the Lakes' license plate number and calls the ATF.

During the course of the investigation, the following statements were made.

1. Neal Atkins said that no one collects that type of revolver because it is of mediocre manufacture. In his experience, the gun is frequently used for home defense or sometimes as a throwaway weapon in a crime.

2. Roger Evans, a customer in the gun shop at the same time, heard that Minerva Lake worked the register at the local pharmacy in the afternoons.

3. Fred Katz said that gun buyers are usually very interested in examining a weapon before they purchase it.

4. ATF agent Betty Kent learned that the car Minerva Lake was driving was registered to her husband, Felix Lake.

5. Ann Lee, a neighbor of the Gun N Tackle shop, thinks that the store attracts "all sorts of suspicious types."

6. Another customer, Brian James, saw Felix Lake wink to Minerva Lake before she went to the counter to purchase the gun.

7. Landlord Benny Miller verified that the Lakes live at the residence Minerva supplied to the gun dealer. Miller stated that the Lakes are quiet, responsible tenants who pay their rent on time every month.

8. In accord with the store's policy, Neal Atkins receives a sales commission for every gun he sells at the store.

9. Minerva Lake said that when she handed the gun to Felix, she was simply asking him to place it in the trunk of the car. She said she wanted to have the gun to protect her and her son when Felix works nights.

10. Upon investigation, ATF agents learned that Felix Lake is a felon, convicted for selling drugs in 1994. It is illegal for a felon to own a gun.

11. Which statement represents an opinion rather than a fact?
   a. Statement 6
   b. Statement 2
   c. Statement 5
   d. Statement 8
   e. Statement 4

12. Which statement is hearsay?
   a. Statement 2
   b. Statement 4
   c. Statement 6
   d. Statement 9
   e. Statement 10

13. Which statement is least helpful to the investigation?
   a. Statement 1
   b. Statement 3
   c. Statement 4
   d. Statement 6
   e. Statement 10

14. Which two statements seem to corroborate each other?
   a. Statements 3 and 8
   b. Statements 4 and 6
   c. Statements 5 and 7
   d. Statements 7 and 10
   e. Statements 1 and 9

15. Which statement indicates an attempt by the speaker to establish innocence?
   a. Statement 2
   b. Statement 3
   c. Statement 6
   d. Statement 8
   e. Statement 9

16. Which statements do NOT implicate Felix Lake in a crime?
   a. Statements 1 and 3
   b. Statements 3 and 6
   c. Statements 5 and 10
   d. Statements 7 and 9
   e. Statements 1 and 10

17. Which two statements along with statement 10 indicate that Minerva Lake may have been purchasing the gun for her husband?
   a. Statements 2 and 4
   b. Statements 3 and 6
   c. Statements 4 and 5
   d. Statements 7 and 9
   e. Statements 1 and 8

18. Which two statements along with statement 10 are most damaging to Felix Lake?
   a. Statements 1 and 3
   b. Statements 1 and 4
   c. Statements 3 and 5
   d. Statements 4 and 7
   e. Statements 6 and 8

19. Which statement indicates that salesman Neal Atkins might not have been as responsible and careful as he should have been in overseeing the sale?
   a. Statement 2
   b. Statement 4
   c. Statement 5
   d. Statement 8
   e. Statement 10

20. Which statement indicates that Felix Lake may attempt to use the gun for criminal purposes?
   a. Statement 1
   b. Statement 2
   c. Statement 5
   d. Statement 6
   e. Statement 8

One morning, police receive a call from a Mr. Albert Fein, who states that he believes his next-door neighbor, Ms. Anabel Hayes, is involved in selling illegal drugs. When police arrive at Ms. Hayes's home, they find the frail, elderly woman outside in her garden, tending her flowers, her three cats stalking butterflies nearby. Ms. Hayes appears shocked by the accusation, and says Mr. Fein has had it in for her for the last two months, ever since she called the dog pound to come pick up his dog who was bothering her cats. They all have a chuckle, and police depart. Several days later, police receive a 911 call reporting that Mr. Albert Fein's daughter, Heather, has found Mr. Fein dead in his breakfast nook, a gun in his hand, an apparent suicide. The autopsy pinpoints the time of death at around 2:00 A.M.

During the course of the investigation, the following statements were made.

1. Heather Fein states that her father was planning to be married in a month to a Mitzi Fork and had purchased two plane tickets the week before, in preparation for a honeymoon to Aruba.

2. Anabel Hayes says that the night she went to make up with Mr. Fein about the dog incident, Mr. Fein was despondent, "as if he had the whole world on his shoulders."

3. Mrs. Miner, a neighbor of Ms. Hayes, says that she didn't hear the shot the night Mr. Fein died because of all the noise the motorcycles were making in Ms. Hayes's driveway. "She has rowdy people in at all hours."

4. Ms. Hayes says that she just loves having young people around because it makes her feel young.

5. Heather Fein states that she has just found out Mr. Fein has taken out a $100,000 life insurance policy naming Mitzi Fork as his beneficiary.

6. Raymond "Hulk" Barnes says that Ms. Anabel Hayes allows him and his friends to hold meetings in her house in an attempt to win them away from drugs.

7. Mitzi Fork states that in the six months she knew him, Mr. Fein never owned a dog, that he hated dogs.

8. Mitzi Fork says that she works only at the cosmetics counter at Macy's in the mall.

9. Heather Fein says that Mitzi Fork works as an exotic dancer in a club downtown.

10. Lance Tarkington, Mitzi's third cousin, reports that Heather told a mutual acquaintance that she was furious at her father giving away her inheritance to "that little tart Mitzi."

21. Which statement represents an opinion rather than a fact?
a. Statement 1
b. Statement 2
c. Statement 5
d. Statement 8
e. Statement 10

22. Which statement is hearsay?
a. Statement 3
b. Statement 4
c. Statement 6
d. Statement 8
e. Statement 10

23. Which two statements together most clearly indicate that one of the speakers is lying?
   a. Statements 5 and 10
   b. Statements 2 and 3
   c. Statements 1 and 8
   d. Statements 4 and 6
   e. Statements 8 and 9

24. Which two statements appear to corroborate each other?
   a. Statements 4 and 6
   b. Statements 1 and 10
   c. Statements 6 and 7
   d. Statements 1 and 7
   e. Statements 1 and 9

25. Which two statements together offer the clearest motive for murder?
   a. Statements 2 and 6
   b. Statements 5 and 8
   c. Statements 4 and 10
   d. Statements 5 and 10
   e. Statements 1 and 4

26. Which statement, if true, points against Mr. Fein's having been planning in advance to commit suicide?
   a. Statement 1
   b. Statement 2
   c. Statement 4
   d. Statement 8
   e. Statement 10

27. Which statement, if untrue, casts suspicion on Ms. Hayes?
   a. Statement 1
   b. Statement 2
   c. Statement 6
   d. Statement 7
   e. Statement 10

28. Which two statements indicate that the speaker is trying to cast suspicion onto a particular person?
   a. Statements 1 and 2
   b. Statements 3 and 6
   c. Statements 7 and 8
   d. Statements 5 and 10
   e. Statements 4 and 7

29. Which statement, besides statement 6, casts the most suspicion on Ms. Hayes?
   a. Statement 2
   b. Statement 4
   c. Statement 5
   d. Statement 7
   e. Statement 9

30. Which statement, taken by itself, is most irrelevant to the case?
   a. Statement 1
   b. Statement 3
   c. Statement 5
   d. Statement 8
   e. Statement 10

Answers

Part A: Verbal Reasoning

1. b. See the second sentence of the passage. The other choices may be true but are not dealt with in the passage.

2. d. The essential information that supports this statement is in the last sentence of the paragraph. Choice **a** is incorrect—it uses a detail from the passage (artists and musicians) but draws a conclusion that is not suggested by the content of the paragraph. Choice **b** is contradicted by the second sentence, which states that creative people can help "increase efficiency." Choices **c** and **e** are outside the scope of the passage. The author does not discuss whether creative workers are loyal nor does it cover how to encourage creativity among workers.

3. e. This idea is stated in the second sentence and discussed throughout the passage. None of the other choices is in the passage.

4. c. The answer is clearly stated in the third sentence. Choice **a** is incorrect because the entire paragraph suggests otherwise. Choice **b** is not mentioned. Choice **d** looks attractive, but the idea of dividing jobs among several people is not mentioned in the paragraph. Choice **e** is not in the passage.

5. e. See the final sentence. The other choices sound reasonable and may be true but are not dealt with in the passage.

6. b. The answer is found in the third sentence. The other choices are incorrect because there is no mention in the paragraph of the sanitation workers' responsibilities or habits at home or at work.

7. c. The essential information is located in the second sentence of the paragraph. Choices **a** and **d** may be true statements, but the paragraph does not support them. Choice **b** is not one of the recommendations offered by the passage. Choice **e** is not a valid answer because it uses the absolute term "100% effective"—the paragraph does not make such an overriding claim.

8. d. Although the last sentence expands on the main point, the rest of the passage explains why hearsay evidence is only admissible when it doesn't matter whether or not the statement is true.

9. a. The first sentence states that skills and abilities of one member may not be known to another. Choices **b** and **e** are not mentioned. Choice **c** is incorrect because even though the paragraph seems to be addressed to one individual reader, it does not say that one member should be assigned the task of discovering everyone's talents. Choice **d** is incorrect for that same reason.

10. d. The last sentence points to the need for balancing responsibilities. The other choices are not mentioned in the paragraph.

11. e. Choice **a** is incorrect because the first sentence suggests that becoming jaded is unavoidable. The other choices are not mentioned.

12. b. This statement is supported by the third sentence in the passage. Choice **a** is incorrect because it is contradicted by the paragraph's first sentence. Choice **c** is contradicted by the paragraph's third sentence, which states that not only the elderly are vulnerable, but also children, people with certain medical conditions, even young and healthy people. Choice **d** makes an absolute claim that staying in air-conditioning is the "best" way to prevent heat illness—a claim not backed up by the passage. Choice **e** is wrong because it introduces details that are not mentioned in the paragraph.

13. e. This statement is supported by the paragraph's third sentence. Choice **b** uses a detail (the image of lie detectors in TV shows) from the first sentence of the paragraph, but it is incorrect because the paragraph does not compare how often polygraph testing is used in entertainment with how often they are used by law enforcement groups. Choice **c** overstates its claim—the paragraph does not infer that poly-graph tests are "completely useless." Choice **e** may be a true statement, but it is not covered by the paragraph.

14. b. The search team leader and the members of the team need to plan in advance. Choices **a**, **c**, and **e** are incorrect, as they are in opposition of information given in the passage. Even though choice **d** is implied, the passage deals with many more aspects of the search than teamwork.

15. b. Choice **b** is the most accurate conclusion because the first sentence speaks of *periods of war*. The other choices, whether true or false, are not addressed in the selection.

16. e. Any of the choices may be a definition of *background*; however, the context of the passage indicates that the word refers to the education and training of the proposed author—that is, the author's ability to write the book.

17. c. The second sentence of the paragraph shows that the author would probably agree with this statement. Choice **a** is incorrect because the author's tone is one of neutrality; she does not make it clear whether or not she believes global warming is positive. Choice **b** is contradicted by the details that the author provides in the second sentence. Choice **d** goes too far in its assertion that human activities are the "sole reason" for the earth's warming, when the paragraph states that they are the "main reason." Choice **e** is not supported by the paragraph.

18. e. This is the main thrust of the paragraph. The other choices either are not mentioned or are refuted in the paragraph.

19. a. The word *increasingly* in the second sentence supports this statement. Choice **b** is outside the scope of the passage, which does not indicate how many schools are implementing bullying prevention programs. Choice **c** is incorrect—the paragraph infers that bullying was once looked upon as a normal, acceptable part of childhood, but that now, that attitude has changed. Choice

d is contradicted by the last sentence in the para-graph, which gives details about how schools can do something about bullying. Choice **e** is too narrow in its scope—the paragraph indicates that bullying includes a range of behaviors.

20. d. The second sentence says parachutists cannot jump over or into a congested open-air assem-bly of persons *unless a certificate of authorization for that jump, issued by the FAA, has been issued*. This refutes choices **a**, **b**, and **c**. Choice **e** is incor-rect because the qualifications of parachutists are not discussed in the paragraph.

21. b. The last sentence of the paragraph implies this statement. Choices **a** and **d** are contradicted by the paragraph—choice **a** by the first sentence and choice **d** by the second sentence. Choice **c** is incorrect—the paragraph does not imply that any one animal's lung system is better than another, merely that dinosaurs and birds share a similar lung system. Choice **e** is also contra-dicted by the paragraph, which cites a "recent analysis" as evidence of the link between dinosaurs and birds.

22. c. The first sentence especially supports this choice, as it speaks of recent *injury to members of the public*. Choices **a** and **b** are contradicted in the passage, which says that hospitals do attempt to deal with the problem of medical waste. Choices **d** and **e** are not in the passage.

23. b. The essential information for this statement is in the last sentence of the paragraph. One can infer that "sound investigative techniques" includes the general ability to "recognize and explore leads." Choice **a** may be a true statement, but it is not discussed in the paragraph. Choice **b** is contradicted by the last sentence, which indi-cates that all investigators must write reports. Choice **d** is incorrect—the paragraph does not compare the danger or difficulty of different types of investigations. Choice **e** is contradicted by the last sentence in the passage that lists two tasks that all investigators have in common.

24. c. The third sentence of the passage says: *The main reason for so many injuries and fatalities is that a vehicle can generate heat of up to 1500° F.* Choices **a**, **b**, and **e** are mentioned but are not stated to be the main cause. Choice **d** is not in the passage.

25. a. The amount of potential data storage in home computers is impressive. Choices **b**, **c**, and **e** are not addressed in the passage. Choice **d** is incorrect, as that is a part of the passage and not the main theme.

Part B: Arithmetic Reasoning

1. d. It takes 5,280 feet to make a mile. To find how many miles are in 33,000 feet, divide: 33,000 feet ÷ 5,280 feet/mile = 6.25.

2. b. The number of trucks loaded per person per hour must be found. Nine trucks divided by (3 hours × 2 people) = 1.5 trucks per person-hour × 2 hours = 3 trucks loaded by Jean = 6 hours.

3. c. If he has a full tank of gas and refills twice more, he has put in a total of 6 gallons of gas. He has 1.5 gallons left. 6 − 1.5 = 4.5 gallons used. 4.5 × 56 gallons used. 4.5 × 56 miles per gallon = 252 miles.

4. e. This is a simple interest problem. $I = P(r)t$; $I = \$3.50$; $P = \$500.00$; $t = \frac{50}{365}$ or, rounded, 0.14. The equation therefore gives a 5% rate, which is none of the possibilities.

5. d. Gary's total with interest is $53.21. Divide the total by 1.06 (that is, 100% + 6% sales tax = 106% or 1.06) and you get $50.198, rounded to 50.20.

6. b. $13,000 × (100% + 20% markup = 120% or 1.20) = $15,600.

7. c. If the salesclerk's overtime pay is $9.00 at time and a half, her regular pay would be $6.00. $6 × 40 hours + $9 × 8 hours = $312.

8. d. The mileage is the ratio of miles traveled to gallons used. A total of (200 + 120) miles are traveled, and the amount of gas used is (200 ÷ 20) + (120 ÷ 15).

9. c. Multiply the cost per acre by the number of acres: $60,000 × $1\frac{3}{4}$ = $105,000.

10. d. Time = distance ÷ rate
Time = 8 ÷ 50 = .16 hour
.16 hour × 60 minutes = 9.6 minutes

11. c. The first car will travel 2 hours × 60 mph = 120 miles. The second car has 2 hours − 20 minutes = $\frac{10}{6}$ hours. 120 miles ÷ $\frac{10}{6}$ hours = 72 miles per hour.

12. a. Two iterations must be done to find the answer:
$A = P(r)t$
$A = \$500 \times 0.08 \times 0.50 = \$20$ (first half-year)
$A = \$520 \times 0.08 \times 0.50 = \$20.80$ (second half-year)
Therefore, the original amount will grow to: $500 + 20 + 20.80, or $540.80.

13. e. The tax rate is $325 ÷ $50,000 = 0.0065 = $6.50 per $1,000.

14. d. To find the answer, you should multiply: 0.15 × $300 × 4 televisions = $180.

15. d. First, subtract the amount withheld from Martha's check every two weeks: $1,100 − $223.00 − $80.41 − $55.20 = $741.39 every two weeks; so one week's net pay is $741.39 ÷ 2 = $370.70.

16. a. If there are 55 men total and 30 have no facial hair, 25 must have facial hair. There is a total of 12 + 22 men from each category. Therefore, the number in both must be the total of the two categories minus the total with facial hair. This gives (12 + 22) − (55 − 30).

17. c. To answer this question, a ratio must be set up: 3:1 = 9:x; x = 9 ÷ 3 = 3; 3 + 9 = 12.

18. d. To solve this problem, work the following equation: $255 ÷ 340 is 0.75, so $255 is 75% of $340. 100% − 75% creates a 25% loss.

19. b. This is an average of the earnings. The total money earned is ($10,500 × 1.23) + ($7,535 × 1.17). The ratio of money earned to capital is money earned divided by capital; 1 must be subtracted from this to find the percent earning. This gives ($10,500 × 1.23 + $7,535 × 1.17) ÷ ($10,500 + $7,535) − 1.

20. e. The ratio of commissions is the ratio of costs of VCRs to televisions. This is $225 ÷ $75 = 3:1. Since three VCRs are sold, 3 × 3 = 9.

Part C: Problems for Investigation

1. d. To figure the amount, divide $66,000 by 4 to get an amount of $16,500. Divide that amount by 12 to get the monthly amount of $1,375.

2. b. Statement 8 presents Mabel Wylie's neighbor's opinion.

3. c. Statement 9 provides a link between the suspects in the case and the registered owner of the handgun.

4. a. Statement 5. If Wylie was planning an action against the government because he was fired, he probably would not wait two years.

5. b. Statement 4. Circumstantial evidence is evidence from which the presence of a fact of the case can be inferred. From evidence of Hanson's proximity to the fingerprint facility, one can infer he was gathering information about the area.

6. a. To convert kilometers to miles, multiply 1,250 by .62. This gives an answer of 775 miles.

7. a. Statement 3 indicates Mabel has driven the car in which the gun was found and is related to the owner of the car. Statements 7 and 9 add the information that the gun is registered to Mabel's ex-husband, indicating she may have had access to the gun.

8. e. Statement 10 indicates that Robert Hanson harbors ill will toward the government and may have believed he was treated unfairly. This is motive for targeting a federal facility.

9. d. Statements 4 and 7 are examples of local law enforcement providing information to federal agents.

10. b. Statement 3 is an attempt to implicate another person as the owner of the items found in the car, even though Wylie is the owner of the car.

11. b. Statement 2 is Ann Lee's opinion; it adds no facts to the case.

12. a. Roger Evans's statement was made without personal knowledge; he simply repeated what others said.

13. c. The fact, by itself, that the Lakes' car is registered under Felix Lake's name adds nothing to the investigation.

14. e. Neal Atkins's statement that the .32 caliber revolver that Minerva Lake purchased is often used for home defense seems to back up the statement made by Minerva Lake that she planned to use the gun to protect herself on nights when her husband was working.

15. c. The amount of $3,250 is multiplied by .10 to get the percentage of expenses ($325). That amount is subtracted from the total sales for an amount of $2,925 for donation to the charity.

16. d. Statements 7 and 9 do not implicate Felix Lake in a crime. The first is a statement by the Lakes' landlord, who states that they are responsible tenants. The second is a statement by Minerva Lake, claiming that she purchased the gun for herself, not for her husband.

17. b. Fred Katz stated that gun buyers are usually very interested in examining a weapon before they purchase it; Minerva never examined the weapon nor did she show any signs of interest in it before buying it. The wink that Brian James saw Felix give Minerva may have been a signal that he had selected the gun he wanted and that she should come to the counter to buy it for him. Statement 10 could also indicate that Minerva was buying the gun for Felix. Because Felix is a convicted felon, he would not be able to buy a gun if he wanted one.

18. a. The first statement casts suspicion on Felix Lake because he claimed to be collecting a type of gun that according to the salesman is too cheap a quality to be a collector's gun. Fred Katz's statement that gun buyers are usually very interested in examining a weapon before purchasing it could suggest that Lake's high level of interest mean he was looking at the gun for his own use. Choice **c** is incorrect because even though statement 3 is somewhat damaging to Lake, statement 5 is merely an opinion that is not based on anything specific.

19. d. The fact that Atkins worked on commission and had a financial incentive to sell the gun might indicate that he had motive not to be as careful as he should have been in overseeing the sale.

20. a. Of these choices, Neal Atkins's statement that the .32 caliber revolver is of a cheap make and sometimes used as a throwaway weapon at the scene of a crime could possibly indicate that Felix Lake might consider using the gun for criminal use.

21. b. There is no way to prove whether Mr. Fein was despondent that day or not. The other choices involve statements that can be proved or disproved.

22. e. Lance Tarkington's statement is secondhand. The other statements are based on the speakers' direct experience.

23. e. Mitzi Fork cannot simultaneously work only at Macy's **and** be an exotic dancer downtown.

24. a. Loving young people and allowing them to hold meetings in one's home are compatible.

25. d. Both these statements offer a large amount of money as the motive. In the other choices, one or both of the statements do not bear on motive.

26. a. Planning to get married and buying plane tickets to Aruba do not seem the likely actions of a man about to commit suicide.

27. c. Ms. Hayes's next-door neighbor has said that motorcycles make noise outside Ms. Hayes' house late at night. If the motorcyclists aren't there for friendly, drug-free meetings, then they are likely there to buy drugs.

28. d. In Statement 5, Heather seems to be trying to cast suspicion on Mitzi by attributing the motive of money; in statement 10, Lance is trying the same thing on Heather.

29. d. If Mr. Fein never owned a dog, then Ms. Hayes's explanation to the police that Mr. Fein "had it in for her" over an incident involving his dog is false and eliminates the alternative motive for Mr. Fein's calling the police on Ms. Hayes.

30. d. The fact that Mitzi says she works at Macy's is irrelevant except in combination with the fact that Heather indicates Mitzi is lying.

Scoring

Evaluate how you did on this practice exam by scoring the three sections separately but using the same method for each. First, find the number of questions you got right in each section. Only the number of correct answers is important—questions you skipped or got wrong don't count against your score. Divide the number of questions you got right by the total number of questions in the section to find your percentage. If necessary, use the tables at the end of Lesson 5 to check your math.

If you achieve a score of at least 70% on the three parts, you will most likely pass the TEA exam.

If you didn't score as well as you would like, once again, be sure to go over the LearningExpress Test Preparation System in Lesson 4 to learn how to avoid the main difficulties. You can also go back to the lessons on each section of the test and review the areas that give you the most trouble.

There's an ancient joke that goes like this: In New York City, a man stops a second man on the street and asks, "How do I get to Carnegie Hall?" The second man answers, "Practice."

The key to success in almost any pursuit is to prepare for all you're worth. By taking the practice exams in this book, you've made yourself better prepared than other people who may be taking the exam with you. You've diagnosed where your strengths and weaknesses lie and learned how to deal with the various kinds of questions that will appear on the test. So go into the exam with confidence, knowing that you're ready and equipped to do your best.

NOTES

NOTES

NOTES

NOTES

Special Offer from LearningExpress!

Let LearningExpress help you ace the Treasury Enforcement Agent exam

Go to the LearningExpress Practice Center at www.LearningExpressFreeOffer.com, an interactive online resource exclusively for LearningExpress customers.

Now that you've purchased LearningExpress's *Treasury Enforcement Agent Exam*, you have **FREE** access to:

- **A full-length TEA practice test**
- **Immediate scoring** and **detailed answer explanations**
- Benchmark your skills and focus your study with our **customized diagnostic report**

Follow the simple instructions on the scratch card in your copy of *Treasury Enforcement Agent Exam*. Use your individualized access code found on the scratch card and go to www.Learning ExpressFreeOffer.com to sign in. Start practicing for the TEA exam online right away!

Once you've logged on, use the spaces below to write in your access code and newly created password for easy reference:

Access Code: _____   Password: _____